The End of Elitism?

With developments such as the gross overcrowding of universities and the student revolt of the 1960s, traditional Humboldtian ideals of German higher education were reassessed and new models, more appropriate to an age of mass education, were conceived. In the subsequent reform programme, different types of institution, at and below university level, were merged as a means of introducing greater flexibility within existing structures, promoting social and regional equality, and stimulating curricular innovation. This study examines the impressive achievements of such *Gesamthochschulen* and also addresses the attendant difficulties which militate against comprehensivisation in Germany today. The advent of European credit transfer and the prospect of a united Germany make it particularly topical to study factors which block change in West German higher education. The present volume is intended as a contribution to such an analysis.

Rosalind M.O. Pritchard is Senior Lecturer in the Department of Education, University of Ulster at Coleraine.

The End of Elitism?

The Democratisation of the West German University System

Rosalind M.O. Pritchard

BERG

New York / Oxford / Munich
Distributed exclusively in the US and Canada
by St Martin's Press, New York

First published in 1990 by
Berg Publishers Limited
Editorial Offices:
165 Taber Avenue, Providence R.I. 02906, USA
150 Cowley Road, Oxford OX4 1JJ, UK
Westermühlstraße 26, 8000 München 5, FRG

Library of Congress Cataloging-in-Publication Data

Pritchard, Rosalind M.O.
  The end of elitism? : the democratisation of the West German
university system / Rosalind M.O. Pritchard.
    p. cm.
  Includes bibliographical references.
  ISBN 0–85496–661–7
  1. Education, Higher—Germany (West)—History—20th century.
  2. Universities and colleges—Germany (West)   I. Title.
  LA727.P75 1990
  378.43—dc20   89-39611
                                                                          CIP

British Library Cataloguing in Publication Data

Pritchard, Rosalind M.O.
  The End of Elitism? The Democratisation of
  the West German University System
    1. West Germany. Higher education
    I. Title
  378.43
  ISBN 0–85496–661–7

Printed in Great Britain by Billing & Sons Ltd, Worcester

To My Parents

Contents

Preface and Acknowledgements

This book is about German comprehensive universities, but it adopts a broad approach placing them within the mainstream of modern higher education, the development of which began with the foundation of the Universities of Halle and Göttingen. Thus it is more than 'merely' a book about comprehensive universities. It is a historically contextualised study of a whole higher education system.

The research for the book was financed by grants from the Economic and Social Research Council, and the University of Ulster's Faculty of Education Research Committee. In Germany, the following were interviewed, and provided me with insights and material: Horst Arp, Gregor Berghorn, Fritz Bohnsack, Friedrich Buttler, Gerth Dorff, Wolfgang Fischer, Peter Freese, Ludwig Gieseke, Helmut Groh, Christian Heichert, Toni Hochmuth, Adolf Kell, Hilde Kipp, Dietfrid Krause-Vilmar, Siegfried Maser, Bernhard Nagel, Peter Neumann-Mahlkau, Aylâ Neusel, Christoph Oehler, Gerhard Rimbach, Jörn Schmidt, Helmut Schrey, Christian Thieme and Hansjörg Wellmer. Drafts of some or all chapters were read by David Archard, Fritz Böversen, Rex Cathcart, Tom Fraser, Bill Hart, Georg Henning, Günther Kloss, Jürgen Klüver, Klaus Peters and Helmut Winkler. None of the aforementioned is responsible for any errors of fact or interpretation which the book may contain. I am particularly grateful to Jürgen Klüver for all his help, to Eberhard Jobst who mediated many useful contacts for me, to Rex Cathcart who gave unstinting support and encouragement throughout the writing process, and to Vincent Nash who read the entire book meticulously and improved the text. Although they were not directly involved in the drafting of the book I should also like to mention Franziska Kirchberg and Petra Mößner, both of whom have done a great deal during the course of my life to imbue me with a love of Germany. Finally, I should like to thank Kilian McDaid for cartographic assistance and Harold McMahon and Denis Kirkpatrick for help with the production of the manuscript.

Rosalind M.O. Pritchard
The University of Ulster at Coleraine

Key to German and English Abbreviations

ABRC	Advisory Board for Research Councils
AUT	Association of University Teachers
BAK	Bundesassistentenkonferenz
BLK	Bund-Länder-Kommission für Bildungsplanung und Forschungsförderung
BMBW	Bundesministerium für Bildung und Wissenschaft
BPS	Berufspraktische Studien
BTEC	Business and Technician Education Council
CAT	College of Advanced Technology
CDP	Committee of Directors of Polytechnics
CDU	Christlich-Demokratische Union
CNAA	Council for National Academic Awards
CSU	Christlich-Soziale Union
DES	Department of Education and Science
DFG	Deutsche Forschungsgemeinschaft
FDP	Freie Demokratische Partei
FHS	Fachhochschule
FOS	Fachoberschule
FRG	Federal Republic of Germany
GB	Great Britain (England, Scotland and Wales)
GCSE	General Certificate of Secondary Education
GEW	Gewerkschaft für Erziehung und Wissenschaft
GhK	Gesamthochschule Kassel
GHS	Gesamthochschule
HRG	Hochschulrahmengesetz
IGHS	Integrierte Gesamthochschule
KGHS	Kooperative Gesamthochschule
KMK	Kultusministerkonferenz
LEA	Local Education Authority
NABLAHE	National Advisory Body for Local Authority Higher Education, later to become –
NABPSHE	National Advisory Body for Public Sector Higher Education
NRW	Nordrhein-Westfalen; North Rhine-Westphalia
OECD	Organisation for Economic Co-operation and Development

PCFC	Polytechnics and Colleges Funding Council
PH	Pädagogische Hochschule
SCUE	Standing Committee on University Entry
SDS	Sozialistischer Deutscher Studentenbund
SED	Sozialistische Einheitspartei Deutschlands
SPD	Sozialdemokratische Partei Deutschlands
SRHE	Society for Research into Higher Education
THES	*Times Higher Educational Supplement*
UFC	Universities Funding Council
UGC	University Grants Committee
UK	United Kingdom
VDI	Verein Deutscher Ingenieure
VDS	Verband Deutscher Studentenschaften
WR	Wissenschaftsrat
WRK	Westdeutsche Rektorenkonferenz

Glossary of German Terms

Abitur	School leaving certificate
Aufbaustudium	Advanced course (sometimes compensatory)
Baukasten	'Construction kit'; modular degree course structure
Bildung	The German concept of education
Brückenkurse	Bridging courses
Bund	Federal government; federation
Bundesrepublik Deutschland	Federal Republic of Germany
Bürgertum	Middle classes
Diplom	University-level academic qualification (cf. British degree)
Durchlässigkeit	Permeability in the educational system; possibility of transfer between courses or institutions at different levels
Einsamkeit und Freiheit	Solitude and freedom; solitary freedom
Fächerspektrum	Range of subjects
Fachhochschule	Approximate equivalent of British polytechnic
Fachoberschule	Technical upper secondary school
Forschendes Lernen	Learning through research
Forschung	Research
Gesamthochschule	Comprehensive institution of higher education
Gesamtschule	Comprehensive school
Grundgesetz	Basic Law (the West German constitution)
Grundstudium	Foundation course; course of basic study
Gruppenuniversität	University governed by a committee structure on which various important interest groups (*Gruppen*) are represented
Gymnasium	Academic secondary school for able students
Habilitation	Post-doctoral thesis
Hauptschule	Non-academic type secondary school

Hauptstudium	Main course of study
Hochschule	Institution of higher education
Hochschulrahmengesetz	Federal Framework Law for Higher Education
Hochschulreife	Matriculation qualification
Innerlichkeit	Concentration on inner spiritual and cultural values
Integrierte Gesamthochschule	Integrated comprehensive institution of higher education
Integrierte Studiengänge	Integrated courses of study
Kooperative Gesamthochschule	Federal comprehensive institution of higher education
Kultur	The cultivation of wisdom and spirituality through humane learning
Kulturstaat	State based on cultural values
Land (Länder)	Federal State(s)
Lehrfreiheit	Freedom in teaching
Lernfreiheit	Freedom in learning
Machtstaat	State based on the power principle
Mitbestimmung	Joint decision-making
Mittelbau	Sub-professorial tier of research and teaching staff (normally untenured)
Notstandsgesetze	Emergency laws
Numerus clauses	Limited admissions quota for university places
Ordinarius	Full tenured professor on the staff of a university
Pädagogische Hochschule	Teacher training college
Praxisbezug	Practical orientation
Promotion	Doctoral thesis
Rechtsstaat	State subject to the sovereignty of law
Rektor	Aproximate equivalent of British Vice-Chancellor
Staat	State
Studium generale	Course of liberal cultural studies
Technische Hochschule	Technical university
Vernunft	Reason
Verstand	Intellect
Wissenschaft	Knowledge; scholarship; science (but can include humanities); learning
wissenschaftlich	Scholarly; scientific; learned
Zwischenprüfung	Intermediate examination

Introduction

In several European countries, student opinion now constitutes an important performance indicator; this trend is relatively new in Europe, although it has long been customary in the United States of America. In a recent issue of the weekly magazine *Der Spiegel* (50, 1989: 70–87), an article was published with the headline 'The New Universities are the Best'. When *Spiegel* asked 6,000 students to assess their own institutions for quality of life, teaching and research, the highest rating was given to the comprehensive university of Siegen. As a group, the comprehensive universities were clearly more positively rated by their student bodies than the respected older universities, the non-comprehensive new universities and the technical universities. Part of the secret of the comprehensives' success is related to the fact that their numbers are modest in comparison with giant establishments like Munich (62,200 students), Berlin (58,900), Münster (45,000) and Hamburg (44,300); moderate size facilitates academic contact between staff and students, and is conducive to good human relationships. Not only teaching but also research is said to be thriving at the comprehensives – a competence now receiving tangible recognition by the award of international prizes and patents.

The findings of *Der Spiegel* confound certain currently-held prejudices and negative stereotypes. Siegen, in common with the other comprehensive universities, has had a hard struggle to gain acceptance and status in the academic community. The very necessity for the new institutions to prove themselves has spurred them on to achievement. In the early 1970s, it was intended to transform the whole of German higher education from an elitist into a comprehensive system; the new comprehensive universities were to be a means of achieving this transformation, and were conceived not as exceptions but as models to be universalised. The expectations held of them have on the one hand prompted disparagement among traditionalists who feared that 'lower level institutions' might dilute standards, and on the other hand aroused hope among those who saw them as harbingers of the new age.

There were, however, powerful factors which frustrated the attempt to bring about comprehensivisation. The German higher education system as a whole exhibits a pattern of strong vertical differentiation; the universities occupy the topmost position in the prestige hierarchy, whereas other institutions such as polytechnics are perceived as subordinate. Conventional wisdom claims that German universities are all of equal merit, and, in keeping with this claim, credit accumulation and transfer have long been permitted in Germany; this arrangement, however, has been confined almost entirely to the university sector. Academic standards in the German universities and polytechnics differ: a striking example of this difference is that, at the time of writing, polytechnics are not allowed to award doctoral degrees.[1] Holders of polytechnic degrees who wish to proceed to research at a university are often required to undertake additional study to upgrade their first degrees. In certain parts of Germany, holders of polytechnic degrees have to put the initials 'FH' after their qualification to indicate the type of institution which awarded it; if they wish to change to a university-type title, they may have to take an additional examination (British Council, 1989). Notwithstanding these difficulties, it *is* possible for students to transfer from one sector of post-secondary education to another, but the problem is that because of the barriers between the different 'columns' of the system, this usually costs a considerable amount of extra time.

The German scenario contrasts with that in the United Kingdom, where universities and polytechnics pride themselves on their intellectual 'gold standard', which is to say that the same academic level is maintained for university and non-university degrees. This consistency has been reinforced and upheld by the work of the Council for National Academic Awards which was set up to validate polytechnic degrees; the fact that the Open University, too, maintains the 'gold standard' contributes to the cohesiveness of British higher education. In the Federal Republic of Germany, the divisions between university and non-university higher education are thus more substantive than in the United Kingdom. It is not until one reaches a sub-university level in the academic hierarchy that serious divisions become operative in the UK: further education is regarded as lower in academic status, and there has been entrenched opposition to conflating it with higher education.[2]

---

1. The polytechnics have expressed their dissatisfaction with this state of affairs, and the matter is currently under negotiation.
2. This is now changing.

Today, however, a number of factors make it imperative to give sympathetic attention to the possibilities of linkages across different academic levels. Both Great Britain and Germany are faced with the challenge of responding to the demands of neo-conservative governments, which insist on opening education to market forces. This means developing courses which are attractive in vocational terms to potential students, and which give good value for time and money; artificial blocks between institutions which cause unnecessary prolongation of study time are seen as counterproductive. In both countries, demographic trends will soon result in falling student numbers; to maintain their viability, institutions will need to provide non-traditional students with means of access to higher education. In addition, the Federal Republic of Germany will be obliged to re-think some of its educational structures and ideas with a view to achieving closer co-operation with fellow countrymen in what is now the German Democratic Republic, but will soon become part of a united Germany. Perhaps most important of all, however, is the prospect of the 1992 Single European Act, which has implications for the very concept of what constitutes 'higher education'.

In 1984, the European Community established a Network of National Academic Recognition Centres (NARIC) which has been extended and consolidated under the ERASMUS programme, designed to boost the mobility of academic staff and students (Green, 1989). In 1988, a pilot scheme was announced for a European Course Credit Transfer System (ECTS); this scheme allows students enrolled at some 80 selected universities to study in more than one country and still obtain their degrees within a specified period by receiving academic credits for course units, intermediate and final qualifications at one institution and continuing their studies at another institution within the ECTS system (EC Journal, 27 July 1988).

These new European arrangements call into question the difference between advanced/non-advanced, and traditional/new-style institutions. In the publication just cited (ibid.), the term 'university' is used very broadly to indicate 'all types of post-secondary education and training establishments which offer, where appropriate within the framework of advanced training, qualifications or diplomas of that level, whatever such establishments may be called in the member states'. In another EC document (COM (86) 257 final), a higher education diploma is flexibly defined as

> any diploma, certificate, or other evidence of formal qualifications awarded in recognition of vocational study at the level of university or non-university higher education by a competent authority of a Member state,

following a course of at least three years' duration open, as a general rule, only to persons holding a certificate awarded on successful completion of a full course of upper secondary education.

Several interesting points emerge from these definitions. Broad, flexible definitions of 'university' education need to be complemented by an equally flexible concept of secondary education. The fact that 'university' education is defined as post-secondary education begs the question of what 'secondary' education is. There is no simple answer to this apparently simple question. The length of a pupil's secondary school career varies in different school types and different countries: it is sometimes eroded by a student taking 'time out'; conversely, it may be expanded by repetition of a failed year; and what constitutes secondary education in one country may form part of the first year university curriculum somewhere else. 'University' education is thus defined in the European Community documents using a point of reference which is perforce inconstant and variable. Such education may take place in an establishment which is a university by nature but not by name; universities may give training as well as education within a framework which is advanced 'where appropriate'; the European documents do not, apparently, insist that university-level education must of its very nature be advanced.

It is a time which impels change in the United Kingdom and in the Federal Republic of Germany. In the former some moves to create merged institutions in higher education have taken place pragmatically and others are envisaged. In West Germany the legacy of the past causes elite institutions, acutely conscious of their own merit and proud of their autonomy, to resist attempts to break the mould of traditional higher education. The German experience described in the present work is significant as a parallel, and rewarding in the lessons which it suggests for reconstructionist planners. It can be considered under three major headings:

(1) *Analysis of the traditional university ethos.* The rigidities from which German higher education suffers impede development towards European credit transfer and accumulation. Since some of these rigidities are philosophically conditioned, the ideology of the traditional German university is depicted at length; the comprehensive universities were a reaction to the classical university ethos, and it is impossible to understand the one without understanding the other.

(2) *The pathology of the traditional university.* Concepts which had once been inspirational became perverted, and even two world wars did not suffice to change the ankylosed structure which had emerged.

However, in the post-war period a gradualist reform tradition was pioneered by the state education authorities so that, once the student revolt of the 1960s provided the necessary catalyst, it was possible to implement reforms relatively quickly. At that stage, the comprehensive principle dominated higher education, and was regarded as the key to educational renewal.

(3) *The implementation of reform and the obstacles it encountered.* The new institutions required new values, new aims, new structures, and even a redefinition of what constituted 'knowledge'. When the new ideas were put to the test of practice, the comprehensive universities were in the vanguard of change. Throughout West Germany, many people by their work and their example tried to democratise the system which they inherited. Some were educational planners with high principles and vision; some were staff and students in the comprehensives, who more than most are obliged to confront equality of opportunity as an important issue in their daily lives. The personal, legal, structural and political obstacles which they have encountered in their drive for democratisation lead on to an analysis of the reasons why the comprehensives did not become the means of transforming the German system as a whole, and an account of what they have to offer Germany and other European countries.

The point of departure in the study is the present situation in higher education in the United Kingdom which has in many respects a latent readiness for some initiatives of the comprehensive kind.

−1−

Mergers and the Search for Cost-effectiveness

> The number 2 is a very dangerous number . . .
> Attempts to divide anything into two ought to be
> regarded with much suspicion.
>
> C.P. Snow, *The Two Cultures*

Since the late 1960s, British higher education has supposedly been divided into two parts. The system, popularly termed 'binary', is said to comprise an autonomous (university) sector and a public (polytechnic) sector. From the inception of the polytechnics,[1] however, it has always been an oversimplification to conceptualise it as merely 'binary'. Anthony Crosland (Secretary of State for Education and Science in 1966, when the White Paper Cmnd. 3006 which created the polytechnic sector was issued), rejected the term 'binary' in favour of the term 'plural', pointing out that there were many bodies apart from universities which prepared students for degrees, and that in setting up polytechnics, he had not intended to give the universities a monopoly of degree-level work (Crosland, 1967). In a similar vein, Shattock (1983:19) argues that there are at least four

1. In the period 1890–1902, town council and corporation funds were used for the creation of 12 polytechnics and technical institutions in London and of 13 in the provinces; some of their students took University of London external degrees, thus helping pioneer the development of higher education outside the universities. Local education authorities (LEAs) were established in 1902, and in 1918 became eligible to receive 50% central government grants for expenditure on post-elementary education. The 1944 Education Act further stimulated the growth of locally controlled third-level education, and tightened central control over the LEAs. The 1956 White Paper on Technical Education introduced a four-tier system of Colleges of Advanced Technology (CATs), area colleges, local colleges and regional colleges. By 1962/63, two-thirds of the full-time students at the 25 regional colleges were involved in advanced work, and it was these which were later to form the nucleus of the modern polytechnics. In 1961, following a recommendation of the Robbins Report, the nine maintained CATs were granted university status. This upward movement of the CATs left a hole in the system, which was filled by the creation of 28 polytechnics (formed from the regional colleges) as a result of the 1966 White Paper recommendations (cf. Oakes Report, 1978: paras 2.1–2.4).

clearly distinguishable elements in British higher education: self-governing universities, institutions maintained by local education authorities, voluntary colleges mainly linked with religious organisations, and other direct grant institutions funded by the Department of Education and Science (or equivalent body).[2] The structure of British higher education was never, in fact, as simple as it appeared, and recent developments have now made the 'binary' concept untenable.

The ostensible basis of the so-called binary system related to funding mechanisms and academic mission. The autonomous sector was not funded directly by the state, but indirectly through the University Grants Committee in a way which simulated a private endowment or gift (Trow, 1983:120). This arrangement was designed to help guarantee academic freedom, and to protect the universities against political interference. The public sector institutions were funded by local education authorities; they were originally intended to be teaching rather than research institutions, to offer vocational rather than theoretical courses, to attract working-class students (or those who had missed out on opportunities for higher education), and to be more amenable to social control than the universities. However, even the distinction in financing was not rigid, since both sectors ultimately received at least ninety per cent of their financial resources from central government (Williams, 1977:12). It was the disparity in the relative degrees of autonomy permitted to the universities and the polytechnics that was of most significance, although Crosland expected that this would lessen in time as the former responded to 'friendly scrutiny'.

The responsiveness of the polytechnics to direct social control was reflected in their interaction with the local education authorities (LEAs). Sometimes this was a rewarding relationship, but all too often it was problematic, due to the tendency of the LEAs to subject their institutions to low-level bureaucratic restrictions and paralysing restraints in some cases (Robinson, 1968). The difficulty was a long-standing one: as long ago as 1966, the Weaver Report had been commissioned to investigate the best way of attaining a balance between freedom and social control in locally managed colleges of education; the Department of Education and Science subsequently took action in an attempt to follow its advice, but failed to achieve a notably successful outcome (Pratt and Silverman, 1988:95). Somewhat over a decade later, the Oakes working group (1978) under-

2. There also exist a number of hybrid institutions which are financed jointly by Local Education Authorities and by the Department of Education and Science.

took an examination of the management of institutions of higher education in the maintained sector generally, and concluded that the LEAs were excessively restrictive. Oakes advocated the creation of a national body to advise on the total resources to be made available for maintained education and to determine the allocation of national funds between authorities and institutions. This recommendation eventually resulted in the foundation (1982) of the National Advisory Body for Local Authority Higher Education (NABLAHE) (Stewart, 1989:206). Later when its remit was broadened to include voluntary colleges, it became the National Advisory Body for Public Sector Higher Education (NABPSHE), which in turn was the predecessor of the Polytechnics and Colleges Funding Council.

Despite the work of the NAB, LEAs' relations with their institutions continued to be problematic. A report commissioned by the Committee of Directors of Polytechnics criticised LEAs for unnecessary interference, and claimed that the system was dogged by petty jealousy, inefficiency and obstruction; small decisions were blown up into politically contentious issues, and some LEAs used financial sanctions as a means of control. Since polytechnics had no standing in law, disagreements could not be referred to an independent body for settlement, and the report therefore recommended corporate status for certain polytechnics 'without losing the polytechnic ethos or public sector base' (*THES*, 19 Dec. 1986:1). This recommendation was adopted in the 1987 White Paper *Meeting the Challenge* (Cm 114) and in the Education Reform Act (1988), in which the government announced its intention of transferring a number of large polytechnics to corporate status, outside local authority control. The new arrangements give certain polytechnics a degree of independence which brings them closer to the university sector.

Not only organisationally but also in their teaching and research, the polytechnics are becoming more autonomous. Formerly, their courses were subjected to rigorous external validation by the Council for National Academic Awards (CNAA), which did much to ensure quality control, and prompted Pratt (1983:118) to write: 'The history of CNAA validation is, one is tempted at times to think, the history of innovation in higher education in the United Kingdom'. Now, as a result of the work of the Lindop Committee (1985), a number of polytechnics are permitted to review and validate their own courses. Although originally conceived primarily as teaching institutions, the polytechnics undertake serious and successful research, and are being given increased freedom to register higher degree students. Lack of employment opportunity in the university system has also brought them able staff, many of whom have built up creditable research records, notwithstanding inadequate research facilities (Whitburn et al., 1976). This trend has been encouraged by the NAB and the CNAA, both of which insist on the importance of research-led teaching at degree level. Scott (1983b:247) points out that the CNAA has done much to develop common academic values across the binary system, and highlights the fact that 'There has never been any attempt to restrict the polytechnics and colleges to sub-degree or undergraduate courses, while preserving postgraduate courses and doctorates as a university monopoly'.

The rising research power of the polytechnics contrasts with a decline in the universities' research capacity, occasioned by government cuts (Kogan, 1983). A report from the Advisory Board for Research Councils (ABRC) to the Secretary of State for Education (April, 1985) noted that the value of government support for the research councils had fallen by five per cent since 1981–82, and was due to fall by at least a further four per cent by the end of the decade. As a result, about one third of the highest-rated ('alpha') research proposals failed to secure funding by 1984–85.

The report states: 'In some universities, the well-found laboratory no longer exists; and throughout the university system it has become very difficult indeed for even the most outstanding young research scientists to secure research appointments'. The Green Paper (Cmnd. 9524: para.5.7, 1985) goes so far as to envisage that greater selectivity and research concentration may result in some departments and even whole universities losing research funding from the UGC.

The growing success and maturity of the polytechnics is concomitant with a crisis of confidence in the universities. British higher education has moved away from the principle enshrined in the Robbins Report (1963: section 31), which advocated admission to higher education of all who were qualified by ability and attainment to receive it and who wished to do so. It is now expenditure-driven rather than demand-led (Neave, 1984:114). Almost independent of state finance at one time, universities have become major consumers of public money. Faith in education as a worthwhile investment in human capital no longer seems fashionable, and universities are widely regarded as insufficiently responsive to social needs. Already at the beginning of the 1970s, Burn et al. (1971) spoke of the growing concern over universities' dependence on public support, and questioned the correlation between the national need for trained manpower and the production of graduates. They anticipated a break-down in the former cosy relationship between the universities and the University Grants Committee (UGC), and predicted that the UGC would become much more interventionist: 'Universities are too important to national development and too expensive to permit the kind of freedom they enjoyed in the past, sheltered by the UGC system. Some critics of the UGC see its role as a buffer between the dons and the government fast becoming obsolete' (1971:66).

This prediction proved accurate, and the universities have now lost the government's favour. Between 1981 and 1984–5, £460 million was taken away from them; the salaries of academic and academic-related staff have fallen by 24% in cost of living terms and 40% in relation to average earnings during that period. Since 1981, universities have lost one in seven of their academic staff, and polytechnics and colleges one in twelve of theirs (AUT, 1985). In some respects, polytechnics and colleges of higher education ben-efited from the universities' misfortunes. The limitations imposed on student numbers by the UGC led to large increases in the non-university sector, first to satisfy disappointed university applicants and then to preserve access (Shattock, 1983: 208).

The mobility of the polytechnics – upwards – and that of the universities – downwards – is leading to convergence of the auton-omous and the public sectors. Dons' conditions of service are be-coming somewhat similar to those of polytechnic lecturers, whom some of them formerly regarded with mere toleration or actual disdain. Whereas tenure used to be awarded to university teachers on satisfactory completion of a probationary period, this will shortly no longer be the case. The Education Reform Act (1988: paras. 202–8) provides for the appointment of Commissioners to investi-gate the best legal means of breaking tenure in each university. Only existing members of staff who stay in the same institution and are not promoted will retain tenure if they already have it, but will lose it if they move to another institution or are promoted. When the present tenured generation of university staff eventually retires, the United Kingdom will be almost unique in western Europe – no academic will have a permanent post. Since this has always been the case in polytechnics, removal of tenure from the universities will narrow the distance between the two sectors still further.

In financial matters, too, there has been a narrowing of the gap between universities and polytechnics. The 1987 White Paper Cm 114 and the Education Act (1988) state that the payment of grants to university institutions is to be replaced by a system of contracting between them and a new body replacing the UGC. The proposed

Universities Funding Council (UFC) is to have broadly equal numbers of academic and non-academic members, and the Secretary of State will have a reserve power to issue directions to it. A considerable improvement in accountability and in the flow of management information from the universities to government via the UFC will be required, and the UFC's arrangements for funding will 'properly reward success in developing co-operation with meeting the needs of industry and commerce' (Cm 114: section 4.43). The demand for accountability is given added weight by the report of the Jarratt Committee (1985) on efficiency in university management; it recommends changes in the management, budgeting, and monitoring of institutional performance. Like the universities, the polytechnics are also to receive a new funding body (the Polytechnics and Colleges Funding Council (PCFC)) and their present system of grant aid is to be replaced by a system of contracting between them and the PCFC. Accountability for the use of public funds is to be sharpened, and the polytechnics are to do everything in their power to attract contracts from outside sources (Cm 114: section 4.17 and 4.20). In terms of the status quo, the changes in funding machinery will further confirm the polytechnics' new-found independence, whereas the universities are steadily becoming less autonomous, and more subject to surveillance or direct intervention by state education authorities. Universities which do not become more vocational and service-oriented in teaching and research will suffer financial penalties; this will bring their academic mission more closely into line with that of their polytechnic counterparts. The similarity in function and powers between the UFC and the PCFC is striking, and may well contribute eventually towards the government's dissolving them both, and establishing instead one overarching body across the binary divide.

Changes in funding levels, conditions of service and academic orientation correlate with changes in the public perception of university staff. If the status of the polytechnics is rising, that of the universities is falling. Withdrawal of public approval is reflected in the hostile portrayals of university dons in modern fiction. Page (1978) in an article entitled 'Academic Man: Seen through Novelists' Eyes' finds that 'Academic men and women . . . seem to have few redeeming traits. We have a collection of petty-minded self-centred poseurs, whose personal lives are as pathetic as their intellectual pretensions'. The decreasing prestige of university teaching can be documented not only in literature but empirically. A firm of management consultants, PA Personnel Services, was commissioned by the Committee of Vice-Chancellors and Principals, and the

Association of University Teachers to investigate the standing of the profession. Their stark conclusion was that: 'The university teaching profession is not being reproduced . . . The brightest and best have no desire to become university teachers arguably because the status of the profession has so sharply declined, and actually because insufficient opportunities exist to build a worthwhile career' (*THES*, 9 May 1986: 32).

Financial stringency, as well as a loss of public support for the universities, has contributed towards narrowing the differences between the public and autonomous sector. The institutions which started life as poor relations of the universities are becoming increasingly self-assured, and impatient with restrictions upon their development. Some of them are now demanding that *de facto* convergence between the two sides of the binary divide be formally recognised by re-naming the polytechnics 'universities'. An increasingly synoptic view of educational goals is being forced by government on polytechnics and universities alike.

In comparison with most continental institutions, the typical British university is small. In terms of students, their size varies greatly, from London with over 40,000 to Lampeter with 740, the average being 6,055 (University Statistics, 1987–88). Smallness is now increasingly seen as a disadvantage. Thus, Swinnerton-Dyer (1988:42) notes that 'one of the UGC's major problems is that of providing in an increasingly parsimonious world a sensible future for small universities'. As an aide to the Vice-Chancellor of an English university put it: 'There is evidence that simply being large helps an institution' (*THES*, 2 Sept. 1988). What research there is indicates that British institutions of higher education are too small to produce graduates at the lowest cost per student (Layard and Verry, 1975; Verry and Davies, 1976). Blaug (1983:20) writes: 'If government policy in higher education accorded top priority to minimising costs per student, it follows that a good many universities and polytechnics should be amalgamated . . .' In research, too, smallness is increasingly considered a handicap. Hall (1987) argues that most of Britain's universities are not of sufficient size to compete in the world league, and that their inevitable decline, especially relative to American universities, can only be arrested by amalgamating them to form federated regional institutions.

In the search for cost-effectiveness and rationality, various forms of co-operation are being explored, and many institutions on both sides of the (now eroded) binary line are coming to the conclusion that it makes good sense for resources such as computer facilities, libraries and staff to be shared. Already, one university is developing a college outpost jointly with a polytechnic, and another university and polytechnic are offering a joint degree course. Pushed to its natural conclusion, the logic of sharing is merger. This can offer an excellent means of making the best use of scarce resources in a climate of budgetary contraction. As a response to crisis, institutional mergers are, in fact, being envisaged more and more often – witness, for example, that between the University of Cardiff and the University of Wales Institute of Science and Technology (UWIST), which has been thrust upon the partners in order to help the University out of serious financial trouble. Most remarkable of all is the merger which in Northern Ireland has led to the present University of Ulster. This is the first transbinary merger in the United Kingdom (although there have, of course, in the past been mergers between universities and monotechnic institutions, such as colleges of teacher training, art or technology). The Ulster merger is particularly noteworthy because of the considerable distances between the campuses which now make up the institution, and because the University involved in the merger was much smaller and less 'successful' than the Polytechnic.

The issues which become salient in any educational merger are similar, whether at school or university level. New courses have to be devised, building upon the strengths of the donor institutions; an attempt must be made to achieve consensus on common purposes and values; a new staff structure is required, with new job designations and new salary scale allocations; usually new leadership styles and management patterns are needed. All these issues have been tackled on a massive scale in the Federal Republic of Germany, where a number of new-style universities have been founded. Their establishment involved merging staff and courses from university and polytechnic traditions for the purpose of bringing more flexibility, democracy and creativity into existing structures. The ultimate objective was to establish a complete system of comprehensive higher education, widening access, abolishing educational cul-de-sacs, and maximising the development of individual talents.

There is good evidence that the British authorities had comprehensive higher education in mind as a long-term objective when they set up the polytechnics. Edmund Short's statement in 1970 showed very clearly that such an ideal was in the air: 'What I hope is that over the years the universities will become increasingly comprehensive, both in the structure of the student body – part-time, full-time, sandwich courses and so on – and also in the level of their courses, having not only degree courses but also sub-degree courses' (quoted by Brosan et al., 1971). The new polytechnics were, in fact, described by Crosland as 'comprehensive' on the grounds that they provided for students at different levels of ability and attainment, and embraced full-time, part-time and sub-degree work (speech at Lancaster University, 20 January 1967). In spite of the politicians' protestations, many people felt that their reforms stopped short of their true goals, and castigated them for apparently lacking the courage to be truly radical. Crosland was criticised for setting up institutions which helped the universities to evade the need for change, and was accused of creating establishments which were in effect 'creamed comprehensives', instead of expanding and diversifying the university system (Pedley, 1977:50). At the time, Crosland believed it impossible to create a unified system of higher education based on comprehensive principles. There were three main reasons for his pessimism: first, the universities' supposed autonomy was a disincentive; secondly, costs might escalate unacceptably in such a system; thirdly, he believed that the universities could not be expected to cope with the huge and growing army of part-time students at all levels.

Now, however, the principle of comprehensive education again seems worth considering. The autonomy of universities is no longer sacrosanct, and there is every indication that the government is unwilling to give them privileged treatment; it has demonstrated beyond dispute that it can demote universities and promote polytechnics, if it so wishes. Although financial resources are scarce, the cost element is less of a deterrent than it was formerly. The principles of comprehensive education are widely understood and accepted. Most secondary level children in Great Britain are now educated in comprehensive schools, and the desirability of segregating them at tertiary level can no longer be taken for granted. Demographic trends will result in a dramatic fall in the number of potential young recruits to higher education. There will, in future, be fewer salaried workers to generate wealth and support an ageing population. This necessitates making the best use of existing talent – reputedly one of the strengths of comprehensive education. Inter-institutional co-operation is on the agenda, even for part-time work. The effect of demography and of economic contraction is thus to unite principle with pragmatism. Comprehensive higher education is attractive to many people in principle; and there is, in practice, an organic convergence between the different types of higher education institution in the United Kingdom.

Certain informed observers therefore look to a non-binary, perhaps comprehensive form of organisation as the pattern of the future:

Sooner or later this country must face a comprehensive reform which will bring higher education out of the ivory towers and make it available to all. This will be achieved through a bloodier battle than for the comprehensive reform of secondary education. In that battle, the grammar school was the victim. In the next, the victim will be the university – the commanding height of British education. (Eric Robinson, 1968)

. . . I want to see a highly varied and differentiated system of higher education; but I also want each part of this system to attract its appropriate talent, and to have no sense of being a second or lower choice. I see no way of achieving this but to make higher education comprehensive. (Charles Carter, 1971)

I have very little doubt that by co-operation, consultation, and much more self-awareness on the part of institutions, the higher education system is growing towards a single but complex system. (Sheila Browne, Principal, Newnham College, Cambridge; *THES*, 11 April 1986)

The current topicality of the theme of merger is in no doubt whatever. It is somewhat more doubtful whether comprehensive higher education will win the day, if for no other reason than that native pragmatism makes the British unlikely consciously to adopt a 'system' of any kind. Nevertheless, it is still immensely beneficial for them (or indeed any people) to review developments in a foreign educational system. The study which forms the major focus of the present work concerns the German comprehensive universities, whose foundation and development has been elaborately planned, studied, researched and documented.

Before going any further, an attempt must be made to define the term 'comprehensive university'. A workable definition that holds good across cultures is obviously hard to find, but a number of general characteristics are relevant to our present purposes. First, a comprehensive university is inspired by an ideology of service to the community, manifested in socially and vocationally relevant curricula. As a corollary of this proposition, it is predominantly (but not exclusively) oriented towards applied, interdisciplinary courses and research. Secondly, a comprehensive university involves a system of multi-level co-ordinated courses. Transfer from one of these 'tracks' to another is possible, allowing the individual to find his or her level through upward or downward mobility within the same institution (or by arrangement with an associated one if a comprehensive national network exists). Every attempt is made to avoid the reproach levelled at most existing certificates and diplomas by Eric Robinson when he claimed that they were 'dead ends in that they are recognised as qualifications in themselves but not as leading to something further – in particular they are not conceived as leading to a degree' (1968:125). Thirdly, the comprehensive university is committed to widening educational access for less privileged social classes, regions and genders (and racial or religious groups, if these are relevant parameters). This does not necessarily imply an institution with a global policy of open admissions, like the British Open University or the City University of New York at a particular period in its history (Hermanns et al., 1983). It does, however, imply one with an admissions policy generally more liberal than the prevailing norm in its parent country. This is a relative criterion; because admissions policies differ from one educational system to another, no inflexible specification can be laid down in advance. The ethos of the institution is a democratic one which sets out to include and facilitate rather than to exclude and stigmatise; in admissions policy and course structure, it therefore seeks to maximise educational opportunity and draw out talent, in whatever sector of the population it may be discovered to exist.

−2−

The Classical University in Germany and the Need for Reform

A Cultural and Historical Background for the Comprehensive Universities

The foundation of the German comprehensive universities is one of the most remarkable, large-scale innovations in modern European higher education. These institutions were set up in a conscious attempt to remedy some of the serious defects which had emerged in the classical German university, and which had become the target of bitter criticism during the student revolt of the late 1960s.

The classical university reached its prime in the nineteenth century during which it underwent a process of reform and reaction. Eventually the latter prevailed and a type of structural organisation developed which tended, paradoxically, to pervert the realisation of the honourable ideals upon which the institution had originally been based. The vested interests of the professors unfortunately frustrated any impulses towards change, either from inside or outside the system. In the twentieth century, academics made a very poor showing when it came to resisting the rise of fascism and it is astonishing that, despite this fact, the near sclerosis which characterised the system lasted for almost two decades after the Second World War. The reform movement which resulted in the foundation of the comprehensive universities in the 1970s was a significant force for change, but owing to the remarkably powerful influence of the more traditional ethos, the newer values associated with the comprehensives never succeeded in ousting the old. Indeed, it would hardly be an exaggeration to claim that the values of the classical university still constitute a normative system to which many academics in Germany and elsewhere give their allegiance. They remain a vital point of reference for all innovation in German higher education and no discussion of reform is meaningful without an understanding of the philosophy upon which they are based. The objectives of the comprehensive universities can only be assessed and their importance appreciated by examining the ideology of the institutions to which they are a reaction.

The classical German university is often called 'Humboldtian', after Wilhelm von Humboldt (1767–1835). He was a Prussian nobleman and career diplomat who represented his country at the Congress of Vienna, and whose assignments included the posts of resident minister in Rome and envoy to Austria and London. He had intellectual gifts of the highest order, and published significant work on linguistics, education, political science, philosophy and the theory of history. It is as Director of Education and Instruction in the Prussian Ministry of the Interior that his legacy has been important for education. During this time, he played a major part in developing the ideas which underpinned the University of Berlin. Many of these ideas were not entirely new, having been pioneered at Halle and Göttingen, but they were consolidated and put into practice by the founders of Berlin; although initially linked with one particular institution, they eventually became a seminal power which has dominated German higher education into the twentieth century.

The aim of this chapter, therefore, is to highlight both the grandeur and the inherent negative potential of the principles upon which the Humboldtian university is based. Its importance as a conceptual framework for the discussion of any innovation in German higher education is emphasised by Böning and Roeloffs (1970:47), writing for the Organisation for Economic Co-operation and Development (OECD), who note that: 'It is one of the remarkable features of the national discussion on university reform that every proposal is advanced with the argument that it presented the only way to re-install and uphold the Humboldt ideal in the modern world.'

The Contribution of Halle and Göttingen to the Concept of the Classical University

The philosophy of the modern German university is usually assumed to have originated with the foundation of the University of Berlin (1810), but unquestioning acceptance of this proposition does insufficient justice to the innovatory contributions of Halle and Göttingen.

The Thirty Years War had greatly damaged universities as institutions; some were discredited because they appeared unprogressive and irrelevant; others had simply ceased to exist or clung precariously to life with a tiny number of students; at the beginning of the eighteenth century, Heidelberg, for example, had only 80 students, and 20 other universities had less than 300 (McClelland, 1980:28).

Halle and Göttingen were shining lights in the midst of this darkness and, for a time at least, very successful, but they did not act as catalysts in bringing about a reform of other universities; however, the torch which they had lit passed to Berlin in the early nineteenth century, by which time political circumstances had changed and become more propitious to general reform.

The University of Halle was set up in 1694. It was the first university in the modern sense of the word not only in Germany but in Europe, and had three distinctive features, all of which tended to encourage intellectual freedom and modernism. Firstly, it inherited the tradition of the old *Ritter-Akademie* (knights' academy), an institution which educated the sons of the aristocracy, training them for service in the army and government. As Paulsen (1908:112–16) points out, the decline of these institutions reflected historically conditioned changes in the social order. In the sixteenth century, the nobility and the bourgeoisie had frequented the same schools, but the Thirty Years War in the seventeenth destroyed the power of the bourgeoisie and opened a gap between the two social classes, whose members henceforth attended separate schools. The *Ritter-Akademie* taught modern languages (especially French), some Latin, mathematics, natural sciences, history, geography, politics, some law and some moral philosophy (ibid.:114–15). Stress was laid upon military skills and social graces. The curriculum was a broad one which promoted modern studies and a worldly orientation, thus contrasting with the narrowly circumscribed curriculum of the medieval university, geared to producing 'clerks'.

A second important tendency which soon emerged in Halle was its commitment to a pietistic theology. Robertson (1959) suggests that Pietism was a protest against the stiffening dogmatism of Protestant orthodoxy; it emphasised personal religious experience and exhibited a Puritan distrust of worldly pleasures; it also stressed an emotional, active commitment in which faith was even more important than works. The Pietists regarded simple Christian belief as a principle for renewal of life, which to them was much more important than dogmatic theology (Paulsen, 1908:104–5; 1919:499). Although Pietism later developed into a hard and fast system of penance, grace and rebirth (Cross, 1957), it at first promoted a practical, realistic outlook which was opposed to the pedantry and abstruse speculations of old-style academics and philosophers. The initial effect of Pietism was to encourage religious tolerance and a concern with personal spiritual development, and this became an important contributory element in the later elaboration of the ideology of *Bildung* (the German concept of education).

A third characteristic of the University of Halle which contributed to the German university ideology was the fact that it championed freedom of thought against dogmatism. This constituted a vital contribution to a modern intellectual outlook. Halle owed its status as the stronghold of rationalism to Christian Wolff, who was called to the University in 1706 and lectured on a wide variety of subjects, including mathematics, physics and philosophy. He pioneered a new development in academic philosophy by upholding the principles of reason, and rejecting dogmatic theological authority. This was considered so revolutionary that he was made to leave Halle in 1723, on charges of atheism. He was driven out by his fellow professor, the pietistic Francke, who in 1702 had excluded the wife of Thomasius (also a Halle professor) from holy communion because he thought her clothing was too gaudy and luxurious. Francke regarded Wolff's departure as the answer to his prayer to be delivered from 'the powers of darkness' (Paulsen, 1919:541) but, despite the machinations of his reactionary colleagues, Wolff won in the end. He worked in 'exile' at Marburg until 1740, but when Frederick the Great came to the throne, he was reinstated with honour at Halle. The validity of his rationalist principles was acknowledged, and theology henceforth took second place to them. Until then, the principle of an approved doctrine which the professors had pledged themselves to hand down in an unaltered form had prevailed at Protestant as well as at Roman Catholic universities (Paulsen, 1908). In Halle, however, Wolff's triumph ensured the victory of the principle of *libertas philosophandi*, which resulted in the university pioneering original scientific research and assuming a role of academic leadership based on free inquiry.

For a time, the various ingredients in the Halle ethos were a powerful stimulus to intellectual creativity but they were inherently incompatible. Although Pietism had begun as a reaction to excessive rigidity in the Protestant religious tradition, it eventually became over-rigid itself and entered into a relationship of tension with rationalism and with the worldly heritage of the *Ritter-Akademie*. These stresses led to quarrels and to the formation of various warring factions. The University became less popular and ceased to flourish as it had once done.

In 1737, another modern university was founded, partly to compete with Halle and partly in imitation of it. The House of Hanover was jealous of the Prussian king, in whose lands Halle was located, and chose Gerlach von Münchhausen to set up the University of Göttingen in its own territory. (McClelland (1980) describes the principles on which this institution was based.) The research ethic which developed at Halle was also cultivated in Göttingen. Scholarship was still valued for its own sake, but the need to cope with growing student numbers helped to forge a link between research and teaching which has since become characteristic of universities in Germany and in many other countries

Göttingen set out to provide an essentially liberal education, and did this by developing the role of the Faculty of Philosophy, which had become reduced to providing a kind of remedial education; it had undertaken the propaedeutic instruction (for example in theology, law or medicine) of students who wished to undertake further courses of study but whose existing skills and knowledge were insufficient. The Faculty's status was enhanced at Göttingen by upgrading the level of teaching, recruiting abler students, encouraging research and paying staff good salaries. Münchhausen saw to it that the history professor was paid almost as much as the law or theology professor, and this helped to secure recognition for history as an important and respectable discipline. The enhanced status of the philosophical faculty further contributed to developing the cult of 'personal' values which had already begun.

At Göttingen, considerable importance was attached to law, and this has continued to be the case in German universities right up to the present day. The type of law then taught was calculated to strengthen the nobles' belief in their rights as against those of the absolute princes. In terms of recruitment, this pedagogical policy paid off. In 1797, sixty-two per cent of the nobles in the University were studying law, which of course helped to enrich the institution and make it self-sufficient (McClelland, 1980:47). Theology was de-emphasised so as to avoid the religious disputes which had recently shaken Halle.

The fact that Göttingen was attractive to the nobility made it, in turn, attractive to the new upwardly mobile middle classes. Almost ruined in the Thirty Years War, the bourgeoisie was able to use education, now an important source of prestige, to assert its claims to high status. Universities such as Halle and Göttingen had a democratising influence in conferring prestige through education, even if this applied only to a small élite. As McClelland (ibid.:95) puts it: 'Göttingen forged a new kind of education that was able to bend the edges of *Stand* [class] limits and prepare the way for a new stratum in German society'.

Looking at developments in Halle and Göttingen, we thus see that certain ideas and principles had already gained currency before the foundation of the University of Berlin: modern studies, intellectual tolerance, rationalism, a research ethic and a commitment to liberal, personal education; in addition, the Faculty of Philosophy had begun to assume a prominence which became even more pronounced later on.

The Foundation of the University of Berlin

The influence of the new leaven upon the rest of the dough was minimal, since new ideas were, it seemed, difficult to introduce into existing institutions. Most of the universities were unresponsive to the new trends and remained stuck in that lethargy and dogmatism which made their very survival questionable. Lilge (1948:2) points out that absolutist governments regarded universities as territorial possessions and expected them to enhance state and dynastic prestige by training an efficient civil service and contributing to the practical development of military and industrial enterprises. These expectations, however, continued to be disappointed, and many people believed the universities antiquated and beyond reform.

Student discipline was erratic. Wilhelm von Humboldt was unimpressed with the quality of university teaching, and to illustrate his criticism, he gives the following account of a lecture by a Marburg professor named Selchow:

> His lecture displeased me altogether. A singsong, clipped tone; total reliance on notes; flat, un-German, ridiculous expressions, . . . stiff 'professorial' jokes . . . endless quotations of pages and paragraphs in such prodigious quantities that no student could possibly have money to purchase all the books nor the time to read them . . . The students, whom I observed closely . . . behaved themselves better than the Frankfurt ones usually do – at least they did not keep their hats on . . . Otherwise they spoke very loudly, laughed, threw written jokes to each other and played pranks of all sorts. There was also a big dog in the hall, who trundled round as he pleased, scratched and made all sorts of noises. (Ellwein, 1985:111)

In 1806 the Prussian minister von Massow called the universities 'anomalous institutions' which the state would do well to replace by separate professional schools. The year in which von Massow attacked the universities was also the year in which Napoleon destroyed the Prussian army at Jena and Auerstadt, with dramatic and momentous consequences for the Prussian state. The Peace of Tilsit, concluded in 1807, deprived Prussia of all its territories west of the Elbe, thus almost halving its former size (Thomas, 1973). Its political organisation was left in almost total disarray; its coffers were drained by the heavy reparations which it had to pay to the victorious French; it lost Halle, its best university, and was left with

Königsberg and Frankfurt-an-der-Oder.

Clearly, the circumstances were most unpropitious for the foundation of a new university. However, Wilhelm von Humboldt sought to cheer the King, Frederick William III, by suggesting that it was morally praiseworthy and politically astute for any individual or state hit by adversity to perform an altruistic act which would contribute to a brighter future (Vossler, 1954:259). It was in this spirit that the decision was made to proceed with the foundation of a university at Berlin, partly to meet the state's educational needs and partly to help restore Prussian self-confidence.

The King agreed that the palace of Frederick the Great's brother, Prince Henry, on Unter den Linden, should be the house of the new institution (Sweet, 1980:58). It opened on 15 October 1810, with a very distinguished professoriate. Humboldt insisted on appointing the best intellects available, believing this to be the key to success. The professorial staff included J.G. Fichte (philosophy), F.K. Savigny (law), F.E.D. Schleiermacher (theology/philosophy) and F.A. Wolf (classical philology) (Fallon, 1980:21). The principle of choosing the best possible men, and the equally important principle of *libertas philosophandi* were personally emphasised by Humboldt in his *Organisationsplan* (1809/10:380) for the University. Beyme, the head of the cabinet, wished to deny the institution the title of 'university' because, apart from Halle and Göttingen, universities then stood low in public esteem. In was Humboldt himself who insisted on the name 'university', believing that this would be most widely understood and most effective in attracting students from all over Germany to study at Berlin. The shortcomings of traditional universities were not, however, intended to return with the old name.

So far as the curriculum was concerned, Berlin did not have to be as creative and as consciously attractive to a certain clientele as Göttingen. By 1810, so many universities had closed or failed that there was less competition to attract students; it was therefore unnecessary for the founders of Berlin to go to an inordinate amount of trouble to give their course offerings appeal. In fact, McClelland (1980: 139) suggests that they did not evolve nearly such a clear set of priorities as the founders of Göttingen.

When one considers that the concept of the 'Humboldtian' university has resonated in Europe and the United States for over a century and a half, it is curious to reflect that Humboldt held his post as Privy Councillor in charge of culture and education for a period of only sixteen months (20 February 1809 to 14 June 1810), and withdrew from his duties five months before the University of Berlin opened. Fallon (1980:13–14) points out that Humboldt spent far less time and effort in setting up the new University than certain other persons, but suggests that like Washington in America, he enjoyed unquestioned authority, and 'imposed a unity of purpose that compelled a successful outcome'. Nevertheless, the eponymous use of the term 'Humboldtian' for 'classical' university ideology is not entirely justified by the facts, because other thinkers such as Fichte, Schleiermacher, Schelling, Steffens, Schiller, Kant and Hegel also contributed to the development of the German university concept. The men behind the founding of Berlin were philosophers who saw the University in philosophical terms; the analysis which follows takes due account of their intellectual contributions as well as those of Humboldt.

The Ideology of the Classical German University

The 'French' Enlightenment and German Kultur   Prussia was under French domination when the University of Berlin was founded. Napoleon, the Conqueror, was no friend of universities; in 1802 he had turned those in France into technical colleges, to provide him with the specialists which he needed for his future projects. Vossler (1954:261) points out that, at the time and from Napoleon's perspective, it must have appeared *reasonable* to abolish such apparently old-fashioned, cumbersome and inefficient organisations and re-place them with modern, professional colleges which would produce the necessary doctors, scientists, architects and so forth. 'Rationalism', states Vossler (ibid.), was 'hostile to the universities'. The crudely utilitarian spirit which had made Napoleon ride roughshod over the French universities shocked the Prussians. To some extent, they defined the ethos of their new university in opposition to things French, for France was not simply the military victor; it was also, in many ways, an ideological opponent.

The German intellectual ethos ran contrary to that of the Enlightenment which emphasised belief in the perfectability of man and of the world (Snyder, 1955). The Enlightenment regarded science as a new gospel, as a way of unlocking the secrets of the universe. Reason was the arbiter of all things and a surer guide than the religious authority accepted in the Middle Ages. The rationalists rejected this authority and turned more and more to the secularisation of knowledge (ibid.:8). The door to understanding was mathematics, reason and logic. Supernaturalism was regarded as an obstacle in the path of tolerance, freedom and scientific discovery. The spirit of the age was utilitarian and practical. That which was useful was good, and human beings were expected to promote their own happiness and welfare on earth. Reason was the major source of knowledge, superior to and independent of sense perceptions and opposed to sensationalism (ibid.:9).

The Germans had their own version of rationalism (in vogue for example at Halle), but they reacted against the Enlightenment for a number of reasons. For one thing, it was associated with the egalitarianism which had helped to bring about the French Revolution. At first, under the influence of the *philosophes*, many liberally minded Germans had welcomed the Revolution as the harbinger of a new freedom for mankind; later, however, they were appalled by the violence and excesses of the Terror and whipped into anti-French feeling by Prussia's defeat at Jena. The egalitarianism of the Revolution came to be regarded as destructive and subversive rather than as a potential force for freedom. In Germany, the divisions between classes were far more marked than in either France or England – in part a legacy from medieval times, when the various Estates were sharply distinguished from each other. This was still the case at the beginning of the eighteenth century and the legal distinctions between *Fürsten, Grafen, Herren, Reichsritter, Reichsstädter* and *Reichsbauern* were jealously maintained till the end of the Reich in 1806 (Bruford, 1935:47). In 1777, the Prussian Minister of Education, von Zedlitz, had issued a paper on patriotic education in which he emphasised the differences between the Estates. Farmers, for example, were born to obey and owed the state manual labour (Ellwein, 1985:118).

The German bourgeoisie remained weak and divided, failing to develop a distinctive class consciousness. Especially after the failure of the 1848 Revolution, the richer bourgeois aped the values of the landed gentry and aspired (with considerable success) to join that class by purchasing land or by intermarriage (Sagarra, 1980:30). In such a hierarchical, status-ridden society, the egalitarian ideals of the Enlightenment would plainly have difficulty in gaining widespread support.

Whereas the French emphasised the brotherhood of man (*fraternité*), the Germans had a much less socialised concept of man, which is reflected even in the cultural connotations of certain abstract concepts. Discussing the philosophy of Kant, Dewey (1915) contrasts the German concept of 'duty' with the French concept of 'rights'. For the French, rights are negotiable, reciprocal and social; they can be discussed and measured; they admit of compromise and adjustment. The German concept of duty, however, lacks the reciprocal element, because command is ranged on one side and obedience on the other; it is not negotiable and thus lends itself more easily to absolutism and fanaticism. Invoking the philosophical terminology of Kant, Dewey (ibid.:90) claims that '. . . . the cat-egorical imperative calls up the drill sergeant'. He admits that 'trafficking ethics' (the negotiable aspect of rights) may not be the noblest morality but shows that it is socially responsible as far as it goes. An ethical theory which allows for practical motives, as does the French concept of rights, is more conducive to a healthy political culture, and may help to explain why the French bourgeoisie suc-ceeded while the German one failed.

Many of the utilitarian aspects of the Enlightenment were un-popular in Germany, and indeed the Universities of Halle and Göttingen were severely criticised for being excessively utilitarian in ethos and general outlook. It was felt that many French and English intellectuals, from the seventeenth century onwards, saw science and learning almost solely in terms of technical progress and control of the environment. In Germany, this seemed a vulgar attitude towards knowledge and was at odds with the German mentality, which valued spiritual 'depth' (Ringer, 1969:84–5). The German version of the Enlightenment was much less empirical and utili-tarian than the Anglo-French version and there was always an underlying sense that the Enlightenment was a West European phenomenon which did not truly 'belong' to the German intellectual and cultural tradition (ibid.).

The emerging national and class consciousness of educated German society defined itself by contrasting its own ideas of *Kultur* with the French cult of *civilisation*. *Kultur* is the cultivation of wisdom and spirituality; in a more general sense, it has been used to denote all of man's civilised achievements in society (cf. Ringer, 1969:87–90). The *Kultur/civilisation* distinction had already been made by Kant in 1784, when he identified civilisation with social etiquette, worldly knowledge, manners and polish, and culture with art, learning and morality. Many Germans had come to resent French influence not only in political culture abroad, but in social life at home where French was the language of the German courts and of sophisticated, civilised living. They reinforced their nascent sense of national identity by contrasting their own *Kultur* (profound, significant and attractive), with the French *civilisation* (external and superficial). German national consciousness had a general tendency to define itself by resisting and criticising French culture. Ringer (1969:89) writes as follows about this phenomenon: 'The Germans finding it difficult and yet desirable to define themselves as a nation, tended to see uniquely German characteristics in their preference of culture over civilisation.'

The utilitarianism of the Enlightenment implied a need for useful knowledge, hence an emphasis upon vocational education. The founders of the new University of Berlin, however, made a distinction between *Berufsausbildung* (education for a career) and *Berufsvorbildung* (education preparatory to a career). The former was vocational-utilitarian. It was only the latter which was compatible with the aims of the new University which had no vocational ambitions, but sought instead to embody modern scholarship in all its purity (Schelsky, 1963:53). This was memorably and neatly epitomised by Schiller in his inaugural lecture for his Chair at Jena (1789), when he distinguished the *philosophischer Kopf* ('philosophical mind') from the *Brotgelehrter* ('bread and butter' scholar); ever since, the term *Brotgelehrter* has been used to express contempt for an *ad hoc* approach to study. Fichte took anti-utilitarianism so far that he wished to exclude from the University of Berlin the traditional faculties of law, medicine and theology, retaining only the faculty of philosophy (preferably to teach his own philosophy!). The university's role was the spiritualisation (*Vergeistigung*) of the world with the professors acting as the high priests of culture and education.

Humboldt's personal reactions to the ideas of the 'French' Enlightenment were somewhat ambiguous. In some ways, he was quite democratically inclined; planning the humanistic *Gymnasium*, for example, he stressed that schools should cater for the whole community, and sought to obliterate the notion that children from different social classes ought to be educated differently (Sweet, 1980:48). By his emphasis upon human individuality, however, he distanced himself from the social ideals of the Enlightenment. He called for the education of the whole personality and saw the essence of man in individualism, which should be developed for its own sake. This concept of education had little to say about social responsibility and indeed ignored the need to earn one's living. In its assumption that an adult who sought to cultivate his individual potential already disposed of a secure financial basis to his existence, it was at odds with contemporary values. Only the landed gentry could afford to disregard the materially useful aspects of education – a disregard which became increasingly hard to maintain as time went on. Once education had ceased to be the prerogative of a certain social stratum, denial of its utilitarian implications became increasingly an anachronism. Humboldt distinguished clearly between general education and vocational training and, in his desire to subordinate the latter to the former, went against the utilitarian spirit of the age. Thus Siebert (1967:34–5) states: 'The Enlightenment, the incipient industrialisation and the commercial State threatened the harmony of introverted contemplative men. His [Humboldt's] struggle for the totality of man for its own sake is a struggle against the demands of the time'.

The effects of emphasising *Kultur* in German higher education were therefore complex. It tended to promote anti-French, pro-German nationalistic feelings; it intensified the anti-vocational bias of the university and it gave the professors added charisma and mystique. This raised both the universities and the professors in the public esteem but also helped to isolate them from a broad stratum of society. *Kultur* came to be regarded as something rare and difficult to attain, well beyond the reach of ordinary people.

Although many features of Enlightenment thought might possibly be criticised as somewhat simplistic, superficial or vulgar, the move-ment still represented progress towards a more open society; it emphasised tolerance, brotherhood, happiness and security of the individual, and freedom of thought; it was a vital force in the development of a liberal democratic social order. The Germans, however, had not achieved national unity and were still a prey to *Kleinstaaterei* ('small statism'). They were extremely critical of the French, but their very criticism betokened envy and attraction as well as repugnance. Goethe was continually comparing his own country unfavourably with France, envying the French the cultural context that gave even young writers the support of an intellectual and artistic tradition (Bruford, 1935:292). This was only possible, however, in a country which had achieved a high degree of unity and developed a great urban centre such as Paris. Germany was still a collection of petty states, with no immediate prospect of becoming anything else in the foreseeable future, and the Germans were still unable to open themselves as a nation to liberalising and democ-ratising influences. Snyder (1955:15) believes that in Germany, Russia and the Near East the 'socio-political order was not changed essentially by the intellectual trends of the Age of Reason', and claims that the tendency in those countries was 'towards a politically vague universalism' and 'an authoritarian uniformity of State and faith'. He associates this with the East rather than the West and with a closed rather than an open society, which relegates the individual to the position of a lackey of the state.

By their ambivalent attitude towards the Enlightenment, German intellectuals set themselves apart from France, which was in 1810 promoting utilitarian values in higher education, and also cut them-selves off from certain forces making for a free and open society. They concentrated instead upon developing neo-humanism and idealism, which have their own beauty and inspirational power, but which were not conducive to a social view of man nor, as it turned out, to democratic values in education and in society at large.

Neo-Humanism   In 1809 the philosopher Hegel, then headmaster of a grammar school in Nüremberg, spoke on the aim and value of teaching the classical languages, in the following terms: '. . . I do not think I am staking too high a claim when I say he who has not known the works of the ancients has lived without knowing beauty' (Scott, 1960:4–5). Men like Hegel, Winckelmann, Lessing, Herder, Schiller, Goethe and Humboldt turned back to classical antiquity, and held up the civilisation of ancient Greece as the model of all that was finest and noblest in human development. A special spiritual relationship was believed to exist between Germany and Greece, not so much in the domain of political and military achievement, as in the ideal world of philosophy and science, literature and art (Paulsen, 1908:162–3). Goethe and Schiller both produced plays and poetry in the classical neo-humanist idiom. The Hellenic world seemed to embody a new religion which idealised humanity in place of the Deity, and contrasted with the Christian striving for transcendence. It also acted as a counterweight to the pre-eminence of French culture. The Greeks, not the Romans or the French, were Germany's true and natural inspiration. As Paulsen (ibid.:164) points out: 'The newly-awakened self-consciousness of the German nation appealed from the French and their pseudo-classicism to the Old Greeks as the true classics, as western civilisation. The rising [middle] classes now also found allies and supporters in the Greeks in their antagonism to the French courtly culture and education of the German nobility'.

Wilhelm von Humboldt was convinced that the study of classical Greek language and literature should be the major civilising and humanising influence for modern German youth. Neo-humanism emphasised individual human development and inner growth; it contributed in a major way to the German concepts of *Bildung* and *Kultur* which are so central to the Germanic educational ideology. It also tended to promote a dedication to the pursuit of 'pure' rather than applied knowledge, because the Greeks regarded technological matters as a concern more appropriate for slaves and foreigners than for free citizens (Förmer, 1987:4). Humboldt's idea of self-mastery derived from the Greeks and he also followed them in believing that states of mind are valuable in themselves as ends rather than means. He spoke of the need to look at the world as a 'spectacle rather than as a concern in which one must actively intervene' and regarded a human being's actions as 'only important for one's private view of things and private evaluation of them' (Bruford, 1975:23). This did not prevent him from becoming a statesman who, as Sweet (1980) has pointed out, had a strong urge to power. But in the midst of military and political turmoil, he still believed that one must 'have a world of one's own within, over which the waves of life roll on, while it quietly grows unseen' (Bruford, 1975:23). This is very much in keeping with Winckelmann's neo-humanist concept of *edle Einfalt und stille Grösse* ('noble simplicity and serene greatness') – grandeur of soul is best seen in the condition of repose.

The neo-humanists believed that great heights of human perfection had been achieved in classical antiquity, and some of them felt that those heights could never be reached again. This amounted to cultural pessimism, condemning the Germans forever to inadequate emulation of the Greeks. Schiller, however, saw three phases in human evolution: (1) Greek antiquity which represented a kind of perfection – but an elementary kind; (2) our own times, characterised by an analytical spirit which is clear but limited and one-sided; (3) a future stage in which perfection will be reached on a higher plane than in classical antiquity (Leroux, 1932:416). Humboldt agreed with Schiller that there had been a quite exceptional cultural florescence in classical times and that modern times seemed almost decadent by comparison, but he did not altogether go along with Schiller's theory of cultural evolution. He believed, rather, that mankind accomplishes ever more complete syntheses as the generations succeed one another, because it builds upon what each of them has achieved (ibid.:418).

Despite the work of sophisticated thinkers like Schiller and Humboldt, the tendency of neo-humanism was to condemn Germany to a position of cultural inferiority. The movement involved narrow concentration upon one particular brand of knowledge and an intense idealisation of classical Greece, which ignored certain aspects of historical reality. Lilge (1948:30) asserts that: '. . . this idealization was largely a historical projection of the humanists' own high esteem of the value of human individuality'. Certainly, the folly of idealising Greece was exposed by the researches of scholars such as Böckh (1817) who worked on the empirical reconstruction of antiquity. There was something spurious and artificial about the German evocation of ancient Greece, even in such great and supposedly 'classical' writers as Goethe. The philosopher Santayana (1916) sees in German literary classicism merely an attempt to recover a dead past in order to sentimentalise over its remoteness, its beauty, and its ruins. He remarks that, in *Faust*, after the Greek Helen has evaporated, the hero revisits his native mountains and reverts to thoughts of the German Gretchen. This, Santayana be-

lieves, is a wise homecoming because the craze for classicism sym-
bolised by Helen alienated the mind from real life and led only to
hopeless imitations and languid poses (ibid.:35). Politically, one
adverse effect of idealising the past in this way was to point up a
negative contrast between ancient Greece and modern Germany, thus
devaluing the present and decreasing any desire which the individual might have to respect, improve and make the most of it.

The strong stress on human individuality had its negative side
too. The social dimension of Ancient Greece, as exemplified by the
polis, had been highly important, but the Germans omitted this
social element in their imaginative reconstruction of the past and
concentrated solely on aesthetics instead. This unsocial and unreal
aspect of neo-humanism has been highlighted by E.M. Butler in her
book, *The Tyranny of Greece over Germany* (1935). She shows that the
ideal 'Hellas' of the German classical writers had very little in
common with either ancient or modern Greece. Because none of the
classicists ever actually visited Greece, they were all the more prone
to make it fit in with their preconceived notions. The German
classical movement gazed dreamily into the past, conjured up an
illusory vision of Greece, and thus failed to recognise the power
innate in even the noblest ideas to wreak havoc in real life. The dark
background which gave rise to the tragic element in Greek poetry
was resolutely ignored and eliminated from the idealised concept of
a golden age of Greece. The Germans, argues Butler, were so
tragically dissatisfied with themselves that for far too long they
idolised an alien Olympian ideal which distorted their natural
'genius': 'If the Greeks are tyrants', she writes, 'the Germans are
pre-destined slaves' (ibid.:6). It was perhaps because she attributed
servility to the *Herrenvolk* ('master race') that Butler's book was
banned by the Nazis shortly after its publication in 1935.

The adulation of humanism has also been criticised by Weinstock
(1956) on both political and educational grounds. The very notion
that there can be a *ne plus ultra* of cultural development implies a
belief in the perfectability of man, but belief in cultural perfection –
past, present or future – is politically unsound because it does not
take sufficient account of the existence of evil. Any belief in the
possibility of a flawless humanity involves a grave degree of self-
deception which Weinstock regards as a kind of intellectual 'original
sin'. He believes that *Schwärmerei* (crazy enthusiasm) for any
cultural or political idea has always been historically disastrous and
that humanistic socialism can free itself from self-deception only by
acknowledging the truth that mankind is fallible and fragile. Only
what Weinstock calls a 'broken' humanism is adequate to the

demands of real life and real politics. If the Germans are to cease alternately glorifying and damning power, then they must renounce *Schwärmerei*, in favour of a consciousness of human fallibility. Although this realism can and should be promoted in the educational system, the curriculum has often been quite inappropriate for such a purpose. After 1918, young people should have been made to engage with political themes and should have been taught about decay and periods of catastrophe rather than dazzled by studying brilliant cultural high periods (*Hoch-Zeiten*) (ibid.:327). Weinstock argues convincingly that most Germans never learned about the real Greece, and indeed that Greece could never have been truly apprehended by a people who cherished ideals of self-glorification and harboured a naive belief in the coming empire of reason. *Realpolitik* and sound educational principles demand a consciousness of the fragility of everything human.

Neo-humanism, then, by its idealisation of the past tends to draw men's forces away from active involvement with the present. By creating a vision of classical antiquity which omits the social, neo-humanism makes it difficult for people to associate freedom of the spirit with freedom of society at large. It thus fails in a major way to contribute to the development of liberal democracy in the body politic of contemporary Germany and in the realm of higher education.

Idealism Since the middle ages, the Germanies had been divided into a multiplicity of political units, contrasting with the relative cohesion of France and Britain, and leading reflective Germans to the rueful observation that 'elsewhere links of language and culture had become the keystones of the most successful political societies yet evolved' (Balfour, 1982:21). The French Revolution fanned the flames of nationalism to white heat in Germany, making the Germans still more painfully conscious of their lack of unity. Frustrated nationalism had an important bearing on the foundation and development of the University of Berlin which, it was hoped, would contribute to the national reconstruction of Prussia after its humiliating defeat by Napoleon. This sentiment was echoed by no less a person than King Frederick William III, when he said that the country must regain in the spiritual domain what it had lost in the material. The very titles of the papers written by the early exponents of the ideology of the classical German university reflect this nationalistic orientation clearly. Thus, Fichte's *Reden an die deutsche Nation* ('Speeches to the German Nation'), Schleiermacher's *Gelegentliche Gedanken über Universitäten im deutschen Sinn* ('Occasional

Thoughts on Universities in the German Spirit'), and Schelling's *Über das Wesen deutscher Wissenschaft* ('On the Nature of German Scholarship') were unashamedly nationalistic in spirit.

Yet the nationalist aspirations of Germany were doomed to frustration for several decades to come, and the genesis of the modern German university was therefore marred to a certain extent by a disparity between the ideal and the real. The foundation and development of the University of Berlin was intended to compensate in some measure for the unsatisfactory character of contemporary political reality. There is irony in the fact that, although it was hoped that the University would be an ornament to the Prussian State (this was its covert *raison d'être*), the philosophical orientation of the new institution was apolitical. The lack of German unity tended to encourage escapist tendencies in intellectual life, with consequent tension between the nationalistic leanings of the University of Berlin and its philosophical underpinnings, as manifested, for example, in neo-humanism and idealism. As Lewis (1954:122) puts it: 'All impulses to reform and emancipation were deflected into spiritual channels, so that . . . the great German thinkers leave the world of politics alone and adventure in the world of the intellect. Liberty is realised religiously, artistically, and philosophically, not politically.'

German idealist thought differs from the empirical tradition in believing that essential reality resides in the mind or the spirit (*Geist*). There are many different variants of idealism. Fichte, for example, regarded the material world as illusory and carried a priori approaches so far that he believed it possible to write history without empirical data, and fell a victim to solipsism. However, the most important proponent of idealistic philosophy around the period when the University of Berlin was founded was Immanuel Kant, whose writings profoundly influenced Humboldt, although he had to struggle to understand them.

Kant's philosophy questioned the common-sense view of experience by distinguishing between the noumenal and the phenomenal; noumena are things-in-themselves which cannot be known in practice or in principle, about which we can only speculate, but which are of fundamental importance; phenomena are things as they appear in perception and are interpreted in reflection. Kant insists that we can know only phenomena, not things-in-themselves, implying by this philosophically pessimistic doctrine that true reality must remain forever inaccessible to us. Even science cannot reach things-in-themselves, since it is limited to the world of space, time and causal necessity.

It is by delimiting the domain of reason that Kant makes room for faith. He argues that there are different 'ways of knowing' and that scientific reason relies on special modes of thinking, which are valid for handling scientific data, but not for investigating a moral or religious problems: 'Scientific thought cannot expect to find God, or freedom or anything belonging to the spiritual life of man' (Lewis, 1954:125). Science and morality each have their separate areas of jurisdiction which do not compete with each other and this dichotomy has led the American educationalist, John Dewey (1915:23, 27), to claim that Kant had helped create the 'two worlds' of German philosophy – a duality which Hitler regarded as debilitating for the German people, and which he set out consciously to overcome through totalitarianism.

So far as duty or moral obligation is concerned, Kant's supreme guiding principle takes the form of the categorical imperative: 'Act only on that maxim through which you can at the same time will that it should become a universal law'. He also insists that one must treat both oneself and others as ends, not *just* as means. These commands are not mere moral maxims; they have just the same commanding force for individuals as the facts of nature, and are known to the higher, rational self which then imposes them upon the lower self. Kant places great emphasis upon the intentionality of the doer in his moral actions and believes that an action prompted by the *intention* of doing what is right retains its value as a moral action, even if it turns out badly as a result of some unhappy chance beyond the agent's control (ibid.:12). An action derives its moral value, therefore, not from its results but from the type of action which the doer intended or hoped to bring about; thus man is (reassuringly) protected by an indwelling pure practical reason expressing itself in conscience.

However, the isolation of the ideal from the empirical and the elevation of the moral to the level of a categorical imperative had potentially pernicious consequences for the development of German thought. Human beings' apperception of the categorical imperative is inevitably filtered by human frailty, and can only be subjective in nature, most especially since it is expected that man should draw his moral precepts out of his own will and not from any external source; the categorical imperative itself, however, is an a priori conception, not open to disconfirming evidence; since the categorical command exists in the high and holy realm of morality, it is also absolute. Putting those three elements together ('subjective', 'a priori' and 'absolute'), it is clear that they constitute a basis for the greatest possible self-sacrifice; the individual may be obliged to follow the dictates of his conscience against all self-interest, in order to comply with the highest possible dictates of morality. His moral intuitions may also, however, become so seriously misguided that they may be sincerely but blindly directed towards unworthy ends. This provides a basis for fanaticism, and Santayana (1916:50) actually argues that Kant's moral doctrine is in principle a perfect frame for fanaticism:

> Give back, as time was bound to give back, a little flesh to [the] skeleton of duty, make it the voice not of a remote Mosaic decalogue, but of a rich temperament and a young life, and you will have sanctified beforehand every stubborn passion and every romantic crime. In the guise of an infallible conscience, before which nothing has a right to stand, egotism is launched upon its irresponsible career . . . If today you are right in obeying your private conscience against all considerations of prudence or kindness (though you are prudent and kind by nature, so that this loyalty to a ruthless duty is a sacrifice for you), tomorrow you may be right in obeying the categorical imperative of your soul in another phase, and to carry out no matter what irresponsible enterprise, though your heart may bleed at the victims you are making. The principle of fanaticism is present in either case . . .

Many scholars have thought it justifiable to implicate idealist German philosophy in the collapse of the universities during the era of national socialism, and indeed in the failure of German society as a whole to resist dictatorship. It is interesting to note that Wilhelm von Humboldt was personally opposed to the neglect of empirical philosophy, which he called *sträflich* ('culpable') (Kaehler, 1953:8). There is, however, nothing intrinsically evil in idealist philosophy; nevertheless, historical circumstances have made cultural idealism a philosophical substitute for effective political action; at a time when German national unity could not be achieved, it tended to divert the Germans from confronting and engaging with contemporary political reality.

In education, the influence of idealist philosophy has been at least partially responsible for a tendency to undervalue practical work at both school and university. Thus, science teaching in German schools does not involve nearly so much clinical and experimental laboratory work as in the United Kingdom. Similarly, courses in medicine and education include much less hospital and school experience than in the UK. This, of course, is partially a function of finance, but since resource allocation is always based on a prior value judgement, it can be argued that lack of money for school laboratory experiments or for supervision of university teaching practice placements is an indication that the education authorities do not attach great importance to these activities. The German tendency to value the idealist tradition far above the empirical tradition is highlighted by Friedrich Schlegel's remark in the 1790s, that Fichte's *Wissenschaftslehre*, Goethe's novel *Wilhelm Meister* and the French Revolution were the most significant influences of his age. How typically German, remarks Sell (1953:136), that idealist philosophy and a book about the harmonious development of the individual are put on exactly the same footing as a political earthquake!

Bildung　The cult of *Bildung* became current during the last third of the eighteenth century; it was highly fashionable by about 1800, but was hardly found in German intellectual life fifty years earlier (Weil, 1967:2). *Bildung* implies the forming of the inner self by the cultural and educational environment; Humboldt attributes to *Bildung* a teleological significance (Spranger, 1928:10), which helps to give purpose to life: 'The true aim of man – not any which is suggested by changing preference but that which is prescribed by forever unchangeable reason – is the highest and best proportional development of all his capacities in order to form a wholeness of himself' (Cowan, 1963:142).

Bildung is something which we undertake for ourselves in a ceaseless attempt at self-improvement. In the process of refining ourselves and intensifying our morality, we are aided by our fellow humans and by the changing circumstances of life. In this connection, Humboldt emphasises that if an individual is to pursue *Bildung* successfully, he must be free to expose himself to a rich variety of situations (ibid.:142–3). Travel, for example, is important in furthering our skill at adapting ourselves to many different circumstances and enabling us to encounter many different types of human being (ibid.:126–7). Education is about the improving of our inner selves; it is a ceaseless turning over in the mind of the results of our experience; we must seek the widest possible experience of life and then try to understand it and distil it into wisdom (Bruford, 1975:24). In his own life, Humboldt hoped to achieve a kind of spirituality through *Bildung* by training his imagination to hold every event in life at a distance, abstracting its essence from its practical effect on him (ibid.:25). At the same time, he did not attempt to shut himself off from life, but tried rather to open himself to experience, and to refine it by exercising his rational and emotional faculties. In a letter to his wife he writes: 'He who can say to himself when he dies: "I have grasped and made into a part of my humanity as much of the world as I could", that man has reached

fulfilment . . . In the higher sense of the word, he has really lived'
(Sydow, 1906–16, vol. 2:262).

Humboldt's concept of *Bildung* is very much an individualistic
one, but he also believes that by attending to one's own education,
each individual benefits the whole community without specifically
intending to do so (Cowan, 1963:143). There is thus a relationship
between individualism and universality, in which the improvement
of the individual contributes to the general wellbeing of society
(Spranger, 1928:11, 14). *Bildung*, however, is not utilitarian; it
derives its value not from its final results but from the intentions and
the efforts of the person who is trying to achieve it. (Surely, there are
echoes of Kant's emphasis upon intentionality here; it will be
recalled that Kant thought the moral will behind an action more
important than the results achieved.) The German concept of *Bildung* stresses the importance of education as a means of forming
moral and independent human beings and this non-utilitarian orientation contrasts with the narrow, 'real', vocational orientation of
French institutions of higher learning at the time when the University of Berlin was being founded (Spranger, 1965:16). It is also, of
course, very much in sympathy with German idealist philosophy.

In literary and social terms, there are two major ways in which
German writers have tended to view *Bildung*: ethically, as the
cultivation of existing moral attributes; and aesthetically, as the
forming of an image or picture. The ethical dimension, which we
shall call the 'cultivation syndrome', is related to inner life and owes
much to Protestantism, which encouraged introspection and led to a
preoccupation with the individual soul. The Protestants tried to
follow the Biblical precept: 'Be ye perfect, as thy heavenly Father is
perfect' and acknowledged no intermediary between man and God.
They turned in on themselves and observed their own emotional and
religious development in detail. Members of the bourgeoisie often
disapproved of the lifestyle of the courtly aristocracy on moral
grounds, but could not rival it even if they had wished to do so;
Bildung enabled them to compensate for their social inferiority by
emphasising spiritual distinction (Weil, 1967:52). The 'cultivation
syndrome' had certain democratising tendencies, which were reflected in a Rousseauesque analogy between the development of
human beings and the development of plants; a person does not
need to be an aristocrat to attain *Blüte* (a bourgeoning of the spirit).
It is significant that Herder in his book *Auch eine Geschichte zur
Philosophie der Menschheit* ('Towards a History of the Philosophy of
Humanity') takes the tree as a metaphor for historical development
(see Gillies, 1959), and Goethe uses the same metaphor in his work

Über die Metamorphosen der Pflanzen ('On the Metamorphoses of Plants'). These democratic and organic aspects of the 'cultivation syndrome' stress 'life' above 'form' – an emphasis which bore within itself the seeds of revolution. All that was 'mechanical' in society and in the human spirit was rejected in favour of 'natural' people, who were sometimes criminals or social outcasts (cf. Schiller's play *Die Räuber*). This helped to encourage the democratic stirrings of the bourgeoisie (Weil, 1967:190–1).

The notion of the blossoming of the human personality can be used to link the 'cultivation syndrome' in *Bildung* with what we shall call the 'picture syndrome'. The blossom symbolises the naturalistic aspect of *Bildung*, and also has an iconic force which connects it to the theme of the beautiful picture. Humboldt calls upon people to develop their character subtly, delicately and meaningfully *'as though it were a free-standing work of art'*[1] (Cowan, 1963:144). The idea of *Bildung* as the making of a portrait (or soulscape) derives from Lord Shaftesbury, whose life and philosophy influenced Goethe, Herder and Wieland (Weil, 1967:36). Shaftesbury was a political individualist and a critic of Locke's reductionist view of the soul as a series of mere impressions and impulses to be scientifically ordered. He developed the aesthetic personality principle of inward form, in which serenity and detachment were regarded as important characteristics of the English gentleman. The bourgeoisie had found *Bildung* a convenient way of asserting their claims to status, and so now did the nobility. The democratising trends in contemporary society made it hard for them to assert their distinction externally, and the aesthetic approach to the moulding of personality and character gave them a welcome opportunity to assert their superiority in cultural terms (ibid.:34–5).

Since the cult of *Bildung* ultimately suggested that salvation could be found through the operations of mind, both learning and the university came to be seen in a semi-religious light. This chimed well with the medieval origins of universities as institutions. *Bildung* acquired mystical overtones and the search for authentic, independent, moral values inspired the *Bildungsroman* – a distinctively German type of novel, of which *Wilhelm Meister* was a prime example. Its theme was a voyage of self-discovery. In some cases, this search took the form of a quest for a Saviour, and this 'Messianic' cult may have made German educated society more receptive to the notion of a leader or 'Great Man'.

---

1. My emphasis (RMOP).

Although *Bildung* is intrinsically a fine and indeed an admirable ideal, its weakness lies essentially in its unsocial and non-political nature. It is the educated German's refusal to sully himself with social reality, especially when that reality becomes ugly and threatening, which many observers have seen as a major cause of the universities' poor showing when Hitler came to power in the land. Academics felt safe from the threat and offered little active opposition until it was too late (Ringer, 1969:443). Many of them defined their position as one of inner emigration (*innere Emigration*) and sought a refuge in self-cultivation. Their indulgence in scholarship and inwardness (*Innerlichkeit*) prevented them from engaging with, and resisting, the dark new forces which were overwhelming their existence.

Given the political situation in Germany throughout most of the nineteenth century, it was understandable that *Bildung* should be non-political, because the German states were still politically separate. For both the individual and the community, *Bildung* provided a kind of compensation. It allowed those nobles who were fearful of losing their wealth and status to believe in their own spiritual distinction, and it also comforted members of the bourgeoisie who had brains but little money, and wanted to move up the social ladder. In addition, it held out the hope of unity on a higher, spiritual plane – a particularly attractive notion in the context of a divided Germany, suffering from frustrated nationalism.

However, the fact that *Bildung* remained essentially non-political has led many people to apportion it some of the blame for the universities' moral defeat in surrendering to Nazism. Thomas Mann's life shows clearly how inadequate and inappropriate *Bildung* had become, as an ideology for the man of principle in the twentieth century. In 1936, Mann's name was deleted from the list of honorary doctors of the University of Bonn. Bruford (1975) traces the changes in the author's outlook and philosophy of life which brought him to that point.

In 1923 Mann had given a lecture to a group of republican students in Munich, in which he dealt with the general question of political involvement and the failure of the middle classes to support the Weimar Republic. He said:

> The finest characteristic of the typical German, the best known and also the most flattering to his self-esteem, is his inwardness. It is no accident that it was the Germans who gave to the world the intellectually stimulating and very humane literary form which we call the novel of personal cultivation and development. . . . The inwardness, the culture [*Bildung*] of a German implies introspectiveness; an individualistic cultural con-

science; consideration for the careful tending, the shaping, deepening and perfecting of one's personality or, in religious terms, for the salvation and justification of one's own life; subjectivism in the things of the mind, therefore, a type of culture that might be called pietistic, given to autobiographical confession and deeply personal, one in which the world of the *objective*, the political world is felt to be profane and is thrust aside with indifference, 'because' as Luther says, 'this external order is of no consequence'. What I mean by all this is that the idea of a republic meets with resistance in Germany chiefly because the ordinary middle-class man here, if he ever thought about culture, never considered politics to be part of it, and still does not do so today. To ask him to transfer his allegiance from inwardness to the objective, to politics, to what the peoples of Europe call *freedom*, would seem to him to amount to a demand that he should do violence to his own nature, and in fact give up his sense of national identity. (Bruford, 1975:vii)

Later, however, in the novel *The Magic Mountain*, Mann makes Clawdia Chauchat castigate the young hero, Hans Castorp, for his commitment to *Bildung* which she sees as typically German and highly dubious: 'It is well-known that you [Germans] live for the sake of experience – and not "for the sake of life". Self-enrichment is what you are out for. C'est ça, you [yourself] do not seem to realize that that is revolting egotism, and that one day you [Germans] will be revealed as enemies of humanity' (Mann, 1927:778). This suggests that the German preoccupation with *Bildung* may well prove catastrophic for the world if it remains self-regarding and uncommitted, causing the individual to neglect his social ties with his immediate environment and the wider world.

By 1933, Mann had come to believe in socialism and was convinced that thinking middle-class people should now side with the workers and social democracy. In a written address intended for delivery at a meeting of a socialist society in Berlin (but never actually delivered because Hitler became Chancellor shortly before the meeting was due to take place), we find the following declaration:

> ... I feel deeply how dishonest and life-repressing it is to look down scornfully on the political and social sphere and to consider it of secondary importance compared with the world of the inward ... It is not admissible, in a world as anti-divine and bereft of reason as ours, to represent man's metaphysical, inward and religious activities as inherently superior to man's will to improve the world. The political and social is one aspect of the humane. (Bruford, 1975:254)

This conversion of a famous writer from being a non-political man to being a political one suggests a new, more socially conscious concept of *Bildung* and a new definition of each intellectual writer's responsibility.

'Solitary Freedom' and Inner Values   The cult of *Bildung* led to a pre-occupation with the inner rather than the outer world and helped to strengthen the German emphasis upon internal rather than external values. Political disunity and the lack of big city culture drove the German intellectual in upon himself. He pursued self-cultivation – but from the highest of motives. The German cult of *Innerlichkeit* is associated with the context in which the individual lived out his existence. Bruford (1935:304) remarks that *'Gemüt* is best cultivated in solitude, not in a courtly or urban society where "the proper study of mankind is man"'. Elsewhere he states that: 'The German writer . . . is satisfied if he understands himself; if others have difficulty in understanding him he is all the more convinced of the depth of his thought' (ibid.:302).

The emphasis upon inner values and the life of the mind was institutionalised at the University of Berlin in the concept of *Einsamkeit und Freiheit* ('solitary freedom'[2]) which has since become part of the German academic tradition. It is a concept which has over-tones of the attitudes which must have prevailed in a medieval monastery (Schelsky, 1963:107). At Berlin, however, it had a socio-political function which was clearly articulated by the founding fathers of the University.

Schleiermacher (1808:281–3, 301) argues that freedom is essential for the intellectual and personal development of young people who are struggling to form their character, find their aptitude and assert their independent existence – in short, to achieve maturity. He stresses that this freedom must include independence from their families and from the state, especially for those who are destined to assume leading roles in society, and to take responsibility for others. They cannot do this successfully if they simply pass from one form of obedience (to their parents, for example), to another (to future employers). In post-university life, they will probably exercise a formative influence on others, and they must therefore have freedom to 'form' themselves at university. They can pass successfully from obedience to influence only if they go through a period in which they are free from pressures, and have liberty in which to develop their own character. Academic freedom should operate to ensure the liberal expression of individual traits within the academic com-

2.   There are several ways of translating *Einsamkeit und Freiheit*. 'Loneliness and liberty' would be a mistranslation. It seems to the present writer to sound most natural in English if the first noun is converted into an epithet – 'solitary freedom'.

munity and, since it is an absolute necessity for the attainment of maturity, must always be protected even at the risk of being abused. It is essential too for the good of the nation, and Fichte (1807:217) looks to the academic body to help educate the German people to clarity of thought and freedom of spirit.

Fichte (ibid.:188–9) also develops the more political aspects of *Einsamkeit und Freiheit* by insisting that students must not be shackled by ties of family, class or party in their search for *Bildung und Kultur*, and must not be drawn into the triviality typical of much human socialising. They need to leave home in order to find their own level in society, and to become valued for what they themselves are worth. While attending university, they should be freed from all material cares, so that they can concentrate utterly upon their pursuit of learning. No one who is constantly tormented by money worries can be really independent, and Fichte (ibid.:192–3) therefore advocates grants, or partial grants for needy but intellectually gifted students. On leaving university, they should go to wherever they fit in best, not necessarily back to the place where they happen to have been born. The democratic implications of these arguments are obvious, since they reflect the assumption that *Bildung* can and will serve as an avenue of upward social mobility for those who are endowed with intellectual and spiritual rather than monetary riches. Yet the meritocratic vision of the young scholar finding his own level in society through education co-existed, paradoxically, with a scarcely veiled contempt on Fichte's part for the bourgeoisie.

Some of the founders of the University of Berlin were so conscious of the need to give the aspiring student a new start and free him from being bound by any narrow class or social interest group that they were reluctant to site the university in a large city. Large cities (*Großstädte*) were thought bad places to study in, both because of their moral laxity and because they were centres of what Wilhelm von Humboldt's brother, the explorer Alexander, called *die Elendigkeiten des bürgerlichen Lebens* (the wretchedness of bourgeois life). Fichte, however, took the view that scattered regional universities were not conducive to the development of German unity and citizenship, and Wilhelm von Humboldt sought to counteract the dangers of the *Großstadt* by emphasising the neo-humanist and idealist ethos of the new establishment. Potsdam was actually considered as a possible location for the university but the choice finally went in favour of Berlin – a decision strongly endorsed by Schleiermacher (1808:301–2). The initial reluctance to opt for Berlin reflected a strain of anti-bourgeois social élitism, which was overcome only by a powerful desire to help restore German self-respect after the war with Napoleon; the ideologues decided that this purpose would best be served by siting the university in the Prussian capital.

The emphasis upon the solitary character of the academic life was very much in tune both with contemporary idealist philosophy and with the Romantic movement in literature. The philosophy of Schelling and Fichte had influenced German Romanticism, which accentuated the cult of the 'solitary', and regarded the gap between aspiration and achievement as unbridgeable. The German romantics rejected the real world, preferring to glory in the divine spirit of poetry, and to escape into the world of dreams, the sub-conscious, fairy tales or medievalism. They revelled in states of mystery, yearning, heightened emotion, extravagant imagination and intuition. Their frequent harking back to a mythical Golden Age reflected a disgust with the present, and their intense subjectivism was strengthened by the fact that political repression would have made it difficult for most of them to play an effective public role in contemporary society, even if they had wished to do so. Tymms (1955:35) writes:

> Escapism, which is the pre-requisite of the romantic mood was encouraged by the suffocating restrictions of the political and social conditions obtaining in Germany during the romantic age. The Germans were free only in the realms of philosophical and aesthetic ideas; there they had carried out their great revolutions, but not in political reality; they 'dreamed their French Revolution'.

Artists took refuge in their art and in lofty flights of aesthetics and metaphysics; sometimes, like Novalis, their escapism took the form of refusing to acknowledge the existence of evil in the world. Ignoring evil did not, however, banish it; it merely ensured that no attempt was made to fight it, and so left it all the freer to flourish unchecked. The effect of Romanticism was to emphasise the discontinuity between the individual and society and to prevent the individual from coming to terms with present reality.

It would, however, be misleading to give the impression that *Einsamkeit und Freiheit* implied *total* solitude for the young student. This was not so. Social relationships within universities were regarded as important; the students formed associations for sporting, political and cultural purposes and Schleiermacher (1808:281–3) stressed that universities ought to contain a collection of people from many different environments who learn to express their own individual peculiarities in a liberal, common forum. The concept of a community of scholars did exist, but it co-existed with a valuing of *Innerlichkeit*.

The dangers of *Innerlichkeit*, not only for the individual but also for the political culture of German society, are explored by the sociologist Ralf Dahrendorf (1965b). He postulates the existence of 'private' and 'public' values and attempts to work out the influence of each on society as well as on the individual. Although he is not the first scholar to do this, he is one of the most famous, and his model can readily be applied to higher as well as to school education.

Dahrendorf contrasts private values with public values. Public values are a necessary condition of the operation of the constitution of liberty; they contribute to the development of the responsible and socially aware 'citizen' as distinct from the dependent 'subject'. Citizenship offers the individual the opportunity to take part in the more inclusive social process, that is, to carry his or her interests to the market of politics. The citizen, states Dahrendorf (ibid.:68), 'has liberated the many [*sic*] from the prison of closed opportunities, and thus marks the turning point of the road from inherited position to autonomous decision, from status to contract'.

Private values, Dahrendorf argues, provide the individual with standards for perfecting the self; in the academic life, perfection may be achieved by striving for *Kultur* through the medium of *Innerlichkeit*, nurtured in *Einsamkeit und Freiheit*. There is, however, something negative about private values: they are antagonistic to the virtues of participation in a liberal democracy. The private individual may go through the motions of taking part in the 'external' public world and in the political process, but he always reserves the right to retreat. This lack of genuine commitment naturally leaves the way open for the 'overlords' to indulge in authoritarian rule, without fear of a concerted or institutionalised opposition. The lack of solidarity among members of the bourgeoisie is exacerbated not only by the cult of *Innerlichkeit* but also by the fact that, sociologically, they have failed to achieve a class-consciousness proper to their group. McClelland (1980:98) has noted the narrowness of the social basis for recruitment to the university in nineteenth-century Germany. Dahrendorf (1965b:52–3) claims that industrialisation in Germany failed to produce a self-confident bourgeoisie; that the aspirations of the bourgeoisie were for individual recognition rather than recognition as a new political class; that it sought feudal prestige but had little impact on the mentality of the aristocracy.

Dahrendorf believes that private virtues are maintained at both school and university because all the essential impulses of education come from the family; the school in Germany, he believes, fulfils largely subsidiary tasks, a fact which makes it virtually impossible for it to bring its own formative force, informed by public virtues, to bear on the education of children.[3] German schools have changed a good deal since Dahrendorf stated his case, and the grounds for his assertions are now weaker, but his contention that 'one of the reasons for the pathology of liberal democracy in Germany is the precedence given to the family over school' (ibid.:327) remains interesting and suggestive.

By relating educational values to political culture in the way suggested by Dahrendorf, we can see how the apparently dignified and 'pure' conception of a university as a collection of self-educating individualists may come to have dire consequences for society. An over-individualised conception of university education involving the deliberate social isolation of the young scholar, in keeping with the classical university concept of 'solitary freedom', does not provide a fertile soil for liberal democracy. On the other hand, of course, the valuing of collectivism over individualism and the ruthless exercise of power on behalf of that collective may lead to totalitarianism. What is needed is, as always, the elusive *via media*.

The Three Unities of the Classical University

So far, we have studied the ideology of the Humboldtian university mainly as it affects the relationship between that institution and society. We shall turn now to look inside the university, and examine the concept of knowledge which is taken to underlie the whole curriculum (the so-called 'unity of knowledge'); then we shall look at a model for a role relationship between staff and students (the 'unity of teachers and learners'); finally we shall attend to the important question of the connection between the creation and transmission of knowledge (the 'unity of research and teaching'). We shall try to show how, during the course of many years, staff structures and patterns of academic organisation developed, which were the antithesis of those originally intended by the founders of the University of Berlin, and which eventually resulted in a desperately unsatisfactory situation. The 'official' response to the structural and organisational weaknesses in the German university system will be outlined in chapter 3.

3. That the formative force of the school can be used for evil as well as for good is illustrated by the book *School for Barbarians* (1938), written by Erika Mann, daughter of the novelist Thomas Mann. In this short work, she shows how the Nazi state used the school to inculcate values of racism, militarism and jingoism while deliberately undermining the authority of the family, lest it should attempt to act as a corrective to the propaganda of a corrupt state.

Unity of Knowledge

It has sometimes been said that the most distinctive feature of German thinking is a sense of the unity of things (*Ganzheitlichkeits-denken*), and indeed this consciousness of unity has profoundly marked the ideology of the classical German university. The obsession with the unity of knowledge is not unrelated to the fact that German aspirations towards political unity were so long frustrated, and the nationalistic significance of the concept is explicitly highlighted by both Schleiermacher (1808:258) and Steffens (1808/9: 312–16); the latter attributes the temporary cultural and military eclipse of the Germans to the fact that they have temporarily lost the sense of wholeness which had characterised them throughout much of their history (ibid.:316).

In the epistemology of the classical university, every new thought and increase in awareness implies the unity of knowledge, because the whole can be seen in the part and the part in the whole (Schleiermacher, 1808:231). All insights are interconnected and belong to a universal structure which integrates and transcends specific disciplines. Fichte, for example, believes that science and philosophy admit of only one unified *Geist*; it is reason which unites all the different branches of knowledge, and it is the function of academic teaching to activate this reasoning power in the search for knowledge (Fichte, 1807:130–2). The organic wholeness of knowledge must be recognised before individual subjects are studied, for the specific has value only to the extent that it partakes of the general.

The concept of the unity of knowledge marries well with idealist philosophy and with the religious impulses which feed the ethos of *Bildung*. Thus Schelling, in his essay *On the Absolute Concept of Knowledge* (1802a:3–12), argues that the beginning of all scholarly activity is realisation of the essential unity of the real and the ideal. Without this realisation, there can be no knowledge. The geometrician, for example, founds his scholarship on the absolute reality of the ideal. He does not prove that the three angles of any triangle together constitute two right angles by referring to concrete or real triangles, but from 'primeval knowledge' or some abstract idea. Knowledge itself, which is both real and ideal, tells him that this proposition is true (ibid.:7). (The argument here is circular – one 'knows' from ' knowledge itself' – but Schelling's insistence on the 'real' character of abstraction is the interesting point.) All knowledge is grounded in perfect, primeval, absolute knowledge (*das Urwissen in seiner vollkommenen Absolutheit*) and our knowledge in its totality is an image of eternal knowledge. Man is a reasoning being, and his activity as a reasoning being must aim at developing that which is necessary for the total revelation of God. He must show how the ideal is divinely transformed into the natural and real. Everything flows together into one – action and knowledge, being and form, the finite and the infinite – for the nature of the Absolute is this: that the ideal is also the real.

Such is Schelling's theory of the unity of knowledge. If it is accepted, then his insistence on the divine origins of knowledge has powerful implications for the role of the professor, making him in effect the hierophant of *Bildung* and *Kultur*. It also has implications for the role of the student; the concept of the unity of knowledge implies that integration and synthesis are the essence of thought, and this makes great intellectual demands of the student, who needs considerable independence of judgement and breadth of knowledge to think in this way (cf. Schelling, 1802b:16; Fichte, 1807:137). The concept of the unity of knowledge even has implications for the university curriculum. It is usually felt in Germany that universities ought to offer a full range of subjects (*Fächerspektrum*), and indeed failure to do so often stigmatises an institution. The strength with which this conviction is held is a measure of the respect traditionally accorded to the 'unity' concept.

The notion of the unity of knowledge helped to increase the standing of the Faculty of Philosophy at the University of Berlin; from having once been low-status, it enhanced its prestige to a point where it actually supplanted theology which had once been regarded as the queen of all disciplines. Philosophy was important in the idealist scheme of things because it was an integrative discipline, enabling people to reflect upon things and make sense of them, and embracing all of knowledge in its organic wholeness. It was believed that all education at third level must take philosophy as its starting point (Fichte, 1807:148, 157). Hence, the Faculty of Philosophy must take precedence, because all the members of the university, whatever their faculty, must have their roots in philosophy (Schleiermacher, 1808:260). It is with speculative thought that intellectual life begins; it is philosophy which reproduces the unity of the cosmos in the unity of knowledge; it is philosophy which reconciles reason and experience, the speculative and the empirical, thus making knowledge possible (ibid.:250); it is philosophy which opens the way to those two great realms of knowledge – nature and history; it is philosophy, better than any other discipline, which represents the unity of knowledge. Schleiermacher is convinced that no attempt to award subject-specific doctorates would 'last' or become 'historical' (ibid.:291). A tangible symbol of the primacy still accorded to philosophy as the keystone of knowledge is that when we confer higher degrees in Britain, we award 'doctorates of philosophy' ('Ph.D.' or 'D.Phil.') in subjects which are not philosophical in nature.

Schleiermacher's strong sense of the unity of knowledge led him to make a proposal which was radical, not to say revolutionary – too much so indeed to be implemented in his own times. He suggests that lecturers from the academies of mining, building and surgery should be allowed to lecture at the University of Berlin, and goes much further than simply proposing a teaching role for them: why not, he asks (ibid.:306–7), integrate these specialist institutions into the University, make their pupils students in the full sense and their teachers professors? This would have a socially and academically integrative effect and the members of the resultant new university community would, without losing their distinctiveness, tangibly symbolise the unity of all parts of knowledge. The kind of institutional merger here advocated by Schleiermacher was a remarkably progressive suggestion in its time, and anticipates by 150 years the basis on which the comprehensive universities of the twentieth century were established. Although some of the men connected with the University of Berlin were socially élitist, this is not true of Schleiermacher. He attaches great importance to the human side of the academic life, and insists that lecturers have a duty to support and help their students outside of lectures; he roundly criticises students who are tempted to consider themselves superior to the 'contemptible' uneducated masses (ibid.:284), and castigates snobbery – both individual and institutional.

The emphasis upon the unity of knowledge which was so important at Berlin was eroded as the nineteenth century proceeded, and this was reflected in a growing rift between philosophy and other disciplines, not just at Berlin but in other universities. This happened in a number of seemingly innocuous ways, of which historiography provides one example. The research ethos, characteristic of the classical German university, had led to a somewhat arid and antiquarian approach to history. The historian Ranke attempted to base historiography on a firm and critical knowledge of the sources, thus integrating history more firmly into the research paradigm, and pushing it away from the humanistic and towards the empirical tradition (Lilge, 1948). This helped to distance a very important discipline from the humane-liberal values of the Humboldtian university (although Ranke himself emphasised the need for imaginative empathy in reconstructing the past).

In science, too, there was a growing tension between moral and empirical values. As a discipline, science contributed to material progress and therefore was increasingly powerful and respected. It was particularly necessary that it should maintain contact with philosophy, thus ensuring that 'progress' was combined with a morally responsible outlook. Scientists, however, were often embarrassed by human values which could not easily be fitted into their scheme of things. They accordingly distanced themselves from the philosophical underpinnings of their work, which in turn meant that they often failed to work out their own preconceptions and assumptions. This state of affairs inevitably led to a mechanistic view of science based on uncritical materialism (Lilge, 1948:63). The growth of positivism, of course, further emphasised the widening gap between science and values, and soon most scientists were making little effort to achieve a coherent world view.

In the twentieth century, subject disciplines have proliferated and knowledge has exploded to such an extent that scholars such as Schelsky (1963:266) now believe the unity of knowledge to be an obsolete notion which marked a relatively primitive stage of development of scholarship. He may be right in this, but our current difficulty in perceiving unity in knowledge must not be taken as an indication that none exists. A growth in our awareness of the complexity of knowledge does not exclude the possibility of an ultimate synthesis nor the possibility that unity does indeed exist.

Unity of Teachers and Learners

In the classical German university tradition, knowledge is conceived as process rather than product, and as such is never 'fixed' and 'given'. It is a form of thinking rather than a catalogue of facts, and must be actively pursued and sought. The professor does not 'possess' a monopoly of truth and wisdom any more than his students and, in the sense that both teacher and learners are always 'searching', they are equal. Neither can be regarded as the custodian or owner of knowledge (Humboldt, 1809/10:377–8). This notion has implications for human relationships within the university. Fichte (1807:141) emphasises the love of learning (which he calls *Kunst*) and states that, like all love, it is of divine origin. It emanates from the lecturer as the initial focus and binds all the seekers after knowledge into an organic whole of 'learning individuals'. Likewise, Schleiermacher (1808:253) believes that if the lecturer is a good human being, and enjoys close personal relationships with his students, then a much broader area of knowledge will become accessible to them.

Related to this democratic view of the essential equality of professors and students are the notions of freedom to teach (*Lehrfreiheit*) and freedom to learn (*Lernfreiheit*). The professors are free to teach what they wish and to communicate their own particular insights to the students. They must also be free to take their own road to the truth, however tortuous, unpromising or even illicit that road may appear. This is the essence of academic freedom, and any attempt to restrict the scholar for political, ideological or even economic reasons may muzzle the truth, thus producing a poorer and less open society. The student, too, must be free to pursue his own studies and to grow existentially as well as intellectually. A meeting of minds should grow organically out of the relationship between teachers and learners; the state cannot pre-arrange it and allocate people to it, because it depends to a considerable extent upon spontaneity and mutual stimulation (Schleiermacher, 1808:266). Nor should there be rigid rules about the sequence of lecture topics (ibid.:262). The student must on no account be subjected to 'spoon-feeding' (*Verschulung*) or be tormented by continually having to show proof of his intellectual progress (through over-frequent testing and examinations). Any proliferation of intermediate examinations is contrary to the spirit of the Humboldtian university, as is the specification of a set number of years of study for a degree-level course. *Lernfreiheit* demands that students be allowed to take their examinations when they feel ready to do so, not when impersonal regulations state that they have to.

None the less, the organisational structure which developed in the course of the nineteenth and twentieth centuries militated against the unity of teachers and learners within the universities. The dominant figure in this structure was that of the full professor or *Ordinarius*. His power was such that it may be more appropriate to speak of the freedom of the *Ordinarius* rather than the freedom of the university or of a subject. He wielded supreme authority over his 'institute', and over research, teaching, personnel and budget within his own domain; once he was established in his institute, equipment and staff were at his disposal for the duration of his career. Control by a Ministry, Vice-Chancellor or faculty was minimal, and he was usually free in practice to promote his own interests, sometimes treating his institute as if it were independent private property. His social status was very high; in a 1951 survey on the relative prestige of 38 occupations, 'university professor' came out top (quoted by Dahrendorf, 1965b:86).

However, Germany achieved its pre-eminence in research not by appointing full professors in large numbers, but by employing young graduate students to teach and to work on research with the *Ordinarien*. These young scholars were allowed to hope that they themselves would obtain Chairs in due course, but their financial position was extremely insecure since they did not have tenure and were dependent on fees – a situation which led either to sycophancy or competition with the established professors. Even as early as 1848, the ambiguity and insecurity of the position of the young temporary graduate assistants were a cause of public concern (Schelsky, 1963:163).

Numerically, the *Ordinarien* were predominant until the end of the eighteenth century. By 1907, however, they were vastly outnumbered by the *Mittelbau* (the sub-professorial tier of research and teaching staff), and this meant that the top positions were held by a relatively small privileged group. The researches of one Fritz Eulenberg revealed that there were 3,866 German-speaking university teachers. Of these, 'only' 1,437 were *Ordinarien*, while there were 79 'honorary' professors, 862 associate professors (*Extraordinarien*) and, apart from 148 lectors and instructors, no fewer than 1,324 private lecturers who were waiting to become full professors (Ellwein, 1985:134). Burn et al. (1971) estimate that in 1966, over two-thirds of all academic positions in German universities were held by *Assistenten* (members of the *Mittelbau*), who, like the private lecturers (*Privatdozenten*), were vulnerable to exploitation (Busch, 1959;1963). Jaspers and Rossmann (1961:221) note the distinction between *Ordinarien* and *Nicht-Ordinarien*, wryly commenting upon the use of a negative in a job designation; although otherwise somewhat conservative, they argue that the position of the junior lecturer (*Dozent*) must be improved and given a separate career structure, since not every *Dozent* can realistically hope to become a professor. Even Schelsky (1969:123), who is not over-sympathetic to students, states that there must be a staff restructuring which incorporates the *Mittelbau* (liberally understood and not restricted to just one category of non-professorial staff).

The staff structure which had evolved was in fact a travesty of that conceived by the founders of the University of Berlin when they advocated unity of teaching and learning. A role relationship originally conceived as extremely democratic – with professors and students equal in their pursuit of knowledge – had been perverted into a thoroughly hierarchical, paternalistic, authoritarian one – the antithesis of what had at first been envisaged. There was a reluctance to face up to the problems of the *Mittelbau*, because creating tenured posts for them would cost the authorities too much money and because the professors feared any such development might threaten their existing high status.

Unity of Research and Teaching

The classical German university combines research and teaching in at least three different ways. First, the institution itself is conceived as having the dual purpose of teaching students and pushing back the frontiers of knowledge. German university professors are expected to do research as a normal part of their duties. Secondly, students are expected to learn by undertaking at least a limited amount of original research, and thereby learning procedures, habits and methods of work in a particular discipline. They can assist the professors by acting as communication partners and providing intellectual stimulus. The unity of research and teaching inheres in the person of the professor himself and contributes greatly to his prestige. Thirdly, the best teaching is conceived as a kind of 'research'. True communication of knowledge involves a recreation of the processes which produced it, and this calls for much more than rote-learning. Liveliness and enthusiasm should characterise the communicative skills of the university teacher and, in the passing on of knowledge, no repetition should take place without a rediscovery and a recombination of elements; this results in learning on the part of the teacher as well as on the part of the pupil (Schleiermacher, 1808:253).

McClelland (1980:104) argues that the notion of the unity of research and teaching was the product of necessity rather than design. Prussia's financial situation after its defeat by Napoleon was so bad that it could not afford to set up separate research institutions, and the unity of the two functions in the new University of Berlin was actually a way of saving money – a *pis aller*. Nevertheless the fusion of research and teaching provided a pattern for the modern university, and the entrusting of research to the classical German university helped to make it a brilliant success, influencing higher education in many other countries, and giving Germany a leading position in the scholarly world. The research-led university was a much-admired and eminently 'exportable' phenomenon (cf. Kwiatkowski, 1980). Haines (1969), Armytage (1969) and Simpson (1983) have described the German influence on British higher education; America also came strongly under its influence, even if the model which it imported was not exactly the same as the 'real' one, which it believed it was importing (Ben-David, 1968–69); Harvard and Johns Hopkins Universities were developed in the nineteenth century in conscious imitation of German models, and it has been estimated that from 1815 to 1916, a total of 6,000 to 9,000

Americans studied at German universities (Max Planck Institute, 1979: ch. 1).

However, the unity of research and teaching can create certain difficulties for students. If they are expected to involve themselves in 'research', they must clearly possess a substantial degree of intellectual independence in order to do so. Many of them, however, particularly those from less privileged backgrounds, may not have the cultural and personal resources to meet the heavy demands made upon them. Furthermore, the *laissez-faire* notion of *Lernfreiheit* is open to abuse by professors. The notion that *Bildung* is transmitted through cultural osmosis rather than through structured curricula may tempt them to shirk their teaching duties. The entire onus of learning may be placed on the student, with a corresponding disregard for skilful and dedicated teaching in higher education. The temptation to teach badly and negligently is inherent in the concept of the unity of research and teaching, particularly if classes are very large and funds are not available to finance the seminars and tutorials needed to counterbalance the anonymity of a large lecture hall. Unless the students are very able and intellectually independent, the whole arrangement breaks down. The ideal itself cannot be sustained in a mass education system.

The Classical University and the State

The ideology of the Humboldtian university set a great deal of store by freedom, and defended the notions of *Lernfreiheit*, *Lehrfreiheit*, and *Einsamkeit und Freiheit*. This reflected the university's desire for autonomy and freedom (*Freiheit*) from state control. Yet it depended to a considerable extent on the state for funding. This tension between state subvention and the scholars' demands for freedom explains why many of them had highly ambivalent attitudes towards their main patron. While emphasising freedom, they were always sharply conscious of state power. Ultimately the university was answerable to the state, and the state reserved the right to intervene if the university did anything to impede the growth of knowledge. Economic and administrative power were vested in a state curator, who exercised state supervision. This supervision was not merely legal but extended to academic matters (Nitsch et al., 1977:27); the university did not have constitutional autonomy.

It is easy to forget that control of the curriculum by academics is a comparatively recent idea, even in Britain (see Lawton, 1980). Before we take an unrelievedly pessimistic view of the relationship between university and state in Germany, we would do well to remember that in Victorian Britain, not only the institutional management but also most of the academic management of universities was in the hands of outsiders (Moodie and Eustace, 1974). Even in Oxford and Cambridge, the role of teaching staff in curriculum matters and examining was strictly limited. Lecturers were not fully in control of either until about 1900, when Birmingham was chartered as a University. Genuine academic control of universities is very recent, and if the current centralist policies continue in Britain, it may turn out to have been only a transient phase in the history of UK universities.

In examining state control of universities in Germany, we are deepening the study of academic freedom, already initiated in connection with the concept of *Einsamkeit*, and are sharpening our perceptions of the relationship between state and university in Germany. An understanding of this relationship is crucial to any study of organisational innovation in German higher education.

The State as a Positive Force in Higher Education

The German state is not normally seen as a liberalising force in higher education, but McClelland (1980) has argued persuasively that in eighteenth-century Göttingen, for example, Münchhausen was amply justified in keeping the important prerogative of professorial appointment in the hands of the government and its agents. At first, this might seem an unwarranted presumption and a threat to academic freedom, but it was in fact the only way of controlling the nepotism, favouritism and seniorism prevailing at most universities. Münchhausen, says McClelland (ibid.: 40), sought to avoid 'divisive quarrels and factionalism in the faculties, especially of the sort that derive from personal interest'.

In the nineteenth century, Humboldt saw the state as a lawgiver which could help to protect academic freedom. The state bestows institutional autonomy upon the university and ensures reform. It can help to counterbalance the one-sidedness and rigidity of scholars, and to shield the university against particularistic threats and pressures. For these reasons, Humboldt (1809/10:358) thought it essential that the state should retain the sole right to appoint university professors, assuming that the Ministry would be sympathetic and reasonable. He did not trust professors to act without self-interest, and in a letter to his wife, Karoline, complained that directing a group of scholars was not much better than dealing with a troupe of actors! In another letter to Karoline, he wrote:

You have no idea what problems I have to wrestle with, especially with the scholars – the unruliest and most difficult to pacify of all peoples. They besiege me with their eternally self-thwarting interests, their jealousy, their envy, their passion to govern, their one-sided opinions, in which each believes that his discipline alone has earned support and encouragement. (Lenz, 1910:210)

Humboldt's sense of the need for state safeguards against the caprices and egotism of the professors even made him consider setting up a state Commission (*theoretische Grundsatzkommission*) to protect culture and education (Schelsky, 1963:152), but this idea was never carried out. It is obvious that Humboldt, like Münchhausen, looked to the state to hold the balance between the sectional interests of the professors. In practice, the state–university connection actually increased the universities' power, since they had a monopoly in training state functionaries, and so could help to mould the ruling caste's mentality. In many cases, the state itself sought to eradicate abuses and create order and regularity. In Catholic areas, it tried to break the stranglehold of such religious orders as the Jesuits on higher education; it introduced modern curricula and trained competent, worldly students. It is true that ministerial wilfulness and arbitrary interference increased, especially as time went on, and particularly when the universities were seen by the state as a subversive force. This was notably the case after 1848 and during Althoff's term of office as head of the universities section (and later also the schools section) of the Prussian Ministry of Education (1882–1907). None the less, without wishing to glorify the state, McClelland (1980) demonstrates that its influence on the universities was, in the fissiparous existence of Germany, by no means always a negative one. Similarly, Blackbourn and Eley (1984) emphasise the beneficent role of the state in Imperial Germany, and Eley (1984:144) argues that the German pattern of revolution, which from 1802–12 and 1862–71 was from *above*, was just as capable of ensuring bourgeois predominance as the very different patterns of revolution which had prevailed in American, French or British history; Blackbourn (1984:178) points out that state authority helped to clear tenacious reactionary forces from the 'backward' enclaves of society, and shows that the state gave German industry and commerce many valuable assets and improvements, such as banking, more efficient railways, a standard currency, patent laws and the beginnings of a national communications system.

The more positive aspects of German state power need to be highlighted as a corrective to the sceptical, negative views frequently expressed about the role of the state in German education. It was often used in very positive ways and, in the twentieth century, the state played a vital, pro-active and often imaginative role in the foundation of the German comprehensive universities.

Tension Between the State and the University

Despite what has been said above, the relationship between university and state in the late eighteenth and early nineteenth centuries was often embattled and fraught with difficulties. Ambivalence and apprehension *vis-à-vis* the state run like a leitmotiv through the writings of the ideologists of the early classical German university, who were deeply conscious of state power as a possible threat to academic freedom. One incident which shows that the university had just grounds for concern was the public reprimanding of Kant for allegedly using his philosophy 'for the purpose of distorting and deprecating several basic teachings of the Holy Bible and Christianity' (Lilge, 1948:7). The Prussian Minister Wöllner, on behalf of Frederick the Great, ordered Kant to use his 'prestige and talent for the realisation of our patriarchal intentions'. This incident took place in 1794 and was related to a royal edict of 1788 which restricted the freedom of teaching and publication, and established a committee to examine the orthodoxy and reliability of future Protestant preachers and school teachers. Such interference deeply alienated many German intellectuals and led Kant to produce his treatise 'The Quarrel of the Faculties', written in 1793/94, in which he called for academic freedom.

Humboldt himself believed the exercise of state power to be necessary in some circumstances, but was nevertheless very mistrustful of it. In the years 1791 and 1792, when he was aged 23–24, he wrote a paper entitled 'Ideas on an Attempt to Define the Limits of the State's Effectiveness' (Burrow, 1969). This document is one of the most important defences of liberal democracy in Germany and influenced John Stuart Mill's essay 'On Liberty' (Lilge, 1948:9). Humboldt had three main reasons for objecting to the exercise of state power:

(1) It tends to sap the vitality of individuals (and ultimately of the nation) by making them over-dependent (Burrow, 1969:25). This dependency is incompatible with Humboldt's conception of the real purpose of human life as the development of man's powers to a complete and consistent whole. Freedom and variety of situation are the prerequisites here, and both are

inhibited by intrusive state action;

(2) It carries with it the danger of indoctrination. Humboldt (ibid.:23) fears that a spirit of national uniformity may develop, and that those who are subjected to state interference may all become alike in what they are and what they do;

(3) It contributes to the growth of a heavy-handed bureaucracy which feeds upon itself and ultimately vitiates the good intentions of the state.

Humboldt's description of the suffocating nature of bureaucracy has such a ring of truth about it that it is worth quoting the relevant passage (ibid.:34):

> . . . . the administration of political affairs itself becomes in time so full of complications that it requires an incredible number of persons to devote their time to its supervision, in order that it may not fall into utter confusion. Now by far the greater portion of these have to deal with mere symbols and formulas of things; and thus, not only are men of first-rate capacity withdrawn from anything which gives scope for thinking, ... but their intellectual powers themselves suffer from this partly narrow, partly empty employment.

Since Humboldt rejects even benevolent state paternalism in this way, it comes as no surprise that he regards national education as very questionable. If there is one thing which requires free activity on the part of the individual, then it is education, whose object is precisely to develop the individual (ibid.:51). The first aim should always be to develop human nature as freely as possible, with minimum reference to citizenship. The person thus freely developed may then attach himself to the state, if he wishes, but the systematic organisation of education, as such, should be considered wholly beyond the proper limits of the state's influence. The state should merely seek to preserve national security against the threat of outside enemies and internal dissensions (ibid.:43).

As it turned out, Humboldt was called upon in later life not only to accommodate himself to state power but to exercise it actively, so he must have been able to overcome his youthful distaste for statism. Indeed he would have found it hard to be a successful educational administrator if he had believed in a stark dualism between the rights of the state and the rights of the university. Schelsky (1963:141) believes that his achievement was to think out the relationship between university and state from the viewpoint of the state. His initial stance was a liberal one, but the authority and power which he enjoyed during the founding of the University of

Berlin ensured that he had to put his ideas to the test. The idealist was forced in some measure to become a pragmatist, and this involved a degree of compromise.

Most of the ideologists of the University of Berlin feared the state as a possible threat to academic freedom. Thus, Steffens (1808/9:323–4) stresses the dangers of the state inevitably seeking to control what it creates; it should recognise its limits and cease to assert its claims over the spiritual or intellectual (*das Geistige*). Schleiermacher too (1808:232) avers that if academic considerations are not to be dominated by political ones, the nobler spirits must seek to be as independent of the state as possible. Members of the university should seek to disengage themselves from the power of the state and, if this proves impossible, then they should attempt to build up their own credibility and public prestige.

The founding fathers of the University of Berlin were constantly on the defensive against possible state demands that the universities should demonstrate economic or practical 'usefulness'. They pointed out that universities were indeed useful, since they had, for a long time, provided people for state service. They also believed, however, that academics would deserve contempt if they concerned themselves merely with the practical. By insisting on this, the state would eventually deprive itself of people who are 'capable of conceiving and executing great things and revealing by their sharp perceptions, the roots and the interconnections of all error' (Schleiermacher, 1808:245). Likewise, Schelling was alarmed by utilitarian demands on higher education. He argues (1802b:17) that the state would be striking a blow against freedom if it turned institutions of higher learning into commercial or industrial schools. Utility is a dangerous criterion, for what is useful today is the opposite tomorrow; this yardstick, rigorously applied, would 'stifle all greatness and energy within a nation' and would mean in effect that the 'invention of the spinning-wheel would be more important than the discovery of a world-system' (ibid.:42). In a similar vein, Steffens (1808/9:342–3) points out that even the gardener must avoid taking a short-term view, if he is to avoid sacrificing the seedcorn of the future to the bloom of the present. The state must recognise that present appearances are not always a reliable guide to future developments; indeed the seed of the future is often inconspicuous and unpromising, which is why it must be cherished and protected with special care. There is nothing which the state should regret so much as the suppression of a budding talent; it follows that it must strive 'to defend and care for the *inner* freedom of the spirit, of which external freedom is only to be regarded as a pale reflection' (ibid.:343). Humboldt, in the following much-quoted passage from his *Organisationsplan*, expresses his view that the state is best served if it adopts a 'hands off' policy towards the universities:

> The state must treat its universities neither as grammar schools nor as specialist schools and must not use its *Academie* as a technical or scholarly appendage. It must in general . . . demand nothing from them that is related immediately and directly to itself but should cherish the inner conviction that if they achieve their aims, it too will achieve its aims and indeed from a much more elevated point of view, which comprehends much more and brings into play quite different forces and levers than it is able to set in motion of itself . . . (Humboldt, 1809/10:381)

In insisting that the universities must not be made to bow to utilitarianism, the founders of the University of Berlin were going against the spirit of the Enlightenment. Their constant preoccupation with the role of the state is a measure of the anxiety which it inspired in them. The state, upon which they depended for sustenance, had something of the monster in its make-up, and would have to be tamed or domesticated if it was not one day to destroy all that they believed in. Philosophers and theorists from the early nineteenth century onwards set themselves to the task of devising new and more tolerable roles for the state, but all the new ideas were still pervaded by the dangerous ambiguities and tensions which had marked the old ones.

Kulturstaat and Rechtsstaat

Many of those who formulated the ideology of the classical German university rejected direct state intervention, but none the less hoped for state protection. It was but a short step from the notion that the state could protect academic freedom to the idea that it could be inspired by moral purposes. If it is permeated by *Geist*, and constantly uses its strength in order to fight for what is right, then we have what has been called a *Kulturstaat* in which the 'power state' is assimilated to a morally superior 'culture state'. Thus Schleiermacher (1808:232) urges the members of the university to try to influence the state by inspiring it with a 'more dignified and more scholarly way of thinking'. The state is fully aware that knowledge and science are wholesome and excellent; the scientific community needs the state's protection and favour, and so both must strive to achieve a positive relationship and to come together in unity (ibid.:226). Steffens expresses a similar idea when he writes that the happiness of the state, like the happiness of the individual, arises from the interrelationship between knowledge and being. The nation which honours wisdom will attain glory (1808/9:329). Just as the soul penetrates the body and is one with it, so the spirit of the higher intellect should animate the state and become one with it.

The state must acknowledge the demands of *Kultur* and in return the academic élite will mould its sensibility (*Gesinnung*), thus spiritualising it. The university will also produce trained officials who are not mere administrators but also sponsors and defenders of the state (Ringer, 1969:116). This understanding was unconscious and tacit, but it allowed German scholarship to come to terms with state power. As Ringer (ibid.:117) puts it: 'The important point is that the nation and through it, the State were defined as creative and as agents of the mandarins' cultural ideas.'

It was the work of Fichte and Hegel, however, which demonstrated how vulnerable academic freedom can be – even in a *Kulturstaat*. For Fichte, it was society, not the state, which embodied the principle of freedom; indeed he took the scholarly community of free spirits as the model of an idealised society, permeated by reason (*Vernunft*). He recognised, however, the need to socialise the individual in a unified system of national state schools; later, devotion and loyalty to the Prussian state became his own moral law (Lilge, 1948:41); in his essay *On Machiavelli*, he asserted that the national state must secure its survival by any means and that it was not bound by common laws or treaties (ibid.:55).

It has been pointed out (Nitsch et al., 1977:16–17) that the mechanical 'means–end' vision of state and society, or state and knowledge, is unsatisfactory since any conflict between the two will leave the state in a dominant position *vis-à-vis* the individual. What if the state having used reason for self-legitimation should then degrade the power of reason, and use it to make people obey perverted ideals? It is clear that Fichte's concept of the state was highly ambivalent and potentially harmful. To quote Lilge again (1948 : 55): 'The conclusion is inevitable that Fichte's philosophy not only suffered from inherent contradictions; it also helped to promote the political abuse of the most valuable of his educational ideas.'

However, the philosopher who really made the state seem admirable in German eyes was, of course, Hegel. In the Hegelian dialectic, the idea or thesis generates an opposing idea or antithesis, and the two are reconciled in a third more comprehensive idea, the synthesis; this thought-structure, with its awareness of oppositions and antagonisms, could be seen as an attempt to overcome the duality which was inherent in Kant's philosophy, and which he bequeathed to his disciples. Hegel believed that in Greek civilisation the individual begins to assert himself (this is the thesis); that in Roman civilisation he is subordinated to the state (this is the antithesis); and that in the final development of the Germanic state individual interest and social interest will be reconciled and freedom will at last be realised (this is the synthesis) (cf. Lewis, 1954:142). Hegel regarded the state as the embodiment of rational freedom, realising and recognising itself in an objective form; the state could become the external manifestation of human freedom, whereas 'society' was an entity devoid of dignity and power – a prey to conflicting interests. A strong state is therefore needed to overcome the conflicts of society and to promote the common good. So far, Hegel's ideas are compatible with the concept of *Kulturstaat*, but he later came, like Fichte, to believe that it was in order for the state to compel the subordination of the individual. In his last years, he abandoned his own truest insights and argued that right must yield to might, that 'necessity is what we must submit to and that only in this submission is our freedom' (ibid.:147). This gave rise to the concept of the 'power state' or *Machtstaat*, which could, and often did, result in a negation of the freedom which Hegel claimed to value so highly. Aiken (1956:80) suggests that Hegel's philosophy of freedom paradoxically combines outward subservience or even servility towards the state with the preservation of one's inner spiritual freedom, and adds: 'His . . . unseemly glorification of the Prussian state ill becomes a philosopher who conceives his whole philosophy, in one sense, as a meditation on the problem of human freedom'.

The concept of the *Kulturstaat* was always more of a myth than a reality. The type of state which eventually emerged was the *Rechtsstaat*, or state based on law. Briefly, this implies that the government must proceed in accordance with fixed rational principles, that these principles must be publicly and clearly stated and conform to ethical requirements (Ringer, 1969:114). The *Rechtsstaat* arose from a demand for justice and predictability in the face of unsystematic and arbitrary government; it echoed Rousseau's insistence on the necessity of championing independent standards of judgement against despotism.

The evolution of the *Rechtsstaat* has been described by Eley (1984:190–5) as follows:

(1) It involved the concept of equality of citizens before the law, thus signalling a transition from the old corporate state to the new bourgeois one. The notion of legal equality was expressed in the Prussian *Allgemeines Landrecht* [General Provincial Law] of 1794 and in the Austrian *Allgemeines Bürgerliches Gesetzbuch* [Gen-

eral Civil Code] of 1811. The process of emancipation was consolidated when the equality of all citizens before the law was expressed in the constitution of both the North German Confederation of 1867 and the German Reich of 1871;

(2) The principle of legal accountability of the bureaucracy marked a further stage in the move towards the *Rechtsstaat*, and this was finally achieved in Prussia in the 1870s, after much effort;

(3) A public sphere (*Öffentlichkeit*), separate from and independent of the state, was developed; it was characterised by such bourgeois freedoms as freedom of association, freedom of the press, and freedom of speech and petition; together, these freedoms worked against corporate presumption and the danger of state arbitrariness;

(4) The property rights of the individual *Bürger* [citizen] were guaranteed. He was allowed to acquire and dispose of property without restriction; these bourgeois property rights were enshrined in the Prussian Penal Code of 1851 and later in the Civil Code which came into effect in 1900 after decades of preparation. Humboldtian humanism is the origin of the individualist values which informed the Civil Code (Eley, 1984:193).

Although these characteristics of the *Rechtsstaat* may appear liberal and in keeping with our present notions of natural justice and human rights, it would be wrong to assume that they implied widespread participatory democracy. In eighteenth-century Germany demands for legality did not imply any sort of popular participation in government, and even in the nineteenth century when the University of Berlin was founded, it was only a small élite, and not a very open one at that, which worked directly with the structures of bureaucratic absolutism. McClelland (1980:89) states: 'It should. . . . give cause for thought that the origins of the modern university in Germany appear to have been bound up with an attempt to stabilise and legitimate the rule of the more flexible part of the aristocracy, with the aid of a small élite recruited from the middle class'.

In the absence of political unity, the legal framework of the *Rechtsstaat* assumed great importance, since it helped to compensate in some measure for the negative effects of German disunity. The peculiarities of German history have led to a reliance on the law which is very marked in comparison with Britain, and which was to become vital in bringing about educational innovation in the twentieth century. The tendency to legislate for many eventualities also, however, has a shadow side which is manifested in legal positivism and legal realism.

Legal positivism implies that law is defined in a prescriptive way in terms of the commands or edicts of a king or other authority, without reference to moral considerations. The theory of legal realism also involves legalisation without reference to moral considerations, and defines a person's legal rights and duties in factual terms as what the courts decide s/he will be allowed to do. In view of these trends, it is not surprising, then, to find that university affairs in nineteenth-century Germany were regulated pragmatically by a bureaucratic monarchy, and that the demand for freedom was expressed by formal *Rechtsstaatlichkeit* (Nitsch et al., 1977:153,164).

The operation of the law has had a crucial effect in determining the success of attempts to found comprehensive universities in the twentieth century. The reason for discussing the *Rechtsstaat* is to show the important part which the law has played in the history of German educational innovation.

Conclusion

The ideology of the classical German university is a noble one which still has its attractions. Some people (Nitsch et at., 1977; Jaspers and Rossmann, 1961:195; Schrey, 1983:84) maintain that the Humboldtian concept has never been tried in its pure form. A mere decade after the foundation of Berlin University it was obvious, say Nitsch et al. (1977:298): '. . . that not even freedom of scholarship (*Wissenschaft*) was to be realised, not to mention *Einsamkeit*. The university always remained a sphere of influence of state and society.'

However, the power, the persistence and the pervasiveness of the Humboldtian ideal are illustrated by the fact that to this very day it is still held up as a standard to which universities should try to aspire, however discouraging the circumstances. When the Germans criticise their own university system, the complaint is not so much that the ideology upon which it is based is intrinsically inadequate as that it is insufficiently realised in practice – the Humboldtian ideal is very far from dead.

-3-

The Genesis of the Comprehensive Universities

Political Developments Affecting the Ideology of the Classical German University

The Failure of the 1848 Revolution

No analysis of Humboldtian ideology can take place without reference to some of the political happenings which have marked German life. Events in the political arena, such as the 1848 Revolution and the manner in which German unity was attained, impacted upon the professors, modifying their educational philosophy and the outlook of the university.

The ideal of the *Kulturstaat*, benevolently disposed towards higher learning, only survived a relatively short time, from about 1809/10 to 1813/15. Thereafter, the relationship between the state and the universities became increasingly tense and ambivalent. Many academics espoused political liberalism, and their demand for a modern constitutional order giving individuals a say in matters affecting them was a threat to the political authorities and to the nobles. Liberal tendencies co-existed and to some extent coincided with increasingly passionate aspirations towards national unification. These were nourished by many different sources: a romantic awareness of German cultural traditions, a drive for economic progress, unease at the archaic, quasi-feudal nature of German society, a dislike of princely paternalism and an instinctive tendency to define things German in opposition to things French. The chauvinistic and often violent expression of nationalism, and the agitation for liberal reforms eventually set academe on a collision course with régimes throughout Germany, and particularly in the north.

The relationship between the universities and the state began to deteriorate towards the end of the Napoleonic War, when young men returned home from military service, and began to form the *Burschenschaften* organisations; these promoted 'old German' dress and manners and had at first some influence in reforming and refining student life (Lilge, 1948:21). Relatively innocent of political motivation to start with, the *Burschenschaften* rapidly became hotbeds of national feeling (Pascal, 1946:20). The young people thought of themselves as heroic conspirators, sanctified by their patriotic feelings; the influence of Jahn (famous for developing gymnastics) soon drove the intellectual ideals into the background and their place was taken by strutting nationalism, which degenerated into coarseness, anti-Semitism and violence (Sell, 1953:88–9).

The Prussian government felt threatened and began to take repressive measures, especially in 1817, when the students celebrated the tercentenary of Luther's revolt against authority by publicly burning symbols of political reaction at Wartburg. Matters took a more serious turn in 1819 when a student named Sand murdered the poet Kotzebue, who had served the Tsar Alexander of Russia as councillor of state in the Department of Foreign Affairs, and on his return to Germany waged a campaign against liberals (Passant, 1959:19). Metternich feared the possibility of liberal and nationalist movements, because his own country had become so multi-national that the acceptance of national rights for all its subjects would have meant dissolution. The Tsar was sufficiently alarmed by the murder to abandon his flirtation with liberal ideas, and no longer sought to influence Frederick William III of Prussia in that direction. Consequently, Metternich had no difficulty in bringing about an agreement between Austria, Prussia and the larger German states to issue the repressive Karlsbad Decrees, stamping out radicalism in universities, censoring academic activities, and hindering the spread of revolutionary doctrines. All publications under 320 pages were subject to censorship and a committee was set up to investigate 'suspect' persons, whether students or professors. Humboldt publicly condemned the Karlsbad Decrees as 'shameful, un-national and rabble-rousing' (Sell, 1953:95) but to no avail.

Intellectuals of a politically progressive stamp did not yet have a groundswell of popular support. The mass of the people were still rural peasants, whose social and national awareness was little developed. They looked to their existing rulers to give them peace and security. Nevertheless, the academics showed occasional flashes of determination and courage in resisting reactionary forces. In 1837, for example, the Göttingen Seven, a courageous group of politically minded professors, publicly protested against the King of Hanover's abrogation of the constitution granted six years earlier. They were exiled as a punishment for their action.

German middle-class liberalism became synonymous with German nationalism. Aggression increased and a constitution was demanded. Pressure for reform was increased by the vacillation of King Frederick William IV of Prussia, who sometimes tolerated and sometimes suppressed the press. The situation eventually came to a head in the Revolution of 1848, which led to the setting up of a parliamentary government. The National Assembly, which met in the Paulskirche in Frankfurt, was nicknamed the *Professorenparlament* because 106 of the 586 members were school or university teachers (Pascal, 1946:39), and 81.6% of the members had a university education (Sagarra, 1980:92). A constitution was worked out, but by 23 March 1849, when the King reasserted his authority, matters had already gone badly wrong; the Parliament was broken up and the Revolution failed.

The liberal government undermined its own position in several ways. 'Germany' still consisted of a network of states; Austria and Prussia were rivals, neither of which was willing to give way to the other in the cause of unity and nationalism. There was a fundamental conflict between those who wanted to include Austria in the new 'Germany' and those who did not (Sell, 1953:389). The Parliament failed to build alliances with a broad variety of interest groups and generally supported Prussia, thus cutting itself off from the democratic movement elsewhere in Germany (Pascal, 1946:37). It failed to win the peasantry by introducing land reforms, and when the Poles revolted, it sided with the Prussian Army. In addition, the Assembly mismanaged its affairs by refusing to build on the power of popular liberation movements in other countries, and when the Czechs, Italians and Poles revolted, it backed the measures taken by counter-revolutionary governments (in the name of 'civilisation') (ibid.:39).

The members' lack of political experience made itself felt in many ways; Sell (1953:157) points out, for example, that the democratic ideal was discredited by the way in which members treated one another; it seemed impossible for people to disagree without great personal rancour or bitterness, and political opposition all too often degenerated into personal hostility. The actual parliamentary business was also managed clumsily. Thus, Pascal (1946:39) writes:

> The political inexperience and timidity of the German middle classes are strikingly evident in the dreary proceedings of [the National Assembly]. Endless debates, coloured by bookish rhetoric, circled round such topics as the fundamental rights of the citizen, the nature of the future constitution, the extent of Germany (should Austria be included or not?). When urgent practical problems arose, the Assembly left their decision often, their execution always, in the hands of the States where the old autocratic

administration and armies were intact.

The forces of reaction very quickly reasserted themselves, and academics were publicly excoriated and penalised for the role which they had played. In 1849, before the dissolution of the Paulskirche-Parlament, the King of Prussia addressed a meeting of seminar directors and teachers in Berlin. He complained that:

> All the misery which in the past year has broken loose in Prussia is your fault, due to the pseudo-learning and irreligious 'humane' wisdom which you propagate as real wisdom, with which you have destroyed faith and belief in the minds of my subjects and turned their hearts away from me. Already as Regent, I hated this puffed-up, peacock mock-learning from the bottom of my soul, and as Regent tried by all means to suppress it. I shall continue to follow this course of action without allowing myself to be distracted. No might on earth shall turn me away from it. (Bungardt, 1965:50)

A long series of repressive measures followed which were calculated to muzzle and demoralise academics and teachers. It was now obvious that national unity would never be achieved by consent. The military establishment grew in prestige and became a considerable power in its own right. Many liberals thought that Prussian militarism offered the only hope of overcoming the disunity which was now putting Germany at such a disadvantage, particularly in comparison with France or England. Freedom could come later. When Bismarck's policy of 'blood and iron' secured the longed-for unity in 1871, although it excluded Austria, there was no denying that the *Machtstaat* had massively triumphed over the *Kulturstaat*. The intellectuals lost confidence in themselves, feeling that they were powerless to influence events, and tended to abdicate responsibility. They withdrew from the political scene and began, more than ever, to take refuge in self-cultivation and *Innerlichkeit*.

Until about 1848, German university staff and students had represented a progressive force in German political life and were, as McClelland (1980:7) puts it, 'breeding grounds for opposition to the established order'. When national unity was achieved by force, constitutional democracy languished. A serious problem was that, in the Empire, the executive was not under political control. Parliaments could not appoint or dismiss the imperial chancellor; no political party could aspire to form the government of the Empire; there were no imperial ministers, only permanent secretaries (civil servants); and the authority of Prussian ministers was either curtailed or bypassed by the Crown's special powers in military matters (Sagarra, 1980:146). Liberally inclined members of the academic élite would have fared better if they had been able to broaden their basis of support among the people, but they feared the extension of democracy to the masses as a potential threat to the power balance in society. Concerning the ability of the universities to strike alliances, Ellwein (1985:125–6) notes that they did have support from the educated middle class (*Bildungsbürgertum*) at the beginning of the eighteenth century and again after 1871, but this bond did not extend to the industrial middle classes. Many professors became alienated from party politics and regarded the whole political scene as unworthy of their attention. They were both snobbish and self-satisfied. Soon they ceased to agonise over politics and concentrated on academic matters.

The First World War

The period between 1871 and 1914 was in many ways the German university's heyday (Ellwein, 1985:227–8). It was extremely successful academically; the social prestige of professors was high, and the university lived at peace with state and society, apart from certain tensions occasionally generated by the professors' arrogance and complacency. Sagarra (1980:30) points out that, whereas the academics had spoken for the middle classes prior to 1848, by the end of the nineteenth century 'they had come to believe that their own special status within the world of university, school and the profession of letters depended on the preservation or rather petrification of the status quo in a rapidly changing industrial society'.

The entry into the 1914–18 war came almost as a relief to German academe (Bleuel, 1968). Party and class divisions disappeared overnight and the professors joined in the general rejoicing. They saw the war as one of 'traders' (the English) against 'heroes' (themselves) and believed that they were defending European cultural values. They were brashly confident of their own victory, and felt called on to create a national German state ideology; however, they were not accustomed to thinking about politics and did it badly – witness the historian Hoetzsch, who divided peoples into 'lords' and 'slaves' and declared that 'might is right'. Even the moderate professors looked to the war to increase their country's power (cf. Bleuel, 1968:84).

It might have been expected that the shock of Germany's defeat would lead to a radical re-evaluation of norms and values in the universities, but this was only partially the case. Carl Heinrich

Becker, the Weimar Republic's famous minister of education from 1925 to 1930, was a humane and highly scholarly man who tried to reinstate the ideals of the classical German university in spite of serious personal misgivings as to whether the old ideals could meet the demands of the present. He declared that the core of the German university was still sound ('Die deutsche Universität ist im Kern gesund'), by which he meant that the inner spirit of scholarship and research was still alive. Many of the organisational features of the German university which Becker (1919) criticised (the problematic nature of the unity of research and teaching, the oligarchic power of full professors, the difficulty of securing appropriate student representation in committees, the vulnerable status of young would-be professors) have remained perennial problems to the present day; he believed, however, that *Wissenschaft* had remained uncorrupted and inviolate throughout Germany's recent vicissitudes, and that Germans would do well to protect this (essentially aristocratic) phenomenon (ibid.:66). Harking back to Prussia's defeat by Napoleon, many people hoped that intellectual progress would once again compensate for material loss; Berlin's role as a cultural capital was consolidated, and between 1919 and 1932 it was the liveliest and most interesting city in the world. There was even an attempt in the 1920s to establish a third humanistic movement; Hans Richert, for example, saw humanism of the kind cultivated in Goethe's time as an appropriate model for contemporary man (Sell, 1953:407). These attempts to resuscitate in the twentieth century an ideology which had served Germany well for a limited period in the nineteenth indicate a lack of political creativity and give German cultural history a curious symmetry.

However, there was no real reform in the universities. Lilge (1948:145–7) points to three factors which militated against the development of liberal ideas in education:

(1) Some inroads were made into academic freedom, allowing the teaching of class and church dogma;
(2) Enrolment increased rapidly without a corresponding increase in job opportunities, and this led to the growth of an academic proletariat;
(3) The university students were overwhelmingly middle-class, which did not augur well for the new democracy of the Weimar Republic.

Becker himself seems to have felt that the universities would benefit from, and the values of reason and science best be preserved by, isolation from the adverse conditions of the time. However, the reassertion of the traditional 'solitary freedom' of academic life and the predominantly non-political orientation of humanistic education did not in the long run serve the country well. Lilge writes: 'This anxiousness to preserve rather than the courage to reinterpret and reenact the values of a liberal education was characteristic of the leading German educationalists of the time' (1948:147).

Kloss, however, (1968:323–4) highlights some of Becker's positive aspirations and achievements. He tried to reform university teaching methods, do away with the oligarchical organisation of the universities, give university teachers better salaries, and the student body a legitimate place in the academic community. Such reforms as were carried out were implemented in the teeth of bitter opposition from the universities, and Becker's hope that these would renew themselves from within was disappointed.

The Second World War and Reassertion of Tradition

All in all, traditionalist thinking thus prevailed after 1918, and the universities did little to reform their position or ideology. Many of the professors did not accept defeat and still wanted to see Germany great. The Treaty of Versailles was greatly resented, and it was widely believed that social democracy had stabbed Germany in the back. Some academics argued that the authoritarian order was naturally suited to their country, and that democracy was incompatible with Germany's historical destiny (Bleuel, 1968:110). The strength of the German people was believed to have been undermined by non-German elements (such as Jews). The students were depressed and destabilised by inflation, unemployment and the general social disruption. This helped to make them an easy prey to National Socialism.

The abject surrender of the German universities to Nazism is too well known to need any description here (see Hartshorne, 1937; Ringer, 1969; Lilge, 1948; Steinberg, 1973). The Nazis were bitterly anti-intellectual, and some of the most gifted university staff, especially Jews, were expelled; as a result, the universities declined from their former eminence. The Swiss theologian Karl Barth, who taught in German universities from 1931 to 1933, provides a vivid description of the attitudes which the typical academic adopted towards the Weimar Republic:

> I found that the professors, as I came to know them socially, in their offices, in meetings of academic senates and elsewhere, were with a few

exceptions completely occupied with the struggle against Versailles that was common at that time, while their stance towards the poor Weimar Republic – far from giving it a chance – was one that even today I can only call sabotage. Not only did they offer no resistance to the political nonsense to which great numbers of students were assenting; on the contrary, they showed a paternal benevolence towards it, and some of them gave it their explicit support. They scornfully dismissed the idea that the year 1918 might have meant a liberation of Germany. (Max Planck Institute, 1979, ch.1:20)

The Nazis treated the universities with contempt and hostility. The student body declined from 124,500 in 1931 to 85,000 in 1935; new appointments were made according to political or ethnic criteria; and 'many teachers ... trumpeted nazi phrases which were the antithesis of scholarship but which flattered the prejudices of their politicised students' (Shils, 1975:1). The prevailing spirit was one which promoted anti-intellectualism in both genders, but a particular effort was made to reduce the status of women by making them concentrate on domestic matters and discouraging them from entering higher education.

After the 1939–1945 war, the Allies devoted themselves to the educational reconstruction of Germany. Their task was set out in the Potsdam Agreement as follows: 'German education shall be so controlled as completely to eliminate Nazi and militarist doctrines and to make possible the successful development of democratic ideas'. In the West, by contrast to the Russian zone, the cardinal principle of the right of Germans to determine the future of their own education was respected, at least in the long run (Hearnden, 1978:39). In January 1947, control of education was handed over to the German authorities, with the Education Branch personnel retaining advisory status. Devolution thus took place very quickly and the Allies did not play a strong, directive role for very long. In the American zone, for example, policies changed with the advent of the Cold War. All thoughts of German 're-education' for the purpose of changing its social and cultural structures was set aside. Instead, Germany was given aid for physical reconstruction, so that it could become a strong and reliable ally in the confrontation with the Soviet Union (Max Planck Institute, 1979, ch.1:48). In any case, strong intervention in the educational sphere would have contradicted the Allies' ideals of liberal democracy and self-determination. This was particularly the case in the British sector, where the British tradition ran counter to the notion that the nature of educational systems should be determined by government action. Re-education would have meant the intellectual reshaping of German society, and this was neither feasible nor desirable (Mark, 1983:43–4). It would have perpetuated a relationship of dependence, and created the risk of a lapse into chaos when support was withdrawn, as it inevitably had to be in the end. Reform in education was, therefore, accomplished by indirect, rather than direct, influence.

From 1947 on, the British zone had an Educational Adviser directly responsible to the Deputy Military Governor. The first of these was Robert (later Sir Robert) Birley, who believed it essential to inculcate democracy into the Germans by example rather than by precept, while at the same time offering them a maximum of help and information. He saw how difficult it was to teach a nation to be democratic through its schools and universities. 'What was really needed in Germany after the war', he states, 'was the development of a sense of personal responsibility for the affairs of State' (Birley, 1978:54).

The British authorities set out to find those staff and students who genuinely believed in a democratic future for Germany, and to encourage them to put their beliefs into practice. This was not always easy. Bird (1978), who helped to reconstruct the University of Göttingen after the Second World War, blamed opposition to this work on '. . . the well-founded suspicion that we were aiming to break the traditional system of oligarchic government of the universities and to make possible the development of democratic ideas' (ibid.:147). Bird felt that he and his colleagues were more successful with the students than with staff, since many of the latter were unwilling to antagonise their heads of departments and so jeopardise their academic futures by expressing views which those heads of departments might not share. Bird concludes (ibid.:150) that '. . . many were not keenly in favour of democracy in the universities', and notes that even the students needed much advice and encouragement in organising their own affairs – they usually tended to wait for orders.

Both students and staff had suffered greatly from isolation during the Hitler period and this had resulted in massive ignorance and naivety, particularly on the part of the students. Beckhough (1983:85) was amazed to find, when he served in his post as University Education Control Officer (UECO) at Cologne, that the Nazis had banned such a large number of the best German writers that many students had not heard of Heinrich Heine or Thomas Mann. In a similar vein, Sutton (1983) was struck by the childlike minds of many of the students at Göttingen. Expecting to find them fanatical and warped, he was surprised that men of twenty and more had apparently stopped growing mentally when Hitler came to power; what he encountered was not a nation of warped minds but a nation of Peter Pans (this was even true of the ex-soldiers; ibid.:112). Staff, too, were deeply marked by intellectual isolation. Post-war reparations included the handing over of German research to the Allies, and Edwards (1983:121) recalls how keen some of the professors were to undergo interrogation in the UK. Not only did the journey open up an intellectual dialogue with colleagues abroad, but it offered a few days' escape from the misery of destroyed German cities.

However, it would not be correct to picture the professoriate in post-war Germany as avidly absorbing the liberal influences of which they had been so long deprived. All too often, they presented a solid, reactionary front (Phillips, 1983:63). In 1948, a Report entitled 'University Reform in Germany' appeared (re-issued in 1949, and also known as 'Das blaue Gutachten' because of its blue covers). It stressed the social, cultural and ethical responsibilities of universities, rather than their role as research institutes. Their mission was not primarily to train specialised professionals, but to help students understand the world in which they were placed; this involved the cultivation of social consciousness, civic/political awareness and psychological insight. Indeed, the higher the degree of specialisation, the greater the need for an understanding of the general relationships of human action and thought. The essential tasks of the university were construed as humane and not just intellectual or administrative. To avoid the danger of technology becoming utterly inhuman and its latent sinister forces being unleashed, technical subjects were to be taught within a broad framework of Western humanistic thought. By this means it was hoped to restore the sense of the basic unity of knowledge which was self-evident to the great engineering generation of the nineteenth century. For non-technical subjects too, there was a need to foster the unity of culture by means of a compulsory comprehensive programme of general education (*studium generale*). In view of the universities' responsibility towards the majority of students who did *not* intend to proceed to research studies, the importance of teaching was stressed. A key concept in the Report was that of the university's duty to society:

If men and women do not learn at the university to fulfil their duty within the social body, it will be impossible to avoid a new political catastrophe . . . We dissociate ourselves from those conceptions which put, not man, but research in the foremost place. We believe that university activity is justified only in so far as it renders service to man. (URG, 1949: 6,10)

Although the German press was enthusiastic about this Report, the German educational establishment was not. In January 1949, a conference of Ministers of Education and university *Rektoren* (equivalent of Vice-Chancellors) met to discuss it. They rejected its emphasis on teaching and they reasserted the university's primary obligation to further knowledge through research. They were also displeased by the emphasis on the need for links between the universities and society because they wanted, above all, to preserve their institutions' autonomy, even in the face of the practical demands of society. It is true that there was some movement towards the promotion of the social sciences, one sign of this being the establishment of guest professorships for academics from Britain (Pingel, 1983:26). In the fifties, these were followed by the establishment of permanent Chairs in political science and sociology. Attempts were made to broaden the social basis of access to the universities and to democratise staff structures, but these were not very successful. Despite new ideas, little lasting reform was achieved. Hellmut Becker (1978:277) believes that if the reform proposals of this period had been given proper, rapid attention, the 1968 student revolt would never have occurred. However, the forces of reaction rather than progress prevailed and the old order – or something very similar to it – took hold once more.

Lilge, writing shortly after the end of the war, voices his uneasiness as follows:

> There is a tendency to resume traditions of teaching, thought and scholarship which, long before the Nazis, had become questionable. There is, too, a tendency towards academic life as usual. German universities still remain practically cut off from the outside intellectual world, and young men who are now entering an academic career under great difficulties say that they are suffocating in the stale air of stagnant traditions. Here and there a professor raises the questions of a new society, a new education and a new type of man. But no new intellectual life has yet begun to stir, and no leadership has come to the front. (Lilge, 1948:168–9)

One could point to four major factors which militated against reform of German higher education in the post-war period.

First, there was a distrust of centralism in education. Central government had proved so disastrous under the National Socialists that there was an understandable reluctance to concede it much power, even in pursuing reform objectives. State action was limited to the provision and improvement of material conditions, and pursued a policy of non-intervention so consistently that there were virtually no federal regulations on higher education until 1976. Many Germans must have been painfully aware that reconstructionist policies were necessarily two-edged since, in a dictator's hands, they could be used for anti-democratic as well as for democratic ends (cf. Pritchard, 1975/6).

Secondly, there was a massive practical problem of rebuilding shattered cities and amenities. Husemann (1978:170–1) points out how difficult it was to find the resources and energy needed for reform when the mammoth task of absorbing 17 million refugees still had to be faced.

Thirdly, the people who might have been able to bring about change were, for various reasons, unlikely to possess a real capacity and motivation to do so. Husemann (ibid.) notes that the people who could be trusted to take a role in public life were those who had been prominent in the Weimar Republic. These, however, were already in late middle age, and were too fixed in their ways or perhaps too lacking in drive and energy to be effective agents of reform; furthermore, the *Rektoren* and professors had a vested interest in the status quo, which gave them certain pseudo-aristocratic privileges. They were thus disinclined to welcome reform, which might deprive them of their privileged positions in society.

Fourthly, the Germans were psychologically on the defensive. Most of them were too shaken and insecure to do more than hold the tattered fragments of their identity together, and were far removed from having the self-assurance which would have enabled them to undertake wholesale reconstruction on their own behalf (Kloss, 1968). Robinsohn and Kuhlmann (1967:311–12) attribute the slowness of change to a desire to recapture material well-being and social stability; they diagnose a general distrust of 'new beginnings' and experiments, and suggest that the experience of total disruption after the Nazi period led many to look to old and trusted traditions for security. A publication by the Max Planck Institute (1979, ch.2:74) refers to a 'defensive nationalism' which made no claims to racial superiority but stressed the existence, rights, cultural heritage and dignity of the German people as a collectivity. This had the effect of lessening cleavages between different political and social factions, but also 'integrated those hidden undercurrents of political thought still close to the fascist past'. It 'contributed to a constellation of forces which made criticism of the educational system strongly suspect as a threat to one of the cornerstones of the reconstructed, fragile, politico-cultural German identity' (ibid.).

So it was that the classical university re-emerged, and continued to exist for almost two decades before it was seriously challenged.

Overcrowding of Post-war Universities

Marxist theory claims that quantitative change, if sufficiently great, becomes qualitative too. So it was with the universities. More than anything else, it was overcrowding which forced a rethinking of their essential nature, objectives and functioning. Overcrowding gave rise to a number of reforms in the 1960s and contributed to the student revolt of 1968, which was probably the most important single factor in bringing about the establishment of the comprehensive universities.

After the Second World War, 60% of the buildings and equipment in the higher education sector had been destroyed and it was a long time before this damage could be made good. Demand for university places was increased by the post-war baby boom. Tradition decreed that every young person who held the school leaving certificate (*Abitur*) was entitled to a university place, and the fact that it was politically and socially unacceptable to impose restrictions (*numerus clausus*) sharpened the disparity between demand and provision.

The exponential growth of the student population is indicated by the fact that in 1970, the total number of students attending universities and other institutions of higher education stood at 510,500; in 1960 it had been 291,100, so the numbers had almost doubled in a decade (BMBW, 1986/87; BW, 1987). Pressure on the system was set to continue for many years after that, because the number of students qualified to enter higher education was continually rising.

The overcrowding of the universities had several serious and far-reaching consequences. First, it caused a crisis in professional relationships which deprived the 'community of scholars' of its basis. This phenomenon is not unique to Germany; it is in fact a typical concomitant of the transition from élite to mass education. Trow (1974:57) notes that a consequence of expansion in any university system is that '. . . there is a loss of a close apprenticeship relationship between faculty members and students', and that

> . . . the student culture becomes the chief socialising force for new (post-graduate) students, with the consequences for the intellectual and academic life of the institution that we have seen in America as well as in France, Italy, West Germany and Japan. High growth rates . . . weaken the forms and processes by which teachers and students are inducted into a community of scholars during periods of stability or slow growth.

One obvious manifestation of quantitative expansion was that staff–student ratios became quite unacceptably large. The situation in German universities at the beginning of the 1960s has been described as follows:

> At the University of Munich, in the Law Faculty, there are 175 students per teacher: in the economic and social sciences in Cologne, there is one teacher to 250 students. In the more popular or 'mass' subjects, the situation is still worse. In 1958, there were two teachers of English to 689 students. . . . Practical work and seminars with several hundred participants have become common. Only students who are outstandingly talented or who are tenacious and insistent can obtain personal contact with their teachers. (*Minerva*, 1962:91)

The adverse effects of overcrowding upon staff–student relationships have been documented in various empirical studies. One carried out by Hitpass and Mock (1972) was based on a sample of 5,396 students in eight universities of North Rhine-Westphalia. The students perceived the professors as distant and autocratic; 67% said that they were 'unapproachable'; 53% said that they were 'self-important', while less than half claimed that they were 'conscientious'. Most students believed that politics and society interested their professors only indirectly in the narrow context of their work and the publicity which was useful for it. Hitpass and Mock (ibid.:17) advocate the comprehensive university as the best solution to the problems of higher education.

In a survey carried out at the beginning of the 1960s and quoted by Bauss (1977:228), it was found that only 8% of the students 'frequently' discussed questions relating to their studies with their professors; 20% did this 'seldom', 24% 'now and again' and 48% 'never'. About 80% wanted personal contact with professors, but only 16% had talked with them 'often' about non-academic questions, 15% 'once' and 69% 'never'. In fact, many professors deliberately avoided contact with their students and regarded teaching as a necessary evil.

Under these circumstances, there was clearly little hope of realising the unity of teaching and learning, or of teaching and research. Education had become mass production and the university a travesty of the 'community of scholars'. The Humboldtian ideal of staff and students equal in their pursuit of knowledge had been lost and replaced by feelings of alienation and frustration on the part of students.

A second major effect of overcrowding was a lowering of standards, both in the work of students and in the quality of academic staff. In keeping with the Humboldtian tradition of *Lernfreiheit*, degree courses are not of a pre-determined length in Germany as they are in Britain. Because conditions at the universities had deteriorated so much, students tended to take longer and longer to prepare themselves for their final examinations, and there were high dropout rates (Oehler, 1985). Between 1950 and 1960, the percentage of students enrolled for four years or more at university increased from 12.4% to 30.5%, and the percentage of those who had been at their studies for five years or more rose from 2.5% to 16.8% (Burn et al., 1971:174). More lecturers were taken on to cope with the enormous influx of students, and because they were sometimes appointed hastily and in large numbers, they did not always possess the high qualifications traditionally demanded of German university teachers. The country's national reputation for scholarship began to suffer.

However, profound and interesting changes in the universities were brought about by democratisation, itself a function of wider access. In 1957, financial assistance was provided for needy students through the 'Honnef scheme', which was supported on a fifty–fifty basis by the *Länder* and the Federal Government. This helped to change the class basis of student recruitment, and led to a reassessment of values in higher education, particularly in relation to the concepts of academic freedom and knowledge.

University autonomy in the nineteenth century had depended on the fact that the *Bildungsbürgertum* was a very narrow élite, and its socially privileged position had made the interests of state and university appear isomorphic. This isomorphism was strikingly illustrated in the idea of the *Kulturstaat*, which became an increasingly threadbare myth as the century advanced. Humboldt and Schleiermacher had both argued that if the state would only desist from excessive interference, then it would ultimately benefit from university autonomy, in terms both of useful knowledge and of competent, well-trained civil servants (Anrich, 1956:244–5, 381).

The insistence of men like Humboldt and Schleiermacher that there is no *necessary* conflict between state and university is entirely in line with the contention of Bourdieu and Passeron (1977:199) that the university need obey only its own rules (that is, act with *akademische Freiheit*), in order to obey the external imperative of legitimising the social order. The theory of social reproduction argues that the ideal of academic freedom serves to mask the academic institution's function in reproducing existing social groupings. The university's apparent independence and neutrality helps it to fulfil its function of social conservation in a politically acceptable manner (in the early nineteenth-century German university, the 'conservation' involved would have been – overwhelmingly

– that of a small élite); its degree of authority is all the greater for seeming to owe little to the state. The educational system actually seems most autonomous *vis-à-vis* the dominant classes when its essential function of conveying knowledge and its function of conserving 'the social order' entirely coincide (ibid.:198).

The democratisation of the university in the twentieth century, however, led to the admission of people who did not belong to the ruling class and did not share its values. Many brought their own value systems with them, and these were often in outright conflict with the values of the Establishment. It was both impossible and inappropriate for the university to exercise its traditional function of conserving the social order by incorporating the newcomers into the social élite. In any case, membership of an élite is by definition limited, and therefore incompatible with the notion of a mass university. The traditional university–state consensus about values could no longer be maintained in the face of a socially diverse and large student population. During the *Bürgertum's* 'heroic' phase in the nineteenth century, the state had found it relatively easy to assent to *akademische Freiheit*, because this was unlikely to be used against the interests of the ruling classes. Despite the fact that there were poor as well as rich students at university (cf. Fichte, 1956:192–3), its typical denizens *were* the dominant classes. By the twentieth century, this was no longer so, and the implications of this change were profound.

It became far more dangerous for the state to accept the reality of *akademische Freiheit*, although the rhetoric is officially enshrined in article 5, paragraph 3 of the 'Basic Law' (*Grundgesetz*). The intellectual development of large numbers of people from outside the ruling classes was potentially subversive, particularly if their expectations of economic prosperity could not be met. The heterogeneous class composition of the student population led to a critical questioning of the traditional concept of *Wissenschaft*, which the Humboldtian university had equated with a culture assuming no contradiction between knowledge, bourgeois society and the bourgeois individual. Once the democratisation of the student population had eliminated this concurrence, it became necessary to reinterpret *Wissenschaft*, bringing it more fully into line with modern economic circumstances and the needs of diverse social strata. A redefinition of the aims and ethos of higher education became essential.

The Reforms of the 1960s

Some Important Advisory Bodies

To explain why German officialdom responded as it did to demands for reform it is necessary to know something of the legal and bureaucratic machinery which helped put plans and ideas into action.

In the period after the Second World War, there had, understandably, been a horror of powerful central control of education. This resulted in devolution of functions to the eleven *Länder*, which were often quite *dirigiste* within their areas of jurisdiction. Co-ordination between the Federal Government (*Bund*) and the *Länder* was at first either left to chance or else deliberately (some would say 'benignly') neglected, until certain developments such as gross overcrowding revealed the increasing need for liaison between the various agents of change. Gradually, two major needs made themselves felt in higher education: a rational basis for the allocation of finance and the streamlining of Germany's research effort.

The Bundesministerium für Bildung und Wissenschaft As soon as the traditional universities were in a position to start functioning again after the War, they turned their attention to research. According to the *Königsteiner Abkommen* (Königstein Agreement) (1949), the financing of research was fundamentally a matter for the *Länder*, but the *Bund* had shared this expense since 1956 (Peisert and Framhein, 1980:36). Space technology and atomic power research began to flourish, and a Ministry for Atomic Energy (Bundesministerium für Atomfragen) was established in 1955. This was followed by the foundation of the Ministry for Education and Science (Bundesministerium für Bilding und Wissenschaft – usually shortened to BMBW) in 1969, from which the Ministry for Research and Technology (Bundesministerium für Forschung und Technologie) emerged as a separate entity in 1972 (ibid.).

The Wissenschaftsrat Research proliferated, in both the public and the private sectors; many commercial concerns set up their own research departments, not infrequently with support from the public purse; the German Society for Research (Deutsche Forschungsgemeinschaft) and the Max-Planck-Gesellschaft did much to promote the development of research. With so many different concerns all working away without necessarily being aware of each other's work, scholars, *Bund, Länder* and politicians all agreed that a co-ordinating body was needed to facilitate long-term planning and funding of research. So it was that the Council for Humanities and Sciences (Wissenschaftsrat) came to be founded in 1957. This was, and still is, the most important advisory committee on the higher education scene in Germany.

Peisert and Framhein (ibid.) emphasise the extreme delicacy of the Wissenschaftsrat's initial position, before it had had time and opportunity to build up credibility. It was the first central committee in which *Bund* and *Länder* worked together. Its high status was demonstrated by the fact that members were invited to their first meeting by no less a person than the President of the Federal Republic; the *Bund* wished to avoid seeming 'heavy-handed', and an invitation from the President was more acceptable to the *Länder* – jealous as they were of their educational prerogatives – than an invitation from a *Bund* official.

The Wissenschaftsrat is an advisory body, but the *Land* and/or *Bund* can enact laws or allocate money to implement its recommendations, once they are accepted. It has 39 members who work in two commissions, one concerned with administrative and one with academic issues. The administrative commission has representatives from the eleven *Länder* plus six representatives of the *Bund* (with eleven votes); the academic commission has 16 scholars or professors, plus six public figures nominated jointly by *Bund* and *Länder*. There are enough governmental representatives to ensure that the commissions know what is financially and politically feasible, and there are enough academics to give the work a creative and scientific impetus (ibid.:37). At first the Wissenschaftsrat (WR) was very cautious in its recommendations but has steadily gained in authority, to a point where Fallon (1980:71) can write: 'Its stable presence . . . and its moderate voice have provided an unseen anchor during a heavy storm that might otherwise have destroyed the German university altogether'.

The Westdeutsche Rektorenkonferenz Another important advisory body, more conservative than the WR, but with a major role to play on the German higher education scene, is the Westdeutsche Rektorenkonferenz (WRK). It was founded in 1949, and corresponds very roughly to the British 'Committee of Vice Chancellors and Principals' (CVCP), although its composition is broader. From the early 1970s, all institutions of tertiary education were allowed to join the WRK, and by 1979 there were 157 institutional members. Establishments with the right to award doctorates have a majority in all the organs of the WRK, thanks to a differential weighting of votes (Peisert and Framhein, 1980:33). The WRK's decisions are not binding on member institutions.

The WRK's brief is as follows: to seek solutions to the problems confronting higher education; to represent the needs and central concerns of higher education to the public; to advise the politicians in matters pertaining to higher education; to observe, document and report on matters relating to higher education; to co-operate with state authorities and other appropriate committees or associations; to collaborate with equivalent or comparable bodies in other countries (ibid.:33–4).

The Kultusministerkonferenz   A fourth body with an important bearing on any study of educational innovation in Germany is the Standing Conference of Ministers of Education of the *Länder* (Kultusministerkonferenz, KMK) set up in 1949. There are eleven *Land* Ministers, and their recommendations, which are advisory only, must be unanimous. While being conscious of the need to ensure supraregional co-ordination and uniformity, the KMK believes that it is in the interests of democracy in education to defend the autonomy of the *Länder*. It is worth quoting a statement on this question which clearly shows its awareness of the disservice done to Germany by false concepts of education:

The Standing Conference of Ministers of Education is convinced that the totalitarian and centralist educational policies of the recent past are partially to blame for the fateful confusion and servitude of spirit, and the vulnerability of many Germans in the face of Evil [*Ungeist*]. It sees therefore in the commitment and attachment to local and historically conferred autonomy, as well as in the diversity of social conditions, the guarantee of the inner healing of the German people and of the organic growth of their native culture . . . The Standing Conference of Ministers of Education will direct its efforts to ensuring that the sovereignty of the *Länder* in education will be maintained in all measures taken by the organs and authorities of the *Bund*, and that their work in educational politics will not be restricted in any way. (Peisert and Framhein, 1980:32)

The Bund-Länder-Kommission   The basic organisational structure of the *Bund-Länder* Commission for Educational Planning and the Promotion of Research (Bund-Länder-Kommission für Bildungsplanung und Forschungsförderung) was set up in 1970. (Its name was amended in 1975 to include a reference to research.) Its task is to develop long-term policies and budgeting strategies, not merely for higher education, but for the entire educational system (Peisert and Framhein, 1980:43). It consists of one representative from each of the eleven *Länder* (usually the Kultusminister) and seven representatives of the Federal Government. One of its first actions in 1971 was to instigate a series of pilot studies of various educational innovations, one of which was a feasibility study of comprehensive higher education.

Other planning bodies with responsibility for German universities exist and are described in Peisert and Framhein (ibid., ch.2), but the ones which have just been described are the most important for our present purposes.

Formulation of Educational Policy

The authorities were conscious that they would have to meet the challenges of university over-crowding. So far as expansion of the system was concerned, the dilemma was: ought the existing universities to be expanded or ought new ones to be founded? The latter course of action was more radical in that it was far likelier to lead to reform. Until the 1960s, however, the emphasis was placed on expansion of the established universities. Schenck (1976:23), taking a justifiably cynical view of the matter, states: 'Since new foundations always give an impetus to innovation, in the restoration phase of the Federal Republic, the view prevailed that additional resources should be used in the first instance for the extension of the old universities'.

The conservatism inherent in the policy of enlarging existing institutions was manifested strongly in the debates of the Westdeutsche Rektorenkonferenz. Hennis (1982:7) reports that the WRK, during the years from 1950 to 1959, bitterly resisted the founding of new universities, blocking even the most modest proposals to establish new institutions or to make polytechnics into universities. It also opposed the elevation of teacher training colleges (*Pädagogische Hochschulen*) into fully scholarly, 'academic' institutions and attempted to maintain the 'purity' of the university domain against intrusion from outside rivals. Hennis states: 'Every conceivable legal device was employed to interpret the concept of *wissenschaftliche Hochschule* as applying only to universities of the traditional kind'[1] (ibid.).

Although the forces opposed to reform were powerful and strongly entrenched, the Wissenschaftsrat began to demonstrate in a series of reports (especially 1960, 1962, 1965, 1966 and 1967) that not only quantitative but also qualitative reform was needed. It gave clear

---

1. The word *wissenschaftlich* here is difficult to translate. It connotes high status and is a coveted hallmark of high institutional rank.

guidelines concerning the traditional elements which should be preserved and the innovations which should be introduced. Some of its basic principles were as follows:

(1) *No élite institutions.* The Wissenschaftsrat carefully examined the idea of setting up élite institutions separate from the universities (cf. the *Grandes Écoles* in France) and decided against it (*Minerva*, 1963:219–20). It did not favour institutional separation of highly talented and moderately talented students, because it continued to subscribe to the democratic Humboldtian belief that the university should be a community of scholars and scientists enjoying equal rights. It also predicted that separate schools of advanced study would attract the best staff and students, thus causing the universities to lose status and financial support. It rejected the notion that teaching and research should be carried on in separate institutions, taking the traditional view that teaching is enlivened by research, and that students must have the opportunity to come into contact with important work and do some research themselves in their later years at university (WR, 1966:9). In its assertion that all higher education must have a scholarly basis, leading to independent critical thinking, the Wissenschaftsrat clearly endorsed the Humboldtian principle of the unity of research and teaching (WR, 1967:119).

(2) *Admissions restrictions.* The question here was whether, in view of the projected increase in student numbers, measures should be taken to restrict enrolments. These would include a *numerus clausus* and examinations to eliminate sub-standard candidates. The Wissenschaftsrat argued that open entrance was in line with democratic principles and the needs of the economy. It accordingly recommended that limitations on admission to colleges and universities be opposed, and that educational facilities adequate for the anticipated student numbers be developed (*Minerva*, 1962:95–6). This desideratum, however, was to be subject to the preservation of academic standards; in certain cases where universities were hopelessly overloaded, or demand for a particular subject greatly exceeded the number of places available, there was simply no alternative to entry restrictions (WR, 1967:65, 107–8).

(3) *The establishment of new institutions.* The Wissenschaftsrat, while arguing the need for an increase in the size of the student body, did not favour an increase in the size of universities. As early as 1960 it argued that new universities should be established (see also WR, 1967:161–4). As we have seen, the Westdeutsche Rektorenkonferenz had bitterly opposed this option, and the Wissenschaftrat's advocacy of this course of action thus constituted a

progressive step, the more so since the WR also proposed certain patterns of innovation for the new establishments. It was concerned to defend and sustain fundamental values, such as the unity of teaching and research, *Lehrfreiheit* making staff independent of political or ideological constraints, and *Lernfreiheit* giving students responsibility for their own affairs. It believed, however, that these principles could be implemented without necessarily reproducing every feature of traditional German university education (WR, 1960:408). It thought that the number of tasks performed by any one institution should be limited, and the scope of its research and teaching activities selectively focused. The full complement of traditional faculties need not exist everywhere. It also proposed that large groups of students with primarily practical talents should be trained in specialised institutions. Furthermore, it called for changes in the system of lecture fees (*Kolleggelder*) and for the setting up of college residences (*Kollegienhäuser*) to help new students to adjust to the intellectual and social aspects of university life (*Minerva*, 1963). These suggestions must have appeared quite adventurous in the contemporary context.

(4) *Modifications to the staff structure.* In several of its reports (1960, 1962, 1965) the Wissenschaftsrat shows an acute awareness that staffing was not satisfactory in Germany's universities, and notes that the staff–student ratio had changed enormously for the worse. This state of affairs jeopardised the Humboldtian ideal of the unity of teaching and learning. The ideal of a 'republic of learning' was, the Wissenschaftsrat found, 'transgressed by the realities of an oligarchy of incumbents of senior teaching posts and the monocratic rule of the directors of institutes' (*Minerva*, 1963:221). It therefore called for a considerable increase in the number of posts available, and recommended that academics who were not full professors (the *Nichtordinarien*) be granted clear organisational and legal rights. In its 1965 *Recommendations*, it set out a proposal for a more diversified staff structure with a number of new positions, which would, it was hoped, prevent the strengthening of the hierarchical system. It wanted all teachers to be 'clearly . . . full members of a community of scholars and scientists' (*Minerva*, 1966:248).

(5) *Structure of degree courses.* In 1966, the Wissenschaftsrat produced a plan for curriculum reform in higher education. It stated that most students wanted to obtain a degree in order to find a job, and in this espousal of the vocational principle moved away from the Humboldtian ideology of study for study's sake (Kloss, 1968:338). It recommended that degree courses be divided into two stages, basic (*Grundstudium*) and advanced (*Aufbaustudium*). The *Grundstudium*

would last no more than four years, and the first two years would be strictly supervised, with individual guidance and instruction in small tutorial groups. The second two years were to be much freer, but the Wissenschaftsrat continued to emphasise the necessity of streamlining course content and limiting compulsory lectures.

(6) *Institutes.* The Wissenschaftsrat was critical of the practice which gave every professor an institute of his own. This was 'often no more than the result of tradition or a concern for prestige' (*Minerva*, 1966:247). Instead, professors in similar or related subjects should be grouped together into common institutes under collegial management (resembling American or British departments).

Resistance to the Wissenschaftsrat's Proposals   Having initially welcomed the WR's proposals for restructuring degree courses, the Westdeutsche Rektorenkonferenz eventually rejected them with some vehemence, perceiving them as a violation of *Lernfreiheit*, hence a restriction on the students' academic freedom. Kloss (1968:339) says that the WRK seemed to think that by rejecting the Wissenschaftsrat's 1966 proposals, it was preserving the research orientation of the German university against the modern onslaught of spoon-feeding, specialisation and vocationally oriented instruction. This controversy introduces us to one of the problems which was to bedevil the development of the *Gesamthochschulen*. Different institutions such as the teacher training colleges and the technical colleges had their own distinctive origins, traditions and ethos. The notion of following a clearly defined and structured course would have been much more congenial to them than to the universities, and would not have involved a significant departure from existing practice. The proposed division of courses into *Grundstudium* and *Aufbaustudium* roused the hostility of the WRK because it was tantamount to imposing an alien ideology on the Humboldtian model of *Lernfreiheit*, and because the 'holy cow' of research had been attacked (Peisert and Framhein, 1980:99). The old tradition was hallowed by time and confirmed by custom; it could not be abandoned without a fight.

The fundamentally 'cautious' nature of the Wissenschaftsrat's recommendations has sometimes been regretted. Thus Kloss (1968:331) points out that the 1960 and 1962 documents are firmly based on Humboldt's principles, and complains (ibid.:334) that the Wissenschaftsrat did not question the stratification of university staff *per se*. Likewise Fallon (1980:68) accuses the WR of being 'forceful and bold when dealing with quantitative considerations such as the need for more student places, but reserved and cautious – even timid – when dealing with such qualitative considerations as university function, organisation and structure'. These judgements seem, however, to the present writer rather harsh. As early as 1960, the Wissenschaftsrat had actually shown an awareness that quantitative change also involved such qualitative changes as the founding of new institutions with specifically delimited tasks. The financial situation in Germany in the early 1960s was favourable enough to permit expansion, in the course of which many of the Wissenschaftsrat's more innovative suggestions were taken up – albeit on a piecemeal, rather than on a whole-nation basis.

The Setting Up of New Universities

From the early 1960s onwards, a number of new universities were founded, and innovatory features owing much to the work of the Wissenschaftsrat were developed in many of them. Between 1960 and 1970, the following institutions were set up (see BW, 1987, 1/2:4): Bochum (1962), Regensburg (1962), Düsseldorf (1965), Konstanz (1966), Ulm (1967), Dortmund (1968), Augsburg (1969), Bielefeld (1969), Bremen, Osnabrück and Kaiserslautern-Trier (all 1970). Since the new foundations of the 1960s were the trailblazers of reform before the *Gesamthochschulen*, it may be worth glancing briefly at the special features exhibited by some of them.

Bochum was the first post-war university and, in many respects, a model for new developments all over Germany. In addition to the classical subjects, it had three engineering faculties (civil, electronic and mechanical). Interdisciplinarity was a basic component of its philosophy; it abandoned the old rigid structure of large faculties, substituting eighteen smaller departments or 'subject schools'. It had a strong commitment to continuing education in which it tried to create a model which would be both scientific and 'applied' (Handbuch NRW, 1986:45). It was planned as a campus university (a novelty in Germany) and, to prevent wasteful duplication, aimed to break down the chairholders' reserve against the common use of certain facilities (Böning and Roeloffs, 1970:22, 129).

Dortmund was the second new university in the Ruhr region, with special emphasis on natural sciences, economics, social sciences and engineering. It set out to cater specifically for the needs of industry, and was particularly conscious of its 'regional mission' as an institution of higher education.

Bielefeld, like Bochum, was founded with a reform mission, and was intended to have a distinctive profile of its own, instead of merely 'relieving' (that is, taking the load off) traditional, established universities in the region. Some of its special features were:

concentration on selected basic disciplines with certain clear emphases, interdisciplinary university-level specialisms, avoidance of 'institutes' within faculties, and the allocation of research grants for
approved purposes from the university budget.

The University of Bremen followed the recommendations of the
Wissenschaftsrat by establishing residential colleges for 80–120
students each, where special discussion sessions and conferences
could be held; this revived the concept of the unity of teaching and
learning and gave life to the notion that the university's function is
social as well as educational – a view 'revolutionary in Germany'
(Kloss, 1968:337). A basic organisational principle of the establishment was the introduction of *Projekt* study, an attempt to bring
academic study more closely into relation with the students' interests
and the 'real world'.

Konstanz is well known as an experimental university. In 1968, it
was specially exempted from the *Land* university law in Baden-
Württemberg so that it could pursue innovations more freely (Fallon, 1980:84). Its early history was marred, however, by strife over
its statutes, which would have increased the power of students and
Mittelbau at the expense of the professoriate, giving the former
representation at every level of decision-making. The row was
prolonged and acrimonious until the *Land* Ministry of Education
intervened to impose new and less democratic statutes, thus removing a 'promising laboratory for university reform' (ibid.:86). Nevertheless, Konstanz could still claim to be innovatory in other respects
– for example by having only three faculties (science, sociology and
philosophy), by keeping student numbers small and by restoring
research (particularly of the interdisciplinary type) to the centre of
university life. One special feature was the creation of a research
commission for the whole university; this tended to erode the traditional position of the *Ordinarius* as a leader of research. The
abolition of institutes was also intended to lead to 'democratisation'
by providing greater freedom in research work for assistants preparing their post-doctoral theses, and for academic staff who already
possessed that qualification (the *Habilitation*) but were still waiting
for Chairs (Böning and Roeloffs, 1970:95–6).

Regensburg, like Konstanz, was plagued before ever its doors
opened by conflicts between the academics and the state representatives. The founding *Rektor* aroused much controversy because he
had hidden his former Nazi sympathies, and was also frequently
accused of incompetence (Kloss, 1968:337). The Bavarian Ministry
of Education was unwilling to dismiss him, and he eventually re-
signed, but by then Regensburg had acquired an aura of conservatism.

The post-war foundations were characterised by an effort to adapt the classical university ideology to changing social conditions and to demands for reform (Peisert and Framhein, 1980:93). The power of conservative lobbies was always strong, however, and there was constant tension between attachment to the status quo and innovatory tendencies. Many of the older universities were scarcely affected by the reform, a fact endorsed by Hennis (1982:17) when he writes that: 'The universities of Cologne and Bonn, despite many years of attempting to follow the legislature's instructions, continued to be governed in the old style; they remained essentially *Ordinarienuniversitäten*'.

There was, however, in the Federal Republic an uneasy consciousness that reform had not taken place after the war, when it ought to have done. Even the new foundations and new ideas of the 1960s were felt to be inadequate to modernise the system. Many people agreed with the slogan coined at Hamburg in 1967:

> Unter den Talaren
> Der Muff von 1000 Jahren[2]

Germans were afraid that their higher education system would be left behind those of other countries. The Soviet Sputnik success in 1957 had shaken Germany as it had the United States, and books like Picht's *Die deutsche Bildungskatastrophe* ('The German Education Catastrophe', 1964) and Dahrendorf's *Bildung ist Bürgerrecht* ('Education is a Citizen's Right', 1965a) exposed the inadequacies of the existing system all too painfully, and alerted public opinion to the urgency of reform.

Although the new universities embodied interesting and important innovations, their numbers were small and their influence correspondingly restricted. By the end of the 1960s, all of them together enrolled only as many students as one average university. Such reforms as had been introduced were mostly confined to a small number of *Länder* or institutions, but nothing was agreed on a national basis. Because of the strong conservative tendencies in the system, it seemed improbable that any thorough-going renewal would be achieved.

Then, at the end of the 1960s, came the student revolt, which was to act as a major catalyst in German higher education.

---

2. *Translation*: 'Under the academic gowns, the mildew of a thousand years.'

The Student Revolt

The crucible of the student revolt was the Free University of Berlin inaugurated on 12 December 1948. It was set up by the Allied Powers, particularly the Americans, in reaction to the unilateral control which the Soviets had imposed on Berlin University in 1945. East German historians naturally wished to emphasise 'Unter den Linden's' continuity with the venerated traditions of the past, and chose to regard its official post-war opening on 29 January 1946 as a reopening rather than as a new creation (Tent, 1988:29). Soon, however, many staff and students concluded that there had, in fact, been a real break with the past. They discovered a tendency to admit politically active students who were members of the (Communist) Sozialistische Einheitspartei Deutschlands (SED); in the medical faculty, young people who were ideologically more malleable than older ones were selected – despite the country's immediate need for trained physicians; at selection interviews, students were asked questions about their future political deportment, and those who said they would concentrate on their medical studies to the exclusion of politics were judged negatively (ibid.:44–8). Professor Else Knake, who had objected to the politically biased nature of the admissions procedures for medicine, was dismissed from her post as Dean of the faculty (ibid.:62). Obligatory lectures in general cultural studies (*studium generale*) were felt by some to be Marxist-Leninist in orientation; and, most serious of all, in March 1947 several students who had been members of the Christlich-Demokratische Union (CDU) were arrested, tried in a secret Soviet court and found guilty of 'covert fascist activities' (ibid.:66). Students who goaded the leadership of the Soviet Zone's Education Authorities were dismissed from the University, and when a bid to make the Communists relinquish control of the University to a four-power arrangement failed, they called for the establishment of a new university 'free' from ideological commitments – hence the name of the institution. Names were obviously felt to constitute political capital for on 26 January 1949, a few weeks after the opening of the Free University of Berlin, the Soviets changed the name of their institution to 'Humboldt University', thus claiming a propaganda advantage.

From the beginning, the Free University was inextricably connected with Cold War politics and assumed great political and international importance. Consequently, in its formative stages it was given a great deal of American money and moral support. Its constitution was an unusually democratic one, which permitted direct student participation, as of right, in academic government. Students had prominent representation in the affairs of the University; they were members of the Board of Regents, the faculty boards and the Senate, thus giving them a say in the appointment of professors (ibid.:162). The entire *Berliner Modell* was based on the idea of partnership, the intention being to realise in modern terms the Humboldtian conception of a 'community of teachers and students'. Equality of students and staff pervaded the constitution of the Free University; it was orientated towards praxis, as well as equality, for it declared that one of its tasks was to prepare students for their future jobs. This has become part of the common rhetoric of education nowadays, but in the post-Second World War period was still a novelty.

Berlin's proximity to the German Democratic Republic made the modification of anti-communist attitudes particularly necessary (Bauss, 1977:18–19), and this distanced Berlin students from the political outlook of the FRG at large (the Communist Party, for example, had a legal right to existence in West Berlin). From 1958 onwards, many young staff were recruited who identified with the students rather than with colleagues, and created a kind of counter university. Habermas (1971:20) has noted that the proportion of politically conscious and liberally minded professors was greater at Berlin than elsewhere and that '. . . students in Berlin have always been able to count on the solidarity of a group of their professors'.

The revolt was triggered off on 2 June 1967 when a demonstration took place against the Shah of Iran. On the previous day, a few thousand students of the Free University had listened to two lectures in which Dr Bahman Nirumand, the historian, and Dr Heldman of Amnesty International had described the arrest and torture of the Shah's political opponents in Persia (Paloczi-Horvath, 1971:255). The Shah himself was portrayed both as an instrument of political persecution, and as a symbol of the bitter contrast between the fabulous wealth of the few and the abject poverty of the many. During the demonstration on 2 June, a student named Benno Ohnesorg (literally translated the name means 'care free' – a curious irony in view of the young man's fate) was shot from behind, by a plain-clothes policeman. This incident was viewed by Günther Grass as the first political murder in post-war Germany. Matters were not helped when the Mayor publicly thanked the police for their restraint, but expressed no regret at Ohnesorg's death, which he blamed upon the demonstrators (Pinner, 1968:138).

From then on, events moved rapidly. An 'alternative' university, the Kritische Universität, was founded at Berlin, and this initiative was copied elsewhere. All these alternative universities were relatively short-lived, but they set out to bring science and learning into contact with political and social realities; they 'attempted to confront science with politics and to judge its value by its social and political relevance and thereby to strengthen the opposition against the academic and political "establishment" which was felt to be authoritarian, undemocratic and repressive' (Böning and Roeloffs, 1970:151).

The students laid part of the blame for the events of 2 June on the Springer press, alleging that it had whipped up feeling against them and sown the seeds of violence. They broadened the basis of their protest, demonstrating against rearmament, atomic weapons, neonazism, the Vietnam war, colonialism and the Colonels in Greece. There was a sense of moral outrage that 'the established social systems are incapable of solving the problems of survival in other parts of the world' (Habermas, 1971:35).

On 11 April 1968, the charismatic student leader, Rudi Dutschke, was gunned down and seriously wounded by an unknown assailant on the Kurfürstendamm in Berlin. Protest escalated into open revolt, helped by the fact that students, living apart from their families, were easy to contact and mobilise (Bauss, 1977:25). The Humboldtian idea of isolating students from the bourgeois workaday world thus had effects which the original champions of *Einsamkeit und Freiheit* had never foreseen or intended.

Fearing wholesale social disruption, the government attempted to deal with the situation by introducing the notorious Emergency Laws (*Notstandsgesetze*). This caused the utmost alarm and moral outrage in many sections of the population. To quote Bauss again (ibid.:123): 'There has, in the history of the Federal Republic, been no theme which has concerned the democratic forces at all levels [of society] so long and so persistently as the Emergency Laws; about no complex of politico-social development of the Federal Republic has there been such detailed, fundamental and continuous argument.'

The Emergency Laws were directed against the existence of trade unions, freedom of assembly, confidentiality of mail, the right to free speech, free choice of job, and parliamentary control of the executive. The threat to freedom of research and teaching implicit in them needs no emphasis. It would not, perhaps, be too fanciful to see in the Emergency Laws a twentieth-century equivalent of the Karlsbad Decrees. Both were a panic response to undesired political activism.

On 11 May 1968, the Star March (*Sternmarsch*) took place. Between 60,000 and 80,000 opponents of the proposed Laws marched on Bonn (including 15,000 students) but the protest failed, and the Laws were passed at the end of May 1968. The student movement had now spent much of its political force, but it continued to make an important contribution to the debate on higher education. It forced the media, the public and the education authorities to discuss reform proposals, and constituted what Sauvageot (Sauvageot et al., 1968:34) has called a 'detonator', triggering change and showing that students could exert considerable influence if they chose to do so.

The students' intellectual critique of higher education had evolved over a considerable period. They had already formulated and published their ideas on university reform at the beginning of the 1960s, and a document called *Hochschule in der Demokratie* was published by the Sozialistischer Deutscher Studentenbund (SDS) in 1961. Originally the official student group of the Social Democratic Party (SPD), the SDS was at that time the most influential left-wing student organisation. Throughout the sixties, its relationship with the SPD was in fact a tense one. Quite early on, the SPD decided that the position and behaviour of the students were unacceptable, and declared in 1961 that membership of the SDS was incompatible with SPD membership; it subsequently excluded the SDS and cut off all subsidies (Pinner, 1968:149). This left the SDS free to move further to the left, and it became the most vocal and effective section of the extra-parliamentary opposition. Towards the end of the decade, the students came to feel that, by participating in the Great Coalition (1966–1969) with the CDU/CSU, the Socialists were collaborating with their opponents, and were no longer in a position to implement their own reform policies. The Coalition conjured up the spectre of a one-party state, suggesting echoes of the Nazi past.

A more conservative organisation was the Verband Deutscher Studentenschaften (VDS), an umbrella organisation based on automatic (therefore compulsory) registration of all students. The VDS, like the SDS, produced a paper on university reform: *Studenten und die neue Zeit* (1960). This was in many respects similar to the SDS paper, but it laid less emphasis on the relationship between the university and society, and was also somewhat less concrete in its suggestions about student democracy. Another reason for its having less influence than the SDS paper may have been the fact that the political mandate of an organisation in which membership is compulsory is open to question (Habermas, 1971:15).

Some years after the publication in 1961 of *Hochschule in der Demokratie*, a book of the same title was published by Nitsch et al. (1977). Some of the authors of this volume had helped to draft the

SDS document, and it is interesting that Nitsch himself, and two of his co-authors, later became university professors. The SDS paper *Hochschule in der Demokratie* contained a thorough analysis of the structure and organisation of higher education, together with suggestions for its improvement. It is thought that the term 'comprehensive university' (*Gesamt-Hochschule* or *Gesamt-Universität*) was used for the first time in this paper (SDS, 1961:154, 63), although Lüth (1983:24) points out that the antecedents of the concept go back to the Weimar Republic.

For a time at least, academic 'assistants' (*Assistenten*), who helped the full professors in their research, teaching and administration, also had a powerful influence on the development of educational ideas. They were part of the untenured *Mittelbau* and formed themselves into a body known as the Bundesassistentenkonferenz (BAK), which often sided with the students on questions of university reform. The BAK members concerned themselves with the conditions of non-tenured and non-professorial staff in general, but their ideas went far beyond such issues as their own salaries and conditions of service. In a series of papers (see especially BAK, 1968, 1969, 1970a, b, c, 1971), they outlined a comprehensive system of higher education for the whole of the Federal Republic, essentially grounded in the notion that knowledge is a means of bringing critical rationality and emancipation into society (BAK, 1968). Two of the BAK's most important papers are the *Kreuznacher Hochschul-konzept* (1968) and the *Bergneustädter Gesamthochschulplan* (1970a). Like many another underprivileged group, insecurity tended to make the BAK creative. In the debate on educational reform, it offered suggestions and analyses which greatly influenced the development of higher education, and which are still quoted in the scholarly literature of today.

Reform Proposals

Marxism provided the students and *Assistenten* with one of their main perspectives in analysing the relationships and organisational structures of the university. It was not the only basis of their analysis, but it was an important one.

The *Ordinarien* were seen as the owners of the means of production; they alone were believed to enjoy real freedom because all the resources were concentrated in their hands giving them total control of the whole academic process (SDS, 1961:122). The professorial institutes were viewed as cell-like configurations, arranged in vertical groupings, which tended to promote atomisation of knowledge and to militate against collegiality and co-operation in research. The students perceived institutes as organs of domination by an academic oligarchy (SDS, 1961:84–5), who sometimes treated them almost like private property; such units were said to be characteristic of a primitive stage of industrial capitalist development, in that they were small concerns, isolated from competition and from neighbouring 'branches' (ibid.:83). The control which the *Ordinarius* exercised over resources resulted in academic work ceasing to be a form of collegial collaboration, and taking on the character of some sort of 'merchandise'. Even if institutes increased in size, they still retained the essential character of a pre-bourgeois guild institution. They did nothing to promote the dialectic of spontaneity (creative individual achievement), competition (critical discussion) and co-operation (co-ordinated planning) (ibid.:118). Essentially, the monocratic institute was, the students believed, 'alien to knowledge, no matter how hard the director of the institute may try to mitigate this impression by tolerance and by the humane exercise of his authority' (ibid.).

The students went so far as to contest the academic expertise of institute directors. They argued that organisational, administrative and social activities distracted them from the real task of research and that, in any case, the increasing complexity of every field of knowledge effectively prevented them from keeping in touch with all the new developments in their discipline. The students believed that it was a myth that directors 'lead' the research done by their research assistants, and that these do merely subordinate routine tasks such as collecting research material. They resented the fact that although it is often the assistants who do the real work, the formal position of the *Ordinarius* allows him to make sure that his name goes on the scholarly paper written by his *Assistent*, thus claiming some or most of the credit; in the eyes of the young scholars, this is tantamount to intellectual theft (Nitsch et al., 1977:57).

Even in the field of teaching, the students believed that the power of the full professors was illiberal and repressive. They felt that genuine freedom of teaching was very limited because most non-*Ordinarien* were pushed into specialised or peripheral areas, while the *Ordinarien* delivered the main lectures at which attendance was compulsory. As a result, students often missed worthwhile lectures by non-*Ordinarien*, while the old-fashioned, authoritarian attendance requirements ensured that many other lectures were overcrowded (SDS, 1961:111). They also drew attention to the power of the *Ordinarius* in choosing his successors and approving candidates for

Habilitation (post-doctoral research); he exercised a form of academic sponsorship, tending to perpetuate a hierarchy which the students likened to the medieval guild (*Zunft*). In fact, Nitsch et al. talk of a 'refeudalisation', in which real freedom is reserved for the *Ordinarius*, while junior members of staff are free only to choose between different patterns of subordination (ibid.:89). The dependence of the *Assistenten* on the *Ordinarius* is such that independent-minded people tend to leave the system. Too much depends on personality, on prejudice, and on how far postgraduate students are prepared to compromise and adapt themselves (SDS, 1961:111).

The dependence of young scholars on the *Ordinarius* is also highlighted by the BAK (1968:31–2). At its best this relationship *may* be grounded in mutual trust, but at its worst may amount to sheer exploitation. As an untenured civil servant, the *Assistent* is bound to loyalty towards his employer, but the state is not bound to protect his employment prospects or social security in return. He can be dismissed without grounds at any time, and is often left far too little time for his own scholarly work (this is especially true of medical students). This unsatisfactory situation creates the danger of a 'brain drain' from the university to other careers or countries.

Both junior staff and students felt that, whatever value the concepts of intellectual freedom and the unity of knowledge might once have possessed, they were now being destroyed by the prevailing constellations of professorial power and unenlightened administrative procedures. In order to restore the intellectual integrity of the university, they advocated the introduction of a system of comprehensive higher education. The BAK and the SDS both agreed on the principle of comprehensivisation, although they differed on details.

The SDS proposed a comprehensive university ('*Gesamt-Universität*') in which *all* disciplines were to be represented (SDS, 1961:63). This reflected not so much a belief in the unity of knowledge as a conviction that the prevailing over-specialisation of subject work could be counteracted only by emphasising *interdisciplinarity*. Universities must be as open and flexible as possible, and the former divisions into 'universities proper', technical universities and colleges of education should be systematically broken down in order to promote the development of new combination subjects. The technical universities and the traditional universities both should incorporate faculties of technology (ibid.:64–5). Colleges of education should be integrated into the universities, and the division of the teaching body into teachers for élite and non-élite schools should be ended (ibid.:66). It is, however, significant that the SDS did not demand the integration of advanced further education into the universities. It is clear that the students associate such institutions with spoon-feeding and authoritarianism (ibid.:15–16). They do, however, insist that if, as they hope, students are to receive grants for going on to third-level education, students from technical colleges and 'academic' institutions should be awarded grants on the same financial basis (ibid.:141).

The BAK (1968; 1969), by contrast with the SDS, had a far broader picture of the type of organisational merger which it wanted as a basis for the *Gesamthochschulen*: it called for the integration of all third-level institutions. Simply co-ordinating the various institutions loosely was not enough; universities, colleges of education and polytechnics (*Fachhochschulen*) must be properly integrated to fulfil their didactic function (1969:68). The following are some of the basic principles enunciated by the BAK (1968:18–19):

(1) Teaching should be shared between *Gesamthochschule* and polytechnic lecturers; there may even be some involvement of comprehensive secondary school teachers at tertiary level and vice versa. There should be no discriminatory or undemocratic divisions between lecturers from different types of institutions;

(2) In the first three years of a degree course, there should be no bifurcation of long and short courses – that is, there should be a common curriculum for all students following a particular programme;

(3) A counselling system should help to shorten the length of time taken to complete courses;

(4) There must be a commitment to continuing and further education; 'distance education' should also be developed;

(5) Teachers for various types of secondary school should be trained together; those doing sixth form work should undertake more advanced courses of study. The BAK advocates a closer interlocking of theory and practice for certain professional courses such as law and education;

(6) Teaching skills in higher education must be improved; special institutes and Chairs in third-level teaching methods should be set up in as many universities as possible. Every effort should be made to use teaching methodologies which promote communication and co-operation; different social forms of education (for example, team teaching) should be explored as a means of overcoming student isolation and an over-abstract curricular bias.

In order to restore the unity of research and teaching, the BAK (1970b) developed the concept of learning-through-research (*forschendes Lernen*), which takes the Humboldtian concept as its point of departure, but goes beyond it. The BAK argued that there should be no division between research and the acquisition of knowledge (or skill); the former should not be deemed to begin only when the latter has been 'acquired'. An academic education should mean participating in the process of creating knowledge; it should be dynamic, systematic, independent, critical work, not the static 'possession' of certain techniques or elements of knowledge (ibid.:9). Learning-through-research is implicit in the notion of unity of research and teaching; *forschendes Lernen* should constitute the core of the teaching approach in the new comprehensive system of higher education advocated by the BAK. It will most often be realised in the form of a student-designed *Projekt*. This is a piece of work oriented to problem solving, the form of which will differ according to the subject involved. It could comprise a survey, simulation, case-study, clinical observation, interpretation of a text, architectural model or analysis of a legal or administrative problem (ibid.:27). This list is by no means exhaustive, but it illustrates that such *Projekte* demand an interdisciplinary approach which is related to praxis and to critical learning.

The *Projekt* helps to relate 'academic' to 'vocational' education, since it brings new topics of inquiry from praxis into research, and from research into teaching. It promotes independence and autonomous activity on the part of the learner who is actively involved, and develops the capacity to *apply* the concepts, principles and methods which s/he can already verbalise so well. The learner is initiated into strategies for gaining knowledge and solving problems, and is moved to reflect critically upon this process (ibid.:29). The BAK regards *forschendes Lernen* as constituting the didactic unity of a reformed university (ibid.:10).

The professorial institutes had done so much to breed frustration and fragment knowledge that both the students and the BAK suggested sweeping changes in the government of higher education. They wanted to substitute collegial self-administration for monocratic directorship. They advocated the setting up of departments to replace the unwieldy faculties (SDS, 1961:68–9; BAK, 1968:22). The BAK demanded that *all* members of a university should have the right to be consulted, and to participate in decision-making about important matters. Students must on no account be isolated, and thrust into the role of mere 'consumers' of education or 'users' of the institution. Administrative responsibilities should be spread as widely as possible, with four groups (professors, assistant professors, graduates and students) being equally represented at both central and subject area level. All members of an electing committee should have the right to vote for all candidates, and not just for their own interest groups. Deans should no longer be *ex officio* members of central committees, nor should there be any *ex officio* members in the executive body generally (BAK, 1968:22–5).

Both the SDS and the BAK demanded a more vocational orientation in higher education. However, despite the fact that the BAK (1968:11) sees preparation for a career as an integral part of the university's task, it resists a purely utilitarian value system. Knowledge should not be regarded merely as a means of boosting production in an industrial system, nor as the private property of some privileged stratum of scholars, who pursue 'pure' knowledge in an institution of higher education screened off from the world (ibid.:13). The search for knowledge ought to bring critical rationality and emancipation into society and serve as a medium of self-enlightenment for individual and society. No rigid distinction should be made between education and training; the BAK sees academic study as a potential source of economic benefit, but also as a refining, emancipatory and even ennobling influence on human beings.

The students, like the BAK, also leaned towards a vocational concept of education but their objections to the notion of 'pure' learning were much more ideological and coloured by Marxist theory. The SDS believed that general education had become a mere superficial adjunct to specialist education (ibid.:28–9). The university in effect delivers an upper-class ideology which guarantees self-confident leadership on the part of the bosses. The very 'uselessness' of such arts subjects as philosophy, history and art turns education into a form of 'conspicuous consumption', which buttresses social prestige, and sets the 'possessor' off from those below him/her in the educational hierarchy (ibid.:29). The same point is made by Bourdieu and Passeron (1977, Book II, 2) when they suggest that universities, like schools, perpetuate the social hierarchy, and that one way of repressing the lower classes is to place a high value upon the ease, style and accomplishments which come from membership of a particular social class rather than hard work. Hence specialisation, trades and business may be disdained, while such imponderables as general culture and social skills are held in high regard. The German students of the sixties were already conscious of the class aspects of the 'general' versus 'vocational' education issue, and it was class consciousness, quite as much as their own material, economic need which made them reject 'pure' learning and general, non-applied studies.

The ideas developed by the SDS and the BAK could be considered at much greater length, but enough has been said to describe their reform proposals, and their reasons for championing comprehensive higher education. Theirs may well prove to have been the most perceptive and vivid critique of the classical German university ideal in the second half of the twentieth century. British or American readers will probably marvel at students engaging so seriously and deeply with educational issues, but it should be remembered that German undergraduate students are generally older than their British counterparts, a fact at least partly responsible for their considerable degree of social consciousness and political maturity. Because they remain at university longer (according to Peisert and Framhein (1980:111), six and a half years in 1976), they tend to have a greater stake in it as an institution and to take a deeper interest in its workings. Longer average periods of study reduce turnover and render the student population more stable than it would be in the United Kingdom; this makes for a greater continuity in student political involvement, and allows the students to develop commitment and intellectual depth.

The point of departure for student protest was anger and frustration at the unsatisfactory nature of the universities, where they found themselves spending several years of their lives. They quickly realised, however, that the university is not an oasis, but a part of society, and this led to general political involvement. As Massialas (1969:124) observes: ' . . . whatever action there is among students, whether rebellious or not, is largely a manifestation of the larger problems that prevail in society'. In the 1950s one of the main concerns of the student opposition had been protest at the veiled continuity of the present with the heritage of the Nazi past (Habermas, 1971:22–3). In the 1960s, students increasingly attempted to combine educational reform with social criticism, and their dissatisfaction erupted publicly in 1967–8.

Admittedly there were certain bodies which were still inclined, even in the face of the student revolt, to drag their feet on reform. The response of the Westdeutsche Rektorenkonferenz was to emphasise university autonomy, and look to the institutions to improve themselves (which they were fairly unlikely to do). The potential strength of the student movement was greatly resented by some of the academic establishment, one of whose members, Helmut Schelsky (1969), complained that Dutschke and the SDS representatives were more 'powerful' than normal professors. He stated:

'today, ideological representatives of the student protest hold mono-
logues with an arrogance, which even the most egocentric *Ordinarius*
would not permit himself' (ibid.:11). He saw the students as tending
to usurp the role of the professors in academic decision-making and
believed that the latter would probably react by taking refuge in
Innerlichkeit, resignation and state-protected research (ibid.:71). He
resented the politicians' apparent responsiveness to student demands for educational reform, and suggested that this was not
wholly unconnected with the fact that students and junior teaching
staff represented a far greater number of potential votes than professors (ibid.:119). His greatest grievance was perhaps that many of the
proposed solutions were too egalitarian. They masked the fact that
the status of certain groups in higher education (for example,
teachers in the proposed *Gesamthochschulen* and the non-professional
staff) would be massively improved if the reforms and restructurings
demanded by the students were implemented (ibid.:116).

The student movement did not die out at the end of the decade,
but it did change its nature (see Webler, 1980, for analysis). In 1970,
the SDS dissolved itself, and the movement was felt by many to have
ended in failure. However, this was by no means the case. It had
succeeded in widening the basis of non-parliamentary opposition,
and constituted an important 'learning process' for the further
development of student activism. So far as university reform was
concerned, the students emphasised the social relevance of higher
education; they showed that it was perfectly valid to criticise the
university as an institution, and that the legitimacy of its ethos
cannot always be taken for granted. The importance of their contribution to the national debate on higher education has been widely
acknowledged. Bauss (1977:228) remarks that the papers produced
by the SDS and VDS were, for a very long time, the only ones which
were academically respectable and thorough. Addressing an American audience, Habermas (1971) affirmed that although 'reform
rhetoric' had been widespread, the only well-developed reform
concepts for higher education in a democratic society had come from
students. Rose (1970) also pays tribute to the role played by the
students in promoting public debate about education, illustrating
his point by showing how the political parties responded by passing
from indifference to involvement. Webler (1980) too emphasises the
importance of the student movement of the 1960s as a political
impetus for academic change. Nagel (1981:42) writes: 'The reform
laws at the end of the 1960s in the realm of higher education were an
answer to the demands of the students and *Assistenten* for the abolition of the traditional university and a reform of the whole edu-

cational system'.

The main effect of the student revolt was to shatter complacency and to make the authorities feel that effective action *must* be taken to increase the democracy and efficiency of the whole higher education system. Their will to reform was further stiffened by the critical reviews of German national education policy carried out by the Organisation for Economic Co-operation and Development (OECD, 1972), and by the International Council On the Future of the University (ICFU, 1977).

Plans for Comprehensive Universities

In 1970, the Wissenschaftsrat published a set of recommendations for the restructuring and development of the higher education system in the Federal Republic. In this document, it argued that both qualitative and quantitative changes were necessary, and called for the development of a system of comprehensive education at university level throughout the entire country. These proposals were meant to be taken in conjunction with others for restructuring the school system, put forward by the Bildungkommission of the Deutscher Bildungsrat; together, the two documents constituted an integrated concept for the reform of the whole educational system throughout the coming decade.

The Wissenschaftsrat recommended the merging of previously separate institutions into a comprehensive system of higher education. The 'organisationally integrated but internally differentiated' *Gesamthochschule* was believed to be the organisational pattern best suited to the needs of the future, because it facilitated the restructuring of courses, and the opening of universities to a larger section of the population (WR, 1970:18). In order to overcome one of the most negative features of German higher education – the impossibility of transferring between courses – the WR advocated intra-institutional co-ordination between different 'tracks', and inter-institutional recognition of various different terminal qualifications. The WR anticipated that about thirty new *Gesamthochschulen* would be needed, and that by 1980, 25–30% of a year cohort would be studying at the new establishments.

The *Gesamthochschule* (GHS) was not, however, intended to encompass *all* institutions engaged in the full-time education of students who had reached the age of 18 or 19. (The WR thus excluded further education from the GHS.) The general criteria for including institutions in the proposed comprehensive universities were that the courses offered should be informed by 'scholarly' (*wissenschaftlich*) concepts and methods, and that those who delivered the courses should be in contact with research (ibid.:19). The intention was to examine each institution on its merits, but the WR judged that teacher education and engineering were already sufficiently well-developed for inclusion in the GHS. It was anticipated that new patterns of staffing would have to be worked out to cope with the large-scale merging of different types of institutions. The overcoming of distinctions between academic staff which 'lack objective justification' was held to be an essential prerequisite for successful development of the GHS (WR, 1970:21). This, namely the achievement of an integrated staff structure, was in fact to prove a serious problem in establishing the *Gesamthochschulen*.

Regardless of whether comprehensivisation was to be achieved by combining existing institutions on a federal basis or by setting up new institutions, merger was still involved, since not even *Gesamthochschulen* set up *ab initio* would start entirely from scratch. New institutions would start by absorbing existing colleges and polytechnics in a given area, and then add a university component to them. Any *Gesamthochschule* would, therefore, encompass a number of different traditions deriving from its component institutions. This was expected to result in richness of tradition, flexibility of course offering, and good use of resources; it also meant that members of staff with very different qualifications and experience would have to learn to work together in mutual respect. Given the diverse patterns of professional socialisation which they had undergone, this would clearly not be easy.

The Wissenschaftsrat based its recommendations for the development of comprehensive higher education on the principle of freedom, both for the citizen and for the scholar. To be intellectually and materially free, individuals must have the highest possible level of education and be given every chance to develop their capabilities in accordance with their levels of interest and motivation. Article 5 of the Basic Law guarantees the scholar freedom in research and teaching. This freedom is, however, threatened by increasing pressure on university resources of staff and equipment; the state has a duty to ensure that the educational system develops in a way which preserves this constitutionally guaranteed freedom of research and teaching. There must be no undue political influence on research, but the universities must also realise that they are not isolated from state and society. The state and the universities must work together to accomplish their joint task (WR, 1970:9).

This concept of freedom has various implications for the organisation of education. The individual should not find himself in a cul-de-sac, trapped by the limitations of his qualifications or perhaps so rigidly trained that he cannot adapt to changing needs and circumstances (ibid.:11). There must be transferability between courses, and no qualification should be 'terminal' or narrowly vocational in character. There should be a system of counselling; recurrent education should be developed to maximise the individual's life chances and provide a more flexible work-force for the state (ibid.:13). The relationship between theory and practice must be rethought, especially as scientific/scholarly knowledge and methods are now extending into areas which were once associated with 'mere' practical training. In general, there should be a concerted effort to expand educational opportunity and to make the most of people's talents.

The case which the Wissenschaftsrat made for *Gesamthochschulen* was a convincing one. A certain slow reform tradition had begun in the 1960s; the WR had advocated some progressive ideas, which had only been tried out in a very limited way. However, the fact that a modest degree of change had already been attempted made it easier for the authorities to act fast once the time was ripe. The planning which had already been undertaken enabled the WR to react very quickly when the student revolt precipitated a crisis. It was felt that the piecemeal reforms of the 1960s were no longer adequate to give Germany a satisfactory educational basis for the future. The disruption and violence of the student revolt were fresh in people's minds and fuelled change. The principle of comprehensivisation appeared ideologically, economically and educationally sound, and was therefore accepted and promoted at the highest level.

Because of the German opposition to centralism, there could be no question of the *Bund* actually implementing the comprehensive principle. Only the *Länder* could do this, and they were usually vigorous in defending their powers against federal encroachment. However, as student numbers grew, so did pressure on their financial resources, and they eventually agreed that the *Bund* might participate in certain carefully defined areas which had formerly been their sole preserve. One of these areas was the establishment and development of institutions of higher education. The Basic Law had to be amended to permit *Bund–Länder* co-operation of this kind (Winkler, 1979:88), and, as we have seen, a joint commission for educational planning (now known as the Bund-Länder-Kommission für Bildungsplanung und Forschungsförderung) was set up as soon as the legal basis had been laid. One of the activities of the BLK was defined in a framework agreement (*Rahmenvereinbarung*) of 7 May

1971, which provided for the planning, execution and evaluation of pilot studies in Education, the results of which would serve as an aid in decision- and policy-making. Over a period of years, a series of pilot studies was commissioned and carried out with a view to exploring the feasibility of establishing comprehensive universities in the Federal Republic.

A formal commitment to the principle of comprehensive higher education is enshrined in the interim report (18 October 1971) of the Bund-Länder-Kommission, which states that:

> The objective of the reorganisation of higher education is to create a flexible system of gradated co-ordinated courses and qualifications which permits transfer. In order to attain this objective, the different institutions of higher education which have up to the present differed in entry qualifications, function and legal standing, must be united in a new higher education system. Existing establishments of higher education are to be developed or merged into *Gesamthochschulen* or else, while preserving their legal independence, should be linked by common organs, especially for study reform [*Studienreform*], into *Gesamthochschulen* . . . In cases in which *Gesamthochschulen* cannot be formed (or cannot yet be formed), assurances should be given that the institutions of higher education co-operate to attain the specified goals.

Two years later, in 1973, the BLK reiterated its commitment to the *Gesamthochschulen* in a formal development plan for the educational system (*Bildungsgesamtplan*, BLK, 1973), which contains this declaration: 'It is the goal of the reform of higher education to create a flexible system of gradated, co-ordinated courses and terminal awards' (BLK, 1973:48).

However, the strongest endorsement of the principle of comprehensive higher education came three years later in the new Federal Framework Law for Higher Education (*Hochschulrahmengesetz* (HRG)), which is of cardinal importance. It committed the entire system of higher education to the development of comprehensive higher education, and it laid down new democratic structures for universities. The HRG came into force in January 1976 and has since been amended several times, with a third and major amendment (or *Novellierung*) in 1985. It sets out general parameters for the development of higher education and, within these parameters, the *Länder* are entitled to enact their own legislation.

The political struggle over the HRG lasted from about 1969 to 1975. The first draft was drawn up by the SPD/FDP and addressed the issues which had been of such burning importance to the students of 1968 and the Bundesassistentenkonferenz. Since the draft was subjected to prolonged party-political mauling, it may well seem remarkable that the text when it eventually emerged was characterised by a considerable degree of liberality. Fallon (1980:92) points out that the real crux of the negotiations was the extent to which universities and other *Hochschulen* would be forced by law to conform to a general national model. The CDU/CSU did not want a national model dictated by the SPD/FDP, and therefore set out to ensure that the *Länder* kept as much control over details as possible, allowing universities in CDU/CSU states to retain and develop more traditional models.

Some of the most important provisions of the 1976 *Hochschulrahmengesetz*, especially as they affected the comprehensive universities and their development, are the following:

(1) *Curriculum and the GHS.* The *Gesamthochschule* was laid down as the basic model for the development of higher education in the whole of the Federal Republic (para. 5). All the different types of institutions of higher education were to be interlinked in a new comprehensive system. The structures to be adopted were either unitary, federal or, if these were not feasible, collaborative (in which case institutions would retain their legal independence). The curricular objectives which were particularly associated with the GHS and some of the new reform-oriented universities were now to apply to the system as a whole (para. 4). These included (1) common study courses, (2) credit transfer, (3) interrelationship between theory and practice, (4) interdisciplinary research and teaching, (5) the development of university methodology, (6) introduction of student counselling, (7) optimum use of resources, (8) research opportunities for professors deprived of them, and (9) regional/supraregional course planning (para. 4, section 3).

(2) *University democracy.* Joint decision-making (*Mitbestimmung*) had long been desired by non-professorial groups such as the BAK and the SDS, and a measure of it was accorded in the 1976 Law. Professors, students, junior academic staff, and other non-academic members of the university were all to be represented and have voting rights on the university's central committees (para. 38, sections 2, 3). In some of the Federal States, these interest groups had already been represented for some time and this gave rise to the term *Gruppenuniversität* ('group university'). At first, when only the three groups of academic staff had parity of representation, the structure was known as *Drittelparität*; later, when non-academic staff were also included to form a fourth group, the term was changed to *Viertelparität*. The 1976 Law, however, did not give parity to all four groups: in matters pertaining to research and scholarship, the professors were to have a majority vote – a rule which was greatly

resented by those parties who found their privileges curtailed.

(3) *Academic organisation*. Formerly, the units of organisation had been Chairs, institutes and the larger Faculty. These units were resourced with staff and equipment according to the reputation of the *Ordinarius*. Now, however, members of one large subject discipline, or several smaller but related ones, were to be bound together into subject areas (*Fachbereiche*) headed by an elected chairman (para. 64). The effect of this reorganisation was to take power and authority away from the *Ordinarius* and disperse it more widely.

The importance of the 1976 *Hochschulrahmengesetz* can hardly be exaggerated. It represented an attempt to overcome the accumulated inertia of decades of non-reform in higher education and embodied a radical rethinking of the purposes and structures of third level institutions. The linchpin of the entire reform concept was the *Gesamthochschule*, which was intended to promote equal oppportunity and to bring a much-needed flexibility into the system.

In some ways, the *Hochschulrahmengesetz* embodied principles which diverged from the Humboldtian ideology. The emphasis upon praxis would have been uncongenial to the founding fathers of the classical university. Likewise, the importance attributed to teaching methodology and student counselling was at variance with more traditional approaches. However, the broadening of representation in university decision-making was certainly compatible with the spirit of the Humboldtian university, which had been essentially democratic in its vision of staff and students equal in their search for knowledge. The fact that undemocratic behaviour and structures had developed around the *Ordinarius* was an accident of history rather than an integral feature of the original conception. The Wissenschaftsrat, as is evident in its reports of the sixties, had long wished to improve the *Mittelbau's* position and devise organisational forms to replace the professional institutes. It was the 1976 *Hochschulrahmengesetz* which constituted the most serious attempt yet made to achieve those reforms.

In a sense, the HRG was a response to the demands articulated during the student revolt at the end of the 1960s. It also marked the apogee of the comprehensive ideal, which was put forward as the model for the development of all existing institutions.

−4−

Structure and Objectives

The Federal Versus the Unitary Model

The intention of the education authorities was to create the *Gesamt-hochschulen* by linking together various institutions. There were two major ways in which such linkages could be accomplished – one conservative and one more radical. The conservative model was the *Kooperative Gesamthochschule* (KGHS) and the more radical variant was the so-called *Integrierte Gesamthochschule* (IGHS). Heated public debate raged round the relative merits of each type of GHS, and fuel was added to the fire by the fact that the same ideas were being applied in the domain of secondary education, where the proponents of the comprehensive secondary school (*Gesamtschule*) had to fight their corner against the defenders of the prestigious grammar school (*Gymnasium*).

The *Kooperative Gesamthochschule* is an association of a number of different institutions which collaborate over degree courses, conduct of examinations, use of resources and exchange or sharing of staff (Cerych et al., 1981a:23). The strongest form of KGHS involves a superordinate *Hochschule* which has corporate status in public law; alternatively, the component parts may retain their legal indepen-dence and their autonomy (Lüth, 1983:30, 31). Co-operation can also take far weaker forms, such as collaboration in committees at *Länder*-level. It is, however, usual to place some upper limit on the number of students and of institutions which are intended to be bound together in the KGHS, otherwise the whole concept becomes so loose and amorphous as to be virtually meaningless.

Cerych et al. (1981a:22–3) attribute the invention of the term *Kooperative Gesamthochschule* to critics of the full-blown comprehensive university, who probably wished to appear 'progressive' without committing themselves to any of the more dramatic forms of insti-tutional merger. Likewise, Lüth (1983:32) shows that the term is used so vaguely, for example, in the Saarland and in Rhineland-Palatinate, that one can only assume that the protagonists wished to distance themselves from the whole concept of comprehensive higher education. It would not be unfair to regard the *Kooperative Gesamthochschule* as a conservative stratagem, giving the appearance of change without the substance.

The *Integrierte Gesamthochschule*, on the other hand, unites different institutions of higher education, which lose their legal independence and form a new entity (Lüth, 1983:28). Not only are different types of institution integrated in the IGHS, but teaching and curriculum are also integrated, as far as possible. Within one subject area, there may be different levels of study leading to different awards; it is characteristic of the IGHS that much of the teaching for these different tracks is done in a 'common core' of lectures or sessions, attended by students aiming at different terminal qualifications. The interpretation subsequently enshrined in *Länder* laws, and taken as the basis of action, includes *both* institutional merger and curricular integration.

Despite the fact that conservative models usually prevail, it is the unitary rather than the federal GHS which has achieved the more enduring success in Germany. Superficially, this may appear surprising. However, Cerych et al. (1981a:79–81) attempt to account for the success of the unitary model as follows. Firstly, the CDU/CSU was much less enthusiastic about *Gesamthochschulen* than the SPD, yet Baden-Württemberg (CDU) was the first *Land* to put forward a plan for the establishment of comprehensive universities and for the restructuring of higher education (the Dahrendorf Plan, 1967). This is not as incompatible with the normal conservative reaction to radical reform plans as one might at first think. The CDU/CSU governments wanted a diversification of higher education, hoping that this would relieve numerical pressure on the élite universities; by promoting an open system with a high degree of mobility, they intended to control costs and to 'cool' the educational aspirations of the masses. The CDU/CSU was, therefore, quite prepared to entertain the comprehensive concept as a part of the total scenario. The SPD and the FDP, however, hoped for different results from educational reform. They wanted to bring about equality of opportunity, further education, socially relevant study and some narrowing of the status differences between terminal awards. So both the major parties were prepared to promote the *Gesamthochschulen*, but for very different reasons.

Secondly, the federal GHS was seen as a 'counter-concept', a sort of non-aggression pact in the realm of educational politics. It seemed to have relatively little of positive value to offer. Its main objectives – making programmes compatible and achieving ease of transfer between systems – were not sufficiently significant to justify a major organisational adjustment. It even seemed open to doubt whether increased ease of transfer would, as had been hoped, make the shorter courses of study considerably more attractive. For the moderate benefits which modest change could bring about, it hardly seemed worth the trouble of introducing the *Kooperative Gesamthochschule*. In the end, experience with the GHS showed that it was ill-adapted to the CDU/CSU objectives of 'cooling out' people's educational aspirations. Instead, it was much more effective at raising them, which was not what conservative politicians wanted.

The *Integrierte Gesamthochschule* thus came out on top, but was established only in *Länder* with SPD governments. The logic of this is evident, given that strong leadership from the state was essential in founding a new IGHS. Such initiatives were far likelier to be taken in socialist than in conservative *Länder*.

The Establishment of the Comprehensive Universities

Hesse and North Rhine-Westphalia, both *Länder* with socialist traditions, were the two major locations for new *Integrierte Gesamthochschulen*. As can be imagined, there was stiff competiton between local towns or cities for the planned new institutions.

Hesse

In Hesse, it was the ancient city of Kassel which succeeded in attracting the new *Gesamthochschule*. Heise (1981:54–64) describes some of the reasons for the city's success. Kassel had already acquired a polytechnic in the nineteenth century, and would have been given the *Technische Hochschule* (which eventually went to Aachen) if it had had sufficient funds to satisfy the Prussians in 1866. It also had an art school which dated from 1777 (although it had been closed for a period, from 1932 until after the Second World War). It had colleges for Mechanical Engineering, Building and Construction, Business Management, Social Pedagogy, Teacher Training and Social Work (the last a denominational institution); in the environs of Kassel, there were also two agricultural colleges. So, all in all, there existed a considerable basis of established institutions to form the nucleus of a new *Gesamthochschule*. There were several libraries (including the old and beautifully situated Murhardsche Bibliothek), and fine museums, which made a valuable contribution to cultural life. As Heise (ibid.:56) says, it was obvious that the new institution of higher education 'would not be built on sand'. Kassel had, after all, been the seat of the Landgraves of Hessen-Kassel, whose palace on the Wilhelmshöhe, with its artificial cascades, had long amazed and delighted visitors. Famed both for their hospitality and as patrons of the arts, the Landgraves often entertained 60 guests to dinner, and had amassed one of the finest collections of pictures in Germany. (Much of this wealth had been achieved by hiring troops to England, France and Holland (Bruford, 1935:39).)

In 1970, Kassel itself had a population of some 214,000, with a substantial catchment area in its hinterland which brought the total to almost one million. Higher educational provision in the area was inadequate, especially in view of the growing pool of working-class students who were being forced to 'emigrate' to study in other cities or *Länder* through the lack of facilities nearer home. Strong in trade and industry and having a complex service sector, it was clear that Kassel would benefit from an institution of higher education with a scientific-technical focus.

The Mayor, K. Branner, spearheaded the GHS campaign. A special body, the Arbeitskreis Kassel, was set up to promote the city's claims to the location of the *Gesamthochschule*. Local industry lent it support, as did established universities in the area. Since the beginning of 1969, the University of Marburg – itself under severe pressure of numbers – had supported the idea of a university in Kassel. The town's own campaign began about November 1968, and was crowned with success in February 1970 when the Cabinet of the *Land Hessen* agreed that the GHS should indeed go to Kassel. This was seen as a triumph for the Mayor, and the *Land* Prime Minister remarked at a press conference that Herr Branner had 'kept at it and at it for 7 years and had at last managed it'! (Heise, 1981:61).

On 18 June 1970, the SPD, CDU and FDP of Hesse approved a law establishing the Kassel *Gesamthochschule* (*Gesetz über die Errichtung der Gesamthochschule Kassel*). This laid the legal basis of the new institution, and allowed the *Bund* to support it. A mere twenty months after the decision to found the GHS, the first students were admitted. The speed with which the institution was established is an indication of the support given it by both the public and the politicians, and of the financial priority accorded to it (Oehler, 1981:23).

North Rhine-Westphalia

In North Rhine-Westphalia (NRW) integrated comprehensive universities were founded at Duisburg, Essen, Paderborn, Siegen and

Wuppertal, most of which are located, broadly speaking, in the Ruhr. This is, of course, the industrial heartland of Germany, and has over five million inhabitants, with heavy working-class concentrations. Until the mid-twentieth century, it was underprovided with universities – a legacy of the old imperial belief that the workers should not be given ideas above their station, lest higher education might make them critical of the social order, with consequent losses of stability and efficiency at work. The lack of universities in the Ruhr was thus calculated to 'keep people down'. The new foundations of the 1960s, like Bochum, Bielefeld and Dortmund, had done something to alleviate the situation, but the demand for places had not yet been fully met.

Planning for the new institutions was carried out by the Ministry of NRW during 1970 and 1971. On 27 April 1971, the NRW Cabinet took a decision to set up new integrated comprehensives in the above-named five cities, and to link together its other institutions of higher education. On 30 May 1972, a law was passed to make possible the founding of the new *Gesamthochschulen (Gesetz über die Errichtung und Entwicklung von Gesamthochschulen im Lande Nordrhein-Westfalen* (GHEG)). The GHEG resembled its equivalent in Hesse, but gave the NRW Ministry greater decision-making powers, even within the projected institutions themselves (Winkler, 1979; Cerych et al., 1981a).

The city of Duisburg had already possessed a university from 1655 to 1818. Its old and new universities are the subject of a book (published 1982) by Helmut Schrey, who from 1972 to 1975 was the founding *Rektor* of the new *Gesamthochschule*. The IGHS was based on the *Pädagogische Hochschule* of the Ruhr and the *Fachhochschule* of Duisburg. In 1984–85, it had 10,500 registered students (Handbuch NRW, 1986:51).

The city of Essen at present has about 630,000 inhabitants, which makes it the fifth largest in Germany. Its association with the Krupp corporation led to 272 bombing attacks during the Second World War, because of the Allies' desire to destroy the Krupp armaments factories. Much of the city has had to be reconstructed, but the environment is now a pleasant one. The IGHS is the only *Gesamthochschule* to have had a university component at the time of its foundation – the clinic for theoretical and practical medicine (at one time attached to the University of Bochum). It also incorporated a *Pädagogische Hochschule* and the Essen *Fachhochschule*, which offered courses in Art and Design, Sociology and Commerce. In 1984–85, it had about 17,400 students (Handbuch NRW, 1986:53). With about 4,000 staff it is one of the largest employers in the region.

The Paderborn IGHS has a particularly attractive setting in a city with an ancient cathedral, a theological college and a fine old town hall. A nucleus was provided by the *Pädagogische Hochschule* of Westfalen-Lippe and the *Fachhochschule*, with outlying departments in Meschede, Soest and Höxter. These outstations are some distance away from Paderborn, and no attempt has been made to establish university courses in them, which means that Paderborn is not really fully unified; however, its four campuses give it a special character . In 1984–85, there were 11,610 students, of whom about 80% came from the *Land* of North Rhine-Westphalia.

The Siegen IGHS is situated in a range of hills known as Siebengebirge. Birthplace of the Flemish painter Peter Paul Rubens, and ancestral seat of the princes of Nassau and Orange, the city is now the focal centre for a regional population of about 600,000. Like many of the other *Gesamthochschulen*, the IGHS was based on the *Pädagogische Hochschule* and the *Fachhochschule*, the latter having been created in 1971 by merging colleges of mechanical engineering, commerce and social pedagogy. With 8,000 students in the winter semester of 1984–85, it is the smallest of the NRW comprehensive universities. About 63.5% of its students come from localities in or close to Siegen.

The last of the five NRW *Gesamthochschulen* is in Wuppertal-Elberfeld (population 380,621) – famous for its hanging railway and as the birthplace of Friedrich Engels. The 'Bergische Universität', as it is known, is situated high on a hill and, with 12,224 students in 1984–85, is the second largest NRW IGHS after Essen. Ninety per cent of the student body comes from the *Land* and every twenty-fifth student is a foreigner. It is particularly proud of its work in teacher training, and carries on a multiplicity of other research activities.

Physically, the *Gesamthochschulen* in North Rhine-Westphalia are all similar, since economic considerations appear to have dictated a uniform architecture. The buildings are, of course, modern – large, and rather impersonal, but solid. Kassel's are less high-rise than NRW's and thus feel more homely, particularly since brick is used extensively. The comprehensives, especially those in NRW, are almost self-contained villages. Libraries are usually efficient and pleasant to work in, with well-organised and cheap photocopying facilities. Although the institutions are very large by British standards, the physical environment is certainly no worse than in modern British universities, once one has learned to find one's way around the very large campuses.

It is curious to reflect that comprehensive universities were intro-

Map 4.1 The German Comprehensive Universities

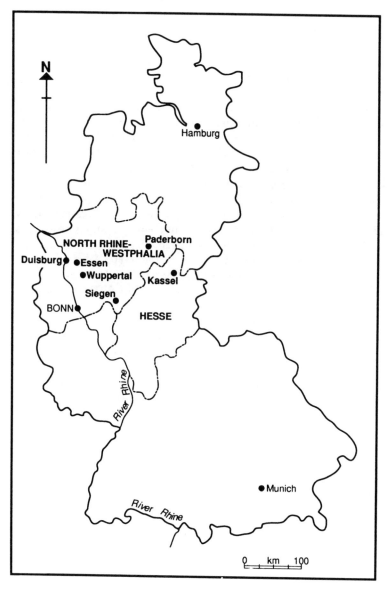

duced as a major innovation in a national education system where comprehensive schools (*Gesamtschulen*) have not been very successful. Such schools existed in the integrated or co-operative forms which we have already examined in connection with the *Gesamthochschulen* and were, for reasons which have already been suggested, much more popular in SPD than in CDU/CSU *Länder*. Nevertheless, they were surrounded by fierce controversy and, by 1980–81, only 8% of all secondary school pupils were attending *Gesamtschulen* of either type (Max Planck Institute, 1979, ch. 10:219).

The six institutions which we have described are the only ones in the Federal Republic which are strictly 'integrated' as defined in this chapter. Peisert and Framhein (1980:21) claim that there were eleven *Gesamthochschulen* in 1977, but Cerych (1981a:23) and Winkler (1979:370) both argue that some Bavarian universities which were called *Gesamthochschulen* did not really qualify, because they lacked some of the distinguishing characteristics. For example, the *Hochschulen* of Eichstätt, Neudettelsau and Bamberg, and the Army *Hochschule* in Munich, did not have different gradations of awards within the same subject area. Winkler (ibid.) suggests that the Bavarian government was merely using the 'GHS' label to appear active and progressive in educational matters, while actually avoiding change and muddying the objectives of the GHS. We should, however, note the existence of a seventh institution which might justly claim to be considered a comprehensive university. This is the 'distance university' of Hagen, founded in 1974 and much influenced by the British Open University. Lessons are broadcast to the students, about 80% of whom are in employment (Handbuch NRW, 1986:57). Because it is not performing the same function nor catering for the same market as the other *Gesamthochschulen* we shall not discuss it further.

The Aims of the *Gesamthochschulen*

One of the great attractions of the comprehensive universities was that they seemed capable of being 'all things to all men'. Thus, Gieseke and Eilsberger (1977:8) state:

> In general, it could be said that the idea of the comprehensive university to a certain extent seemed to offer something to everyone, to the 'progressives' as well as to the 'technocrats' or the 'conservatives'. The many-sidedness and attractiveness of the comprehensive university idea during the first stages of the discussion cannot be over-emphasised.

The general aims of the *Gesamthochschulen* were laid down in the 1976 *Hochschulrahmengesetz*, but within these parameters the *Länder* were entitled to make their own laws. Since most of the new institutions were located in North Rhine-Westphalia, we shall turn to a *Land* document of NRW, *Gesamthochschulen in Nordrhein-Westfalen* (MWF NRW, 1979), which gives a clear, succinct account of what comprehensive higher education hopes to achieve. In 1979, of course, the *Gesamthochschulen* were already operational, so the formulation of the aims is not a priori and over-optimistic; it is a realistic definition of what the institutions were, and still are, trying to bring about. Broadly, the same principles apply in Hesse, except that there is somewhat less emphasis upon the social objectives of university education and no mention of regionalisation of efficiency (Cerych et al., 1981a:29).

(1) *Organisational merger.* The essential principles involved in the amalgamation of institutions are set out in MWF NRW (1979) as follows:

(a) Autonomy: The *Gesamthochschulen* have the right to their own organs of self-administration, and to supervise doctoral and post-doctoral research;
(b) Merger of Institutions: They comprise universities, *Pädagogische Hochschulen* and *Fachhochschulen*, merged in a unitary system, and should fulfil the functions that each of these had hitherto fulfilled separately;
(c) Merger of Subject Areas: They form new, integrated research and teaching units which are conducive to interdisciplinary work;
(d) Merger of Staff: They bind the academic staff together into a functional unity for the purposes of teaching and research.

(2) *Social justice.* There are two major ways in which the *Gesamthochschulen* are intended to increase equality of opportunity. The first is *regionalisation*, that is by making education available in previously disadvantaged regions. The *Gesamthochschulen* are intended to relieve pressure on existing universities, and to offer greater chances of third-level education to local youngsters, especially in areas where educational provision has not been adequate. They are meant to help contribute to the reform of study structures, content and objectives which has been demanded since the 1960s; in a word, they are expected to renew higher education (ibid.:14). The second way is *broader access*, by making university-level courses available to students who lack the traditional matriculation qualification – that is, *Abitur*. A novel feature of the *Gesamthochschulen* is that they allow

students with different levels of entry qualifications to study together, both having the same chance to decide upon their areas of specialism. The academic curriculum consists of co-ordinated long and short courses which allow for transferability from one to the other and, within a subject area, are graded according to length and differentiated according to subject emphases. They terminate with the award of a degree (*Diplom*)[1] (ibid.:16). These common courses, known as *integrierte Studiengänge*, are intended to contribute to equality of oppportunity, ease of transferability between courses (*Durchlässigkeit*) and promote job mobility.

(3) *Compensatory education.* Bridging courses (*Brückenkurse*) are to be offered to students who are in the *integrierte Studiengänge*, but do not have *Abitur*. There is always a danger that students with leaving certificates geared to polytechnics (*Fachhochschulreife*) will be unable to keep up with the *Abitur* holders, or that the latter will be held back. The bridging courses are intended to level out differentials and are an essential part of the *integrierte Studiengänge* (ibid.:21). (It should be noted that the bridging courses are peculiar to North Rhine-Westphalia and are *not* required in Hesse.)

(4) *Promotion of applied and vocational studies.* The GHS must help to overcome the dichotomy between theory and practice. Professional activity in the world of work now demands flexibility and the ability to develop one's work independently. For this reason, practice *and* theory must both be consciously embodied in higher education, even if the emphasis varies from course to course.

(5) *New degree courses with flexibility of transfer between types.* Much is hoped from the *integrierte Studiengänge*. Under the existing system it is very hard for a student who has chosen the wrong course to correct the mistake. Many of the short courses are cul-de-sacs and the initial choice is more or less determined by the type of school leaving certificate the student holds (ibid.:14). Because young people are steered towards the practical or the theoretical 'track', and urged to start specialising as soon as they enter secondary school, early errors of judgement can be corrected only with great difficulty. The co-ordination of courses possible in a *Gesamthochschule* system will keep choices open much longer – vital for the life chances of

1. Caution must be exercised when talking of a 'degree' course in the German higher education system. Traditionally, the doctorate was the only *degree* awarded. Most students study for qualifications awarded by the state (*Staatsexamen*) rather than by the university; the so-called *Diplom* is perhaps roughly equivalent to the British Bachelor's degree (although the Germans study for much longer, range more broadly, and have to prepare a dissertation which is equal or superior in standard to most UK Master's ones); the *Magister* is the structural equivalent of the Master's degree (although often academically more advanced).

students, since income, social prestige and security all depend to a considerable extent upon the type of school leaving certificate one holds (ibid.:14).

It is intended to take special measures to increase the popularity of the short courses (three rather than four years). Traditionally, only the longer courses have been regarded as truly *wissenschaftlich*, and the new structures of the GHS mean that it has to work hard to dispel public reservations about the quality of a six-semester degree. However, it is hoped that the new concept of *Wissenschaft*, as the interrelationship of theory and practice, will achieve widespread acceptance (MWF NRW, 1979:20); moreover, the development of more advanced modules (*Aufbaustudium*), available on top of a three-year course, should help to make the new system more attractive (ibid.:22). The *Land* government of NRW is aware that these important objectives cannot be achieved to order: 'The state can . . . only stimulate, accompany and support, thereby respecting and protecting the freedom of research and teaching as the core of autonomy in higher education' (ibid.:16). There are surely clear echoes here of Humboldt and the *Kulturstaat*. The entire tone of the document (NRW, 1979) is one of commitment to what is being attempted. While the writers regret that reforms to promote equality of opportunity (for the benefit of both individual and society) can be achieved only step by step and not in one great leap forward, they clearly believe in these reforms and really want them to 'happen' (ibid.:22). They also realise, however, that the GHS has been regarded as a kind of panacea for all the ills of higher education, and that no single institution can possibly satisfy these expectations.

Some of the objectives of the *Gesamthochschulen* are quite radical, if one compares them with the perverted structures which had actually evolved in the traditional university system, but are much less so when compared with the 'real' original Humboldtian ideology. The notion of institutional merger would not have seemed very strange to the founders of the University of Berlin – as we have seen, Schleiermacher had long ago suggested an institutional merger as the concrete expression of the unity of knowledge. The *Gesamthochschule* commitment to interdisciplinarity is in fact very much in keeping with the traditional concept of the unity of knowledge; likewise, the intention to extend the opportunity for research to a greater number of teachers in third-level education can be viewed as an endorsement of the principle of unity of research and teaching. The attempt to broaden the social basis of recruitment to the *Gesamthochschulen* would not have been uncongenial to the original proponents of the Humboldtian ideal; after all, Fichte, although in many ways a stern disciplinarian, had called for a system of state aid for needy students who wished to enter university.

In some respects, however, the aims of the *Gesamthochschulen* were a departure from German educational orthodoxy. The attempt to quantify and shorten study times was an encroachment on *Lernfreiheit*, and the bias in favour of applied courses was too much like *Brotstudium*[2] to have pleased Humboldt or Schiller. The policy of regionalisation was directly contrary to that attempted in the foundation of Berlin University. There, the intention had been less to serve a particular narrowly defined geographical area than to escape from provincialism by maximising the appeal of the institution throughout the Germanies (which was why the widely understood term 'university' was used in naming the establishment). It was, above all, the utilitarian and applied approach which differentiated the *Gesamthochschule* from the classical university. In the 1960s, the Wissenschaftsrat had already attempted to promote applied studies, but for the principle to command more widespread support had to await a change in the spirit of the age. This was created by overcrowding, and above all, by the student revolt.

The Main Institutional Components of the *Gesamthochschulen*

The integrated comprehensive universities in North Rhine-Westphalia and Hesse were formed by merging existing non-university institutions and gradually recruiting staff from the established traditional universities. To understand the political aspects of the merger, it is necessary to know something of the history and ethos of the institutions which combined to form the *Gesamthochschulen*.

The *Gesamthochschule* staff were drawn from the universities themselves, the newly formed 'polytechnics' (*Fachhochschulen*), the teacher training colleges (*Pädagogische Hochschulen*) and certain other specialist colleges of higher education. In Hesse, a college of art (*Kunsthochschule*) was included (Blase, 1981). Staff from these institutions differed in their qualifications, experience, self-images and professional expectations.

The Classical University

The history and nature of the classical university have already been described at length in chapter 2. It is a highly prestigious, élite

2. *Brotstudium* – A course to enable one to earn one's daily bread.

institution in which most of the permanent staff have had to struggle hard to attain their positions. Even competent and experienced scholars have difficulty in securing tenure, and evidence of substantial academic achievement is needed to become a professor. It is not at all unusual for a man or woman called to a Chair to have already published a book from his/her doctoral thesis, a second book from the post-doctoral thesis, and two or three dozen articles as well. It would be unthinkable for someone to be appointed to a Chair with only a primary degree and no book to his/her name – yet this happens quite often in the British system, particularly in certain departments, such as adult and continuing education. In 1981, the average age at which the *Habilitation* was completed was 38.1 (Knopp, 1984:69), and this means that people in the German university system are rather older than elsewhere before they can embark on a serious, institutional academic career. They need the *Habilitation* just to get their feet on the bottom rung of the university ladder. Clearly, people of whom so much is demanded will hesitate before conceding parity of esteem to academic staff from other types of institution.

The 'Polytechnics'

The history of the German *Fachhochschulen* (roughly equivalent to the British polytechnics) is traced in the Handbuch NRW (1986:31–9), upon which the following account is based.

The *Fachhochschulen*, like so many other innovations in German education, resulted from agitation during the student revolt. Their immediate predecessors were the *Ingenieurschulen*, which derived from the old schools of mechanical engineering and building construction. The evolution of the *Ingenieurschulen* is an interesting socio-economic study in its own right, reflecting the dissolution of the old guilds, the introduction of freedom of trade and the decay of the corporate state (*Ständesstaat*). These developments offered hope of social betterment to new sections of the population and increased their need for a standard of education commensurate with their aspirations (ibid.:31–2).

The schools of mechanical engineering originated in Prussia, which had no polytechnic schools until 1866. Higher technical education was carried out in the Trade Institute (Gewerbeinstitut) and the Academy of Building (Bauakademie). The Berlin institutions were incorporated in the Technical University of Berlin-Charlottenburg (1879); the provincial ones offered two-year courses which attempted to train craftsmen and technicians, and also to prepare students for entry to the *Technische Hochschulen*. They proved unequal to this double task and their numbers fell. In 1882, they were transformed into *Oberrealschulen*, preparing students for entry to the *Technische Hochschulen*.

In 1889 the Association of German Engineers (Verein Deutscher Ingenieure, VDI) worked out a series of principles for the development of mechanical engineering, and in 1898 the corresponding Prussian institutions were re-named 'Advanced Schools for Mechanical Engineering'. Many new foundations followed. In 1901, the duration of the course was fixed at four semesters, the entrance requirements being an upper secondary school leaving certificate plus two years of practical experience. By 1931, the course had been lengthened to five semesters, and the schools had again been re-named, as 'Higher Technical Teaching Establishments'.

The building schools were the other progenitor of today's *Fachhochschulen*. The building trades have always required a considerable degree of theoretical knowledge, and the master mason's examination was divided into two parts – theoretical and practical – in 1819. By 1913, the Reich had 67 building schools, whose standards and organisation were determined by the Guild of German Master Builders (Innungsverband Deutscher Baugewerksmeister), a body similar to the VDI, mentioned above.

From about 1930, the building schools increasingly came to resemble the Advanced Schools for Mechanical Engineering, and the Reich Education Ministry, therefore, streamlined the system by turning the different types of school into a unified *Ingenieurschule* (1939). The subjects which it taught gradually diversified to include such disciplines as economics, social work, design and agriculture. Its standards continued to rise as Germany increasingly realised that in order to remain competitive in the modern world, it was essential to have well-qualified technical personnel.

Student numbers at the *Ingenieurschulen* increased rapidly from 27,000 in 1950 to 73,000 in 1970 (Oehler, 1985:90). Until the 1960s many of the students were recruited from the *Hauptschulen* (the least 'academic' and prestigious of Germany's three types of secondary school). In the 1970s, the Engineering Schools were still modelled on the authoritarian tradition of Prussian Cadet Academies. Students were treated much like schoolchildren. There was a 32-week academic year with end-of-term reports; they could be made to repeat a year if their progress was unsatisfactory; they were taught in class groups, attendance was compulsory and latecomers to class sometimes had their names taken down in a punishment book. Some lecturers even insisted on students standing up to answer questions in class, and addressing them as 'Herr Oberbaurat' (an untranslatable term meaning something like 'Mr Chief Building Officer') (Scheuerer and Weist, 1981:92). The lecturers themselves were rigidly controlled by their superiors and had very heavy teaching loads. Twenty-four hours a week was the normal teaching requirement (WR, 1981:8) and this sometimes rose as high as 38–40 hours (Rotenhan, 1980:13). There was no tradition of academic democracy in decision-making, and it is clear that the *Freiheiten* so characteristic of the Humboldtian university were not accorded to the *Ingenieurschulen*.

Two major factors combined to change the status of the *Ingenieurschulen*. One was student unrest; the other was the need to conform to the directives of the European Economic Community (EEC). The two were actually connected, because part of the students' dissatisfaction stemmed from the fear that their qualifications might not be recognised within the Community. Under the Treaty of Rome (25 March 1957), citizens of member states were to be given the right, within twelve years (that is by 1969), to move freely and settle in any Community country (Rotenhan, 1980:15). This necessitated mutual recognition of degrees and other qualifications, and it forced the Germans to raise the status of their *Ingenieurschulen*.

In the 1960s, intensive discussions took place with a view to integrating the *Ingenieurschulen* into the realm of higher education, and raising the qualifications required for entry to them. As a result, the *Ingenieurschulen* were authorised in 1965 to award a degree, the '*Ingenieur (grad.)*'. The EEC also required higher school qualifications for admission to degree studies. Twelve years' schooling (Lüth, 1983:26) was now the official requirement and this led to the foundation in Germany of technical schools, the '*Fachoberschulen*'. Both staff and students campaigned on a massive scale for upgrading of the *Ingenieurschulen* to meet international standards.

Rimbach (1983:67) describes how students at the *Ingenieurschulen* boycotted lectures in the summer of 1968. Their initial motive was anger at the thought that their qualifications might not be recognised in other EEC countries, but this soon broadened into a call for total reform and culminated in a country-wide, term-long boycott of lectures in the summer semester of 1969. The students' dissatisfaction was articulated in the following vivid statement by Ulrich Kill, spokesperson for mechanical engineering students at Siegen:

> We are all more or less stuffed with material which is transmitted to us in strict accordance with the timetable, and which cannot be categorised like the three states of matter as solid, liquid, or gaseous, only as cold and

dry. Many of us today, perhaps unconsciously, are cranks who know nothing outside our subject – number-crunchers, 'boot-lickers', bundles of nerves, people who are all twisted up or suffer from other spiritual deformities. Many of us are indeed willing to increase and pass on our knowledge, but far too many are also ready to lick boots and force others to do the same. It is a lamentable cycle in which we are caught, a cycle born of an old-fashioned school system, authoritarian thinking and lack of spiritual freedom. We must face up to and analyse this situation, and do everything in our power to break this vicious circle. (Quoted by Rimbach, ibid.)

The Association of German Engineering Students (Studentenverband Deutscher Ingenieurschulen) further contributed to the public debate in September 1968 by suggesting that the proposed *Fachhochschulen* should engage in applied research as well as teaching.

On 5 July 1968, the *Land* Prime Ministers reached an important agreement. They decided that the *Ingenieurschulen* (and educational establishments of similar rank) should be institutions of higher education (called *Fachhochschulen*), and a special commission was set up to lay down principles for outline legislation applying to all the *Länder* (Handbuch NRW, 1986:36). The commission reported, and in due course (31 October 1968) all the *Länder* approved an agreement laying a formal basis for the establishment of *Fachhochschulen* throughout the country. The underlying principles were the following:

(a) the *Ingenieurschulen* (and institutions of similar rank) would be raised to *Fachhochschulen* as part of the third-level education sector;
(b) a special subject leaving certificate (*Fachhochschulreife*) would be introduced as entry qualification;
(c) the length of study would be three years (no change);
(d) transfer should be possible between the *Fachhochschulen* and the *wissenschaftliche Hochschulen* (and vice versa) (ibid.).

The massive criticism of the existing *Ingenieurschulen* had caught both politicians and bureaucrats unawares, and prevailed against all resistance. In a short time, the old regimented system was liberalised and brought into line with the normal higher education values. The authorities now recognise that the *Fachhochschulen*, like the universities, need a proper theoretical basis for their work. A mere 'bag of tricks' is no longer good enough for FHS graduates. Thus, the Handbuch NRW (1986) proclaims that the FHS student should be enabled to apply scholarly insights and methods, subject knowledge and skills in a free, democratic, social *Rechtsstaat*:

The *Fachhochschule* student not only learns about the structures and procedures of his future profession, but is also introduced during his course to the methods used in specific scientific fields. A critical knowledge of scientific methodology combines with subject knowledge to lay the basis of a qualification which allows the holder either to work in his chosen professional field or to undertake further study at tertiary level.

The status of courses and terminal awards has been redefined by extending the *Fachhochschule*'s educational task to include research and development, and by confirming and re-inforcing its practical orientation [*Praxisbezug*]. The conferring of degrees corresponds [to this redefinition]. (Handbuch NRW, 1986:39)

Education in *Fachhochschulen* is now far more than the mere rehearsal and development of practical skills. The new *Fachhochschule* student is intended to receive an education which is scholarly, critical and liberal, and which allows him or her to pursue advanced studies if s/he so wishes. As institutions, the *Fachhochschulen* are now becoming upwardly mobile; Raupach (1970:97) shows that they are raising their entry qualifications, thereby becoming more like universities. The Wissenschaftsrat (1981:15) notes a substantial increase in the number of recruits entering the FHS with *Abitur*. In 1977, the proportion was one third (although this varied greatly according to courses and institutions).

In some respects, however, the working-class background of many FHS students still influences their values and outlook. Rotenhan (1980:42) suggests that they are likely to have strongly marked regional accents and to have some difficulty in formulating abstract thoughts and ideas. Like many working-class people, they are focused on the present, and are usually not motivated by deferred gratification (ibid.:39). They are used to working alone and are not keen on discussing their difficulties; they like concrete, tightly constructed courses of study, with clearly visible goals, which can be quickly reached (ibid.:40). They are not used to thinking in innovative, lateral ways; this means that indirect or intuitive approaches to problem-solving are not congenial to them (although rote learning often is). They tend to be afraid of failure and to have less expectation of upward social mobility than those born into more privileged circumstances, but are usually prepared to work hard to succeed. They tend to expect people 'higher up' to take significant decisions affecting their academic career (for example, what they should learn). Rotenhan (ibid.:43) quotes data from the Munich FHS (1978–9) which show that 23% of future *Fachhochschule* students had 'failed' at secondary school (usually in the first five years, perhaps by having to repeat a class). This may support the suggestion that the FHS provides a safety net for those who have gone to the academic type of secondary school (*Gymnasium*) but have not been able to keep up. However, a high percentage of FHS students have had experience of industry, commerce and administration before entering third-level education and thus know much more about life than if they had come to the FHS directly from the *Gymnasium*.

Rose (1970:140) has suggested that a major function of the *Fachhochschulen* is to siphon off demand for access to the more scholarly (*wissenschaftlich*) institutions of higher education; it is indeed true that producing an FHS graduate is cheaper than producing a university graduate (Rotenhan, 1980:35). The fact that the *Fachhochschulen* are much more flexible and responsive to market forces and the needs of the economy than the universities (Handbuch NRW, 1986:38) helps to make them a useful part of the higher education scene. One of the factors which makes them good value for money is their lack of a university-type commitment to research.

The first *Land* laws to establish *Fachhochschulen* all refer to research, but interpret it as applied research or as development work. Staff at these institutions are permitted, but not required, to conduct research, and a leave of absence scheme has been in operation since 1976. It is not intended, however, to enable staff to carry out pure research; instead, they are required to return to the world of work and practise their specialism for a certain time. The FHS recruits staff directly from the workplace, and so no *Mittelbau* has developed. It does not have the right to confer doctorates, and in North Rhine-Westphalia, FHS graduates wishing to do doctorates are required to do an additional four terms at a university before undertaking doctoral research. Rotenhan (1980:78) points out that the reasons why *Fachhochschule* staff might wish to do research are complex. On the one hand, they argue that it is functionally necessary, because their institutions cannot satisfactorily perform their educational mission without it. On the other, research is associated with claims for high status and prestige. A 'proper' professor is one who does research, and the *Fachhochschulen* are gradually becoming more involved in such work.

The growing self-confidence of the *Fachhochschulen* in this area has led some to suggest that they will increasingly resemble the university as time goes on. The supporters of this 'convergence theory' are unwilling to acknowledge a distinctive and independent role for the *Fachhochschule* (WR, 1981:19). The Wissenschaftsrat (ibid.:23–5) argues, however, that the various institutions of higher education should neither be uniform nor form a hierarchy; the FHS should not merely reproduce the university, but should have a distinctive role, characterised by tightly structured three-year courses, further education, scientific-advisory or technology-transfer services and a predominantly applied orientation. The fact that the *Fachhochschulen* are different from universities should in no way invalidate their status as scholarly institutions; the rank and prestige of an establishment of third-level education cannot be derived solely or primarily from research. Vocational education is important, and the WR draws attention to the fact that the employment chances of FHS graduates are, on the whole, good (ibid.:24).

Whereas the *Handbuch Nordrhein-Westfalen* emphasises the scholarly, theoretically grounded basis of the work now done at the FHS, the institutional profile and development pattern drawn up for them by the Wissenschaftsrat departs from the Humboldtian university tradition. Since this tradition is so prestigious, it seems a little disingenuous for the WR to suggest that 'different' does not necessarily mean 'inferior'. It is extremely difficult for the *Fachhochschulen* to achieve a status 'different' from but 'equal' to that of the universities when there are clear indications that they do not rate so highly. Examples of such inequalities are the barring of FHS graduates from recruitment into the highest grades of the civil service, and the gross disparities between the teaching loads of FHS and university staff. Whereas the traditional German university is of patrician lineage, the *Fachhochschule* has been called a 'bastard' (Rotenhan, 1980:9), yet it is the *Fachhochschulen* which have formed the nucleus of the comprehensive universities in North Rhine-Westphalia and Hesse. A marriage of two traditions has taken place in the *Gesamthochschulen* which, as we shall see, has often been fraught with difficulties.

The Teacher Training Colleges

A third and very important constituent of the *Gesamthochschulen* was the college for teacher education (*Pädagogische Hochschule* (PH)). These institutions had evolved from teacher training establishments (*Lehrerbildende Anstalten*) and by the end of the 1960s there were about 100 of them (Peisert and Framhein, 1980:19). The *Pädagogische Hochschulen* were given the status of institutions of higher education in 1958, and in the 1960s became self-governing, like the *wissenschaftliche Hochschulen* (Oehler, 1985: 85–6). They thus have a far longer history as institutions of higher education than the *Fachhochschulen*.

The task of the colleges of education is to educate primary and lower secondary school teachers (*Hauptschullehrer*). Although they have now been recognised as belonging to the topmost tier in the institutional hierarchy, their struggle for status has been a long and bitter one (see Bungardt, 1965; Pritchard, 1983; 1986a). Some *Länder*, however, have been less élitist in their attitudes to the training of primary school teachers than others; Hamburg, for instance, has trained primary teachers in association with the university since 1926, and made this sector an integral part of the university in 1967/68. The 1960s were a time of great shortage – a fact which smoothed the way for many reforms in teacher training, professionalising it, making it non-denominational, relating it to theory as well as practice, and integrating its first and second phases (Oehler, 1985:86–7).

At the beginning of the 1970s, about thirty of the independent colleges of education were linked with *wissenschaftliche Hochschulen* and some were entirely integrated into the universities, with staff being incorporated into subject schools or kept as discrete organisational entities within the larger institution. The general tendency was to raise the prestige of teacher training, and make it attractive by basing it upon subject specialisms rather than a practical 'apprenticeship' model. Some but not all *Pädagogische Hochschulen* have the right to award degrees and doctorates. Most of them are of medium size, with between 1,000 and 3,000 students (Peisert and Framhein, 1980:19).

Certain other institutions, such as colleges of business studies, were also absorbed into the *Gesamthochschulen*, but the types described above are the most significant in terms of the firmly established, clearly defined traditions which they brought with them. Staff from different institutions had diverse and distinctive professional norms, assumptions and aspirations, which materially affected the success of the *Gesamthochschulen* in achieving curriculum reform and a unified, harmonious staff structure. The comprehensive universities were to find it very difficult to bring out of this diversity the unity originally dreamed of by the planners, and implicit in the very word '*gesamt*' (whole).

$-5-$

Teaching and Research

The Integrated Degree Courses

The integrated degree courses are the most distinctive feature of the comprehensive universities.[1] Not only are they a major curriculum innovation in Germany; they also constitute a very serious attempt to democratise higher education. If we want to investigate how the *Gesamthochschulen* are performing their social mission, then it is to the operation of these special courses that we must direct our attention.

The integrated degrees are not offered in all subjects, either in Hesse or in North Rhine-Westphalia; they are offered only in subjects which have traditionally been taught at both universities and *Fachhochschulen*. The *Gesamthochschulen* also offer straight FHS-type courses, straight university-type degree courses and teacher-training courses, in addition to the integrated courses. The proportion of students registered for integrated degrees varies from one institution to another but is (roughly) about one third of the total (Cerych et al., 1981b:22).

Entrance Qualifications

One of the major objectives of the *Gesamthochschulen* is to help overcome the vertical divisions in the education system. It is therefore essential to be able to recruit students with non-traditional entry qualifications to university-level degree courses. German legal stipulations make this quite a complex matter, and indeed the rigidity of the German university admissions system contrasts strongly with the fluidity of the British system. In the United Kingdom, most conventional universities will accept a wide variety of entrance qualifications, such as awards from the Royal Society of Arts or from the Business and Technician Education Council (BTEC). In a traditional British university, an eighteen-year-old school leaver could theoretically be admitted to degree level study

---

1. The committee structure, financing and governance of the *Gesamthochschulen* do not differ from those of other universities in Hesse and North Rhine-Westphalia and so we shall not devote any particular attention to these matters.

without any formal qualifications whatsoever (SCUE, 1987). That universities demand entrance qualifications at all is simply a convention. Each university is free to make its own decisions on entrance qualifications, and is not bound by national legislation because none exists.

In Germany, by contrast, the situation is much more tightly regulated. Would-be recruits to the integrated degree courses in the comprehensive universities must hold either the leaving certificate from the upper technical school (*Fachoberschule* (FOS)) or from a grammar school (*Gymnasium*). The first of these is called *Fachhochschulreife* because it qualifies the holder for entry to a *Fachhochschule*; the second is known as *Abitur* or *Hochschulreife* because it entitles the holder to study at a *wissenschaftliche Hochschule*, and can be of two types: either general or subject-bound, both involving thirteen years of study. The general certificate (*allgemeine Hochschulreife*) is more prestigious than the subject-bound certificate (*fachgebundene Hochschulreife*), which limits the range of subjects which may be studied at either the GHS or a traditional university. The *Fachhochschulreife* takes twelve years of study and admits its bearer either to a *Fachhochschule* or to an integrated degree course in a GHS. It does not normally provide direct entry to university and, even if later 'converted' to a form of *Abitur* by additional study, is still subject-bound and therefore less negotiable than the *allgemeine Hochschulreife*. The young people who take the *Fachhochschulreife* tend, on the whole, to come from lower down the social scale than those who take the general *Abitur*, and their more limited range of options illustrates a statement made by Bourdieu and Passeron (1977:229) on social reproduction in higher education. These authors were referring to data for France in 1961–62, but their comment also applies to present-day Germany: 'In short, the lower a student's social origin, the more his access to higher education had to be paid for by a restriction on choice ...'

It will be clear from the above that the *Abitur*, particularly the non-subject-bound variant, is a much more powerful and versatile qualification than the *Fachhochschulreife*. This should not blind us to the fact that the FHS certificate is still a very substantial, solid and estimable qualification, involving, after all, twelve years of study. It would be quite wrong to equate it with GCSE.

It is perhaps because of the traditional German emphasis upon *Bildung* and non-utilitarian education, that the *allgemeine Hochschulreife* is so highly valued by both students and university staff. The empirical study by Hitpass and Mock (1972) illustrates students' attitudes to this qualification. Most students in their sample

(N=5,396) were opposed to the *fachgebundene Hochschulreife* and to early specialisation. Only one third wanted to specialise at sixth form level (ibid.: 41), while two thirds desired a broad education at school and an 'academic' education at university. They generally saw the *Hochschulreife* in idealistic terms as a broad preparation for third-level study, leaving them a free choice of career (certainly a point of view which derives from the ideology of the Humboldtian university). Already strongly held, this general attitude was accompanied by pragmatic considerations which, if anything, served to reinforce it still further; the *allgemeine Hochschulreife* would give them enough flexibility to switch to an acceptable alternative, if restrictions on admissions barred them from their first course choice or if that course proved uncongenial or excessively difficult. It is significant that as many as 20% of Hitpass and Mock's sample reckon that they started by choosing the wrong subject. Many students did not know what they wanted to do at university; only 55% had decided what they wanted to study by the time they took their *Abitur*, while about 40% made that decision between taking *Abitur* and registering at university. Hitpass and Mock's survey thus illustrates the practical value and high prestige of the *allgemeine Hochschulreife* and enables one to appreciate how radical and daring the notion of allowing non-*Abitur* holders to study for university-level qualifications at the *Gesamthochschulen* must have seemed. It appeared to some that 'ordinary cows' were being allowed to associate with 'sacred cows'!

Structure

An important aim of the GHS is to promote social justice by attracting new sections of the population into university-level education. A distinction is made between 'long' and 'short' courses at the GHS: 'long' courses are of traditional university degree standard; 'short' courses are those usually offered at institutions such as the *Fachhochschulen*, which have traditionally had a larger working-class intake. The long courses are more expensive and prestigious than the short courses and would not normally be accessible to non-*Abitur* holders. By introducing short courses into the *Gesamthochschule*, and facilitating mobility between short and long courses, the authorities hoped to go a long way towards democratising higher education. They wished to move away from a vertical system, in which each institutional type had its own particular function, and transfer between institutions or courses was almost impossible. They also hoped that a tighter structure and, perhaps, student counselling, would reduce the time needed to complete the long courses.

Thus the long and short courses are not merely 'innocent' alternatives, but are overlaid with economic and sociological significance. The way in which the two are interrelated in the education system points up the socio-political implications of course design. To illustrate this, we shall look at some of the major prototype patterns for degree structure. Some genuinely open broad horizons to students without *Abitur*, while others tend to leave them in a cul-de-sac from which there is no easy exit. The power of some of the patterns to open up new options is more apparent than real. The following principles may help us to assess the true democratising potential of different course designs:

(1) Transferability between long and short courses is likely to be facilitated if these courses are offered within one institution rather than at separate institutions;
(2) Transferability between long and short courses will be facilitated if students undertake a period of academic study in common, or if a common pool of units is available to everyone;
(3) The longer the courses can remain common, the more democratic the structure is;
(4) It is generally more democratic if advanced courses are developed by adding them to previous components ('consecutive' model) instead of diversifying into qualitatively different options ('branching' model).

Four main designs were considered as possible models for the integrated degrees in the *Gesamthochschulen*. These will now be explored in detail.

The Construction Kit Model ('Baukasten')   This structure (associated with Ernst von Weizsäcker et al., 1970) was a modular one in which students could combine various units of study according to their own wishes. Six- to eight-week study modules would be offered not only in subject disciplines but in interdisciplinary and problem-orientated blocks, leading to certificates or university-level degrees. Practitioners from the world of work would teach alongside university lecturers (Peisert and Framhein, 1980:104). There was to be a framework of recurrent education and credit transfer (cf. Raupach, 1970). However, this design was subjected to some of the same criticisms that have been made of proposals for de-schooling at secondary level; it tended to result in courses which were not coherently sequenced, and although suitable for independent-minded students, well enough informed to make a wise choice, it tended to disadvantage those who were immature or lacking in self-confidence; it was probably too radical to be widely acceptable, and so failed to secure consensus.

The V-Branching Model   A more influential model was the V-branching model in which short and long courses are differentiated from the beginning.

Figure 5.1 The V-branching model

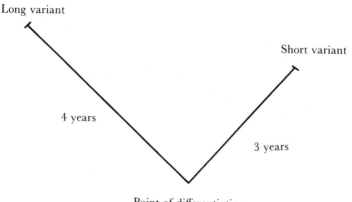

Point of differentiation

An important example of a V-branching model occurs in the *Hochschulgesamtplan* (1967) of the *Land* Baden-Württemberg, popularly known as the Dahrendorf Plan after the eminent sociologist, whose articles in *Die Zeit* (later published in book form as *Bildung ist Bürgerrecht*) had given the education debate in Germany such an impetus. Dahrendorf's demonstration of the extent to which working-class children are underprivileged in higher education had immediate practical impact. The government declared (25 June 1964) that it would do everything in its power in the years ahead to make it easier for working-class children to attend academic secondary schools and institutions of higher education. In June 1966, Dahrendorf was invited to chair a special working party for the planning of higher education in Baden-Württemberg. He likens this mode of working to a British Royal Commision, which he believes to be much more efficient than the usual German Standing Committee, with its alarming fluctuations of interest and energy. His own 'no-nonsense-committee' (Dahrendorf, 1974:147) had to achieve specific objectives in a limited time, and this was conducive to concentration, thereby greatly increasing effectiveness.

Dahrendorf developed a differentiated concept of higher education on the model of the American multiversity, with a number of campuses, rather like Columbia University (Kerr, 1963). It was intended to combine the functions of research and teaching, with the Humboldtian ideal realised in a graduate school for the more advanced and gifted students. Teaching, research and academic levels would be clearly differentiated and the gradations of levels reflected in staff salaries. (The working party had not hesitated to grasp this nettle.) There was to be a short, three-year course with its own terminal qualification (Baccalaureat), and a long course of at least four years duration (with an intermediate examination after two years) leading to a Master's Degree. Advanced studies of various lengths were proposed (e.g. doctorates) and the mechanisms of transfer between courses were described.

However, a shortcoming of the model was that it only allowed the students to keep their options open until they entered the *Gesamthochschule*. They were then obliged to opt for one of the branches of the V-model. There was no real common core teaching from the point of differentiation onwards, so this model lends itself to vertical rather than to horizontal differentiation, and is thus conducive to the preservation of élite tracks within an institution. It only satisfies the first of the four principles enunciated above for enhancing the democratic potential of courses. Equal opportunity exists only at the point of differentiation, and freedom of choice, although allowed for by transferability between courses, diminishes as the students' academic careers proceed.[2] The V-branching model effectively pushes the point of differentiation back to the stage of secondary school, because that is where different curricula are chosen with a view to obtaining different school-leaving certificates. Mobility and flexibility rapidly decrease once individuals embark on third-level education, based on the V-model. Students on the long branch cannot easily shift to the more practical short courses, while those on the short branch usually need supplementary instruction if they are to transfer to the longer course variant and complete it successfully. This costs extra time and money, which working-class students, in particular, can ill afford. This is not, therefore, a model optimally

2. It has been pointed out by Lüth (1983:114) that Dahrendorf's concept of the *differenzierte Gesamthochschule* agrees in many respects with that of the CDU. The Martin-Plan (Martin, 1968), which was supported by the CDU/CSU, features parallel courses, different in rank and with correspondingly different types of entrance qualifications. The courses are to be delivered in different institutions and there is to be co-ordinating machinery to ensure transferability between institutions.

adapted to increasing equality of opportunity.

The Dahrendorf Plan was influential but was not, to its author's chagrin, adopted in Baden-Württemberg. Dahrendorf himself (1974:160–2) blamed this on the fact that the *Land* University Law was being finalised just as his own Plan was nearing completion; the Law tended to confirm existing structures, while the Plan sought to introduce new ones; the Law was geared to the existing situation, whereas the Plan sought to create a new one. Every effort was made to speed up completion of the Plan, but it still came too late to be integrated in the Law, and so was reduced to a mere 'think-piece'. It did, however, have the effect of introducing the concept of the *Gesamthochschule* to a wider public and promoting thought about higher education.

The Y-Branching Model   This model proved more successful than the ones previously described. It features a common period of foundation study, after which degree courses diversify into long and short variants.

Figure 5.2 The Y-branching model

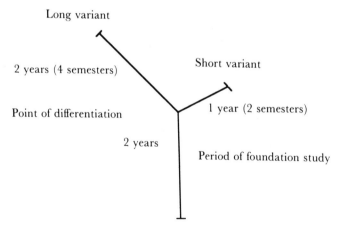

This model was championed by the SPD, whose education experts believed that the *Abitur* was not a good enough predictor of later achievement to 'stream' people into long and short courses as soon as they entered the institution. Versions of it exist in which the period of foundation study (*Grundstudium*) is taught partly, rather than totally, in common. Evers (1968:11) argues that the curriculum for the first two years cannot be designed to serve both as a terminal qualification and as an optimal basis for the longer degree course (*Hauptstudium*) which may follow the *Grundstudium*. It is socially and educationally desirable, however, that the period of common study should be curtailed as little as possible, since such curtailment hastens the process of selection and thus erodes equality of opportunity. It is unfortunately difficult to reconcile equality of opportunity with freedom of choice. Offering the same curriculum to all students during the early part of their course limits their freedom to choose what units of study they please.

Despite the difficulties of organising a common *Grundstudium*, the Y-branching model received the support of the Wissenschaftsrat. It now constitutes the basic design for the integrated degree courses in North Rhine-Westphalia, and is organised as follows (see MWF NRW, 1979:34–48):

(1) *Theory and practice.* An attempt is made to give courses an applied orientation. It is recognised that in developing courses related to professional fields of activity, a balance must be reached between interdisciplinary work and subject-specific study. At the more advanced levels, there may be some subject specialisation.

(2) *Entrance qualifications.* The holders of *Abitur* and of *Fachhochschulreife* are admitted on equal terms to the integrated degree courses (ibid).

(3) *Grundstudium.* The *Grundstudium* lasts for two years (that is, four semesters).[3] About 70% of its content is common to all students, regardless of whether they are aiming at the long or the short course variant. Students can expect to study together for about three terms; in the early stages, the interdisciplinary nature of the work makes it easier for them to transfer to other related degree courses, if they so wish (ibid.:37–8).

(4) *Intermediate examination (Zwischenprüfung).* This takes place at the end of the fourth term, and students must pass it to proceed to the next phase of their studies. This second phase consists of *Hauptstudium* 1 (two semesters) or *Hauptstudium* 2 (four semesters) (ibid.:38). The *Zwischenprüfung* corresponds to the preliminary degree examination (*Diplom-Vorprüfung*) at universities and *Technische Hochschulen*. It is intended to be diagnostic, rather than a mere delayed selection procedure (ibid.:38–9). It indicates aptitudes and achievement, thus helping students to decide on a course of further study.

(5) *Hauptstudien.* The *Hauptstudien* (HI and HII, or as they are

---

3. A 'semester' in German universities is a period of study amounting to half an academic year. When the word 'term' is used in the German context, it should be understood in the same sense as 'semester'.

sometimes known, *Diplom* (D) I and II) are differentiated in content and in duration, yet related to each other. Theory and practice are features of both DI and DII; they are not specific or exclusive to either, although a predominantly theoretical or practical bias is possible and appropriate in certain circumstances. Every effort is made to avoid the old situation, in which university courses needed to be massively supplemented with practical experience, while applied courses needed a much better theoretical foundation. To put it in a nutshell: 'The professional education at the *Gesamthochschulen* cannot be applied or practical unless it is also scholarly' (MWF NRW, 1979:40). The duration of study depends to some extent on subject-specific academic and theoretical factors, and may also vary with the specialist profiles which students aiming at particular careers are attempting to build up. Specialist areas should, however, be chosen with the intention of completing one's studies inside the recommended period (four years) (ibid.:39–40).

(6) *Higher degrees.* A doctorate may be undertaken on the basis of DI provided that the student completes a course of advanced, supplementary studies (*Aufbaustudium*) (ibid.:40).

Relating the Y-branching courses in NRW to our four principles, we see that by offering both long and short courses within one institution, the first is satisfied. The second principle, referring to a common academic study period is also satisfied, but the third, which advocates the preservation of the common period for as long as possible, has been threatened by developments in the last decade. At an early point on the stem of the 'Y', students are already being divided according to 'practical' or 'theoretical' dispositions and the trend is, unfortunately, to force the point of differentiation back further and further until the structure increasingly tends to resemble a V- rather than a Y-branching model. According to the fourth principle (which contrasts consecutive and branching models) North Rhine-Westphalia has not chosen the more democratic of the two models. Its structure does include a consecutive element, however, namely the advanced study module which can be added to DI as a prelude to doctoral study.

The Consecutive Model This model features a prolonged period of common study, culminating in an examination taken by all. Some students may leave the system at this point, with a basic degree. Others may go on to more advanced studies on the basis of the common core which they have already completed.

It is this fourth model which constitutes the basis of the integrated degree courses at Kassel. The development of this consecutive

Figure 5.3 The consecutive model

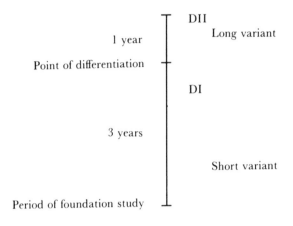

model, known in Hesse as the *Kasseler Modell*, was begun by a project group in 1972 and was subsequently modified by curriculum work groups and pilot studies. A ministerial decree, the *Eckdatenerlass*, made it official in the summer of 1975. As one might expect after such a long debate, it represents a compromise between many different concepts and objectives.

The first phase consists of a *Grundstudium* (two academic semesters plus a work-study placement) followed by a *Hauptstudium* (four academic semesters plus a work-study placement). This three-year course culminates in the award of a basic degree (*Diplom* (D)I). The second phase is that of postgraduate studies and leads to a second degree ((*Diplom* (D)II). It is equivalent to the long variant of the North Rhine-Westphalian Y-branching model. *Diplom* II is intended to permit in-depth study of a subject specialism selected by the student, and is supposed to take two semesters (Neusel, 1981:83). Unlike North Rhine-Westphalia, Hesse does not require non-*Abitur* holders to follow bridging courses, but it does demand that students for the integrated courses should at least have done the *Fachhochschulreife*. There was at one stage a 'brave new world' intention to treat work experience as equivalent to school experience, to bring in (shop-floor) workers alongside *Abiturienten* and to make both groups do a propaedeutic course before moving on to the degree course proper, but this proved impracticable, especially in view of the growing number of *Abitur* holders (ibid.:73). Some of the subject areas for which integrated degree courses on the *Kasseler Modell* have so far been designed are: Architecture, Town-planning, Economics,

Agriculture and Social Pedagogy.

In a consecutive model of this type, it is clearly inappropriate to call for transferability (*Durchlässigkeit*), since there is nothing to transfer to (except, of course, another subject or institution) and the student's only choice is between leaving the system on completing the basic phase and proceeding to the next phase. S/he does not have to make qualitative choices, as for example, between the long and short variants of a Y-branching model.

Since students take a common core of study, this model does circumscribe freedom of curricular choice. It is egalitarian, however, and the Wissenschaftsrat (1962) at first rejected it because it would have equated *wissenschaftliche Hochschule* and *Fachhochschule* courses for a protracted period. However, only four years later, the WR declared itself in favour of the consecutive model (Lüth, 1983:424). It provides the best basis for equality of educational opportunity, and satisfies all of our four principles for enhancing the democratising potential of higher education. It is interesting to recall that a similar structure was proposed by the BAK in the 1960s.

The Bridging Courses

Since some students enter the integrated degree courses with twelve years of secondary school study and others with thirteen, the authorities have expressed concern that *Fachoberschule* students may experience difficulty in coping with university-level work, whereas *Abitur*-holders may not be sufficiently challenged (MWF NRW, 1979:21). There may also be problems with recognition if a student with *Fachhochschulreife* wishes to move from an integrated degree course in NRW to a traditional university in his own *Land* or elsewhere. The solution adopted by North Rhine-Westphalia (but not by Hesse) is to introduce special bridging courses (*Brückenkurse*) for non-*Abitur* holders. These courses are intended to help students cope more effectively with their studies, to level out intergroup differences in standards of attainment, and to overcome any 'credibility gap' affecting NRW students with only *Fachhochschulreife* who want to change to another university or study in another federal state. Hesse has not deemed it necessary to offer *Brückenkurse* but North Rhine-Westphalia has promulgated a decree detailing the procedures (Handbuch NRW, 1986:434–41).

These supplementary courses are 'recommended' to all students but are compulsory for holders of the *Fachhochschulreife*. They are to be taken during the *Grundstudium* (lasting for about two years), and are a prerequisite for entrance to the post-foundation section of their courses. A successful *Grundstudium* is not regarded as a substitute for the bridging courses. Three subjects, one of which must be Mathematics or English, are compulsory; teaching input in these three subjects used to be 300 hours, but has now been reduced to 240 hours, of which practical sessions (*Übungen*) amount to 50% of the total (ibid.: para. 3, section 2). Performance is assessed by a four-hour examination which can be repeated twice by unsuccessful candidates. Success is equivalent to the *fachgebundene Hochschulreife* which entitles students to proceed to the next part of the course at their own university although they must also pass the intermediate examination (*Zwischenprüfung*) which is compulsory for all students, including *Abiturienten*. Alternatively, they may transfer to another *wissenschaftliche Hochschule* in NRW if they so wish. A list of the various topics which candidates are entitled to study on the basis of their subject-bound examination is provided (ibid.: enclosure 1). For example, Computer Studies open the way to degree courses in Electrical Engineering, Mathematics, Physics (as well as Computer Studies, of course), while Psychology opens the way to Sociology, Pedagogy and Psychology.

It can be seen from the above description that the *Brückenkurse* involve a considerable commitment of time and energy on the part of ex-*Fachoberschule* students. However well they are coping with their degree course, proven competence is not enough. They are still required to compensate for the thirteenth year of school study which *Abiturienten* have done but they have not.

Evaluations of the Integrated Degree Courses

Long and Short Variants Comparing the numbers entering the long and short courses in the *integrierte Studiengänge* of the GHS, it is estimated that about 80% of students take the long, university-type course as opposed to the shorter *Fachhochschule*-type course (Cerych et al., 1981a:58). An interesting question is whether *Fachoberschule* (FOS) students have more of a tendency than the *Abitur*-holders (ABI) to end up taking the DI qualification. There is no evidence that FOS students gravitate especially towards DI, and indeed, in an empirical study of economics students (N=213), Endemann and Klüver (1983:87) discovered that 96% of their sample had decided in favour of DII by the fifth semester. Only a very few students, in the eighth and tenth semesters, opt for DI in economics and these have probably failed to gain entry to the DII track. Klüver and Krameyer (1981) found that 55% of chemistry students who went for DI had originally wanted to do DII, but had not been able to do so. This implies that the majority of students begin by aiming at DII, with DI as a safety net. It is obvious from these data that the objective of creating two equally attractive options has certainly not been attained. There are two ways of interpreting this.

Those taking the positive view argue that the *Gesamthochschulen* have provided an excellent avenue of upward mobility for students who might otherwise not realise their potential to perform at university-level; by providing structures and conditions for such a large proportion of students to transcend their own limitations, the comprehensives are fulfilling their social and educational mission.

Those taking the negative view argue that the short courses have 'failed' to become attractive in their own right. This view is, however, based primarily on economic pragmatism. In the early stages of planning for the *integrierte Studiengänge*, there was a conviction that Germany needed as much qualified manpower as possible, and must therefore utilise its people's talent to the maximum. Then when demographic trends and the structure of the labour market changed, there was a corresponding alteration in attitudes to the 'pool of talent' (see Cerych et al., 1981a:58–9). A fear of graduate unemployment (the so-called 'academic proletariat') developed. Because the economy needed less skilled manpower, it no longer seemed so important to devise ways of educating people to their full potential. The emphasis on transferability (*Durchlässigkeit*) in the educational system was questioned. Suddenly the attitude towards those taking the long courses changed: instead of hailing their success, planners complained that the short courses were 'failing' to attract large numbers of students and become appreciated as intrinsically valuable for their own special emphases.

The fact that so many non-*Abitur* holders succeed in completing the long variant of the integrated degree courses has been viewed as a type of academic drift which is not always welcomed by the authorities, especially since students who would normally have studied at *Fachhochschulen* and who take DII courses at the comprehensive universities are thereby receiving a more expensive and longer education. Hence, Gieseke and Eilsberger (1977:12) write in the following terms:

No solution has yet been found for the problem inherent in the Y-model of how to deter a large majority of students from choosing the longer four-year main course of study, because they expect more prestige and a higher income from this degree. In a sense, this is quite understandable and cannot be condemned as far as educational policy is concerned. Nevertheless, problems would arise with regard to capacity, if the comprehensive university were to lead to an increase of study time, through those students who formerly would have studied for only three years at a *Fachhochschule* now studying for four years at the comprehensive university.

This observation may be motivated purely by concern that the longer courses may prove unable to accommodate all who wish to take them, or by the fear that the labour market will not absorb all the people with the higher level qualifications. However, Bourdieu and Passeron (1977:177) argue that technical requirements are always to some extent social requirements; they believe that technocratic measurement of 'output', based on response to labour market needs, is simplistic because it takes no account of the way in which educational systems and class structures interact (ibid.:181). Their central argument is that scholastic hierarchies tend to reproduce social hierarchies and that turning social distinctions into academic distinctions is one way of bringing this about. The ideology of academic 'giftedness' secures recognition of the legitimacy of pedagogic action (ibid.:180), and is acknowledged both by those who succeed and by those who do not. People who fail to measure up to this model of 'giftedness' are excluded or downgraded – that is, they receive the sanctions reserved for the dominated classes (ibid.:205).

The fact that so many young people from the *Fachoberschulen* win the right to enter the long courses at the comprehensive universities is bound to affect the value of these courses in what Bourdieu and Passeron (ibid.:182) describe as the 'economic and symbolic markets'. The profitability of high qualifications on these markets is in inverse ratio to the number of people allowed to attain them. By taking the long courses, many GHS graduates believe they are doing the maximum to enhance their life chances. Unwittingly, however, they may be ensuring that the degrees for which they have worked so hard are in some way tainted or stigmatised – by virtue of the very fact that they have been able to achieve them. They are, after all, non-*Abitur* holders and therefore not members of the top flight. By performing well, they obviously create economic problems for the planners because their education costs more than it would have done at the *Fachhochschulen*. By laying claim to high status qualifications and actually achieving them, these students are disrupting the traditional balance of the reproduction of social hierarchies, and threatening the status monopoly of the classical university. The least one might expect is that the GHS graduates from the integrated courses would be sanctioned in some way, either by having social approval and recognition withheld from their degrees, or by a redefinition of the academic boundaries which they had disturbed;

this would involve a restructuring of the social and academic hierarchy to ensure that the position of the GHS graduates remained inferior to that of the traditional élite.

Academic Reputation and Performance   An important indicator of the economic and pedagogical performance of the *Gesamthochschulen* is the time taken by students to reach degree standard (both *Diplom* I and *Diplom* II). The times normally given in official documents are three years for DI and four years for DII, but these are usually exceeded. As we have seen, it is part of the ideology of *Bildung* in the traditional Humboldtian university that students should not be pressured to take examinations at set times. For an insider's view of the contrast between elastic, German-style courses and the goal-directed British approach, we may quote the conclusion of a paper written by two students of Paderborn GHS who studied at Trent Polytechnic in the United Kingdom on an exchange scheme (Menke and Ott, 1984). They were studying engineering and were able to compare the British degree structure with its German counterpart. Their English is not perfect, but what they say conveys the spirit of the Humboldtian university quite vividly and shows why German students think it important that the length of degree courses should not be fixed.

> The obvious question is, which system results in better education? This cannot be answered definitely. In our opinion, the English way to become an engineer is much shorter and too straight. There is too little time left to be spent on flowery lawns on the way to the top of the hill. This circumstance causes a more comfortable way without interruptions. The industry will receive well-educated engineers. Then, they might see (in our opinion) that even for technicians, it is necessary, and not only worthfull [*sic*], to know about the 'flowery'. Nevertheless, we prefer our system of education, because you have more freedom to develop your own personality and you receive the chance to find your own way. (ibid.:8)

This is an eloquent plea for *Lernfreiheit* and shows that the *Gesamthochschule* has taught these two students to value theory as well as practice, the aesthetic as well as the vocational. It is clear that they do not regard engineering as a mere 'bag of tricks'. For them, the 'flowery' is of primordial importance and, in the end, of practical value too.

Now, if we look at the current situation in the Bundesrepublik, we find that the average length of study at German universities is about six years, compared with the officially recommended four years (Wilms, 1986). According to a Federal Ministry report of 1976,

GHS students study for 4.90 years on average (quoted by Cerych et al., 1981a: 67). This lower figure, however, is derived from an aggregate of long and short courses, so we must suspect that comprehensive universities do not differ significantly from traditional universities for equivalent subjects and degree levels. Cerych (ibid.:68) suggests that study times at the GHS could be cut only if the curriculum were rigorously pruned and restructured, or if the prestige of the short courses in the world of work increased greatly. However, the fact that long courses at the GHS are probably not significantly shorter than those at a traditional university may also seem reassuring, since it suggests a kind of parity between the two types of institution.

So much for length of study as an institutional performance indicator. Let us turn now to the question of standards attained by individuals. Two empirical investigations into students' academic performance (Hitpass et al., 1979; 1980) were commissioned by the Ministerium für Wissenschaft und Forschung and were carried out at the Essen GHS.

The main hypothesis tested is that *Abitur* holders and non-*Abitur* holders at Essen have the same chances of succeeding in their studies, in spite of the difference in their entry qualifications. The studies cover students doing integrated degree courses in Mathematics, Physics, Civil Engineering, Economics, Chemistry and Mechanical Engineering.

In both studies, Hitpass et al. use a 'scholastic aptitude test' which indicates a clear advantage in favour of the *Abiturienten* (ABI), and remains remarkably stable as the students' academic careers proceed. Despite these measured differences, however, they show that the *Fachoberschule* (FOS) students have the same chance of success as the ABI students and do just as well in the end. They suggest that the FOS students' study capacity may be enhanced by such cognitive or non-cognitive personality traits as 'creativity' or 'productive thinking', with which they seem more endowed than the ABI students.

Likewise, in an empirical study of attitudes among chemistry students at the Essen GHS(N=1,001), Klüver and Krameyer (1981) can find no support for the notion that entrants from the *Fachoberschule* are less well equipped to pursue their studies than those who have done their *Abitur*. On the contrary, ex-FOS students are superior to ABI students in subject-specific tests. Because many of them have been laboratory assistants, they actually know more chemistry and physics on entry to the GHS than ABI students (ibid.:49), and this subject-specific knowledge is arguably more important for a successful *Grundstudium* than 'general aptitude for study'. The schooling and vocational experience of the FOS students is more homogeneous than that of the ABI students. They have done a year less mathematics at school, but the test results indicate that they know as much as the ABI students, and there is no difference in mark averages between the two groups (ibid.:54–5). The FOS students experience no special difficulties in their work; this is corroborated by Endemann and Klüver (1983:13 and 1981:11).

It is true that there is a small majority of ABI students (the 'high-flyers') who score higher than FOS students in the fourth semester, but the relationship subsequently alters to the advantage of the FOS students, who are more goal-directed (ibid.:85). Their commitment to their course is demonstrated by the fact that they drop out less often (Klüver and Krameyer, 1981:61). The dropout rate for ABI students in chemistry was 37% against 25% for FOS students. Most of the FOS group had apparently made the right choice of subject straight away (ibid.:33), whereas almost one third of the ABI group had really wanted to study another subject (e.g. medicine or pharmacy) but had been prevented from doing so by the *numerus clausus*. (Note: there is, however, no evidence that these *Abiturienten* constituted a 'negative selection'.)

ABI students also drop out more frequently than FOS students in civil engineering (Endemann and Klüver, 1981:39). It is not easy to collect precise information about course dropouts in the Federal Republic (because many students do not formally indicate that they are leaving), but it must be remembered that ABI students have a more versatile qualification than FOS students and may suddenly choose to pursue a different option. FOS students are restricted to a particular cluster of subjects, whereas ABI students are not. The fact that ABI students have more options may partly account for their apparent lack of commitment to courses for which they register (cf. Hitpass and Mock, 1972).

Let us turn now to the important matter of the *Brückenkurse*. How do FOS students perceive these 'remedial' courses? Are they really helpful in bringing about qualitative parity between FOS and ABI students? In view of the fact that, at the beginning of the degree course, FOS students in chemistry at Essen do at least as well in mathematics tests as ABI students, it is clear that the bridging courses are not functionally necessary (Klüver and Krameyer, 1981:73). Yet FOS students who want to take the long course are not allowed to do so unless they have taken and passed the bridging courses. Some of them suspect that this rule has been introduced to keep them out of the long courses (ibid.:72). Both ABI and FOS students find the bridging courses of only marginal benefit, but ABI students can withdraw from them, whereas FOS students are not permitted to do so. Both ABI and FOS chemistry students believe that the main function of the bridging courses is to compensate formally for a missing year of school, and they are supported in this view by *Fachhochschule* lecturers. University staff, however, are more 'agnostic' about the function and value of the bridging courses (ibid.:73), claiming that they cannot judge adequately how necessary (or otherwise) they may be. Staff generally take a more favourable view of the bridging courses than students. The FOS students in both economics and civil engineering at Essen share the ambivalent or negative attitudes of the chemistry students towards the bridging courses. Both ABI and FOS students believe that these are intended to ease the initial difficulties of 'settling down' in their degree courses or overcoming subject knowledge deficits, but they do not believe that in practice they accomplish this successfully. The overwhelming majority would attend voluntarily the bridging courses in the earlier stages of the course, but resistance stiffens as the courses proceed, so that by the fifth semester 37% of ABI economics students indicate that they would be unwilling to attend, while 48% of ABI civil engineering students are already unwilling to participate (see Endemann and Klüver, 1983:13–14; 1981:11–12).

One fairly serious side effect of the *Brückenkurse* is that they tend to prevent the ABI and the FOS groups from integrating socially. Thus, in economics, 53% of the FOS students worked predominantly with non-*Abitur* holders (Endemann and Klüver, 1983). That the students themselves were clearly aware of differences in entry qualifications is demonstrated by the fact that only one tenth were unaware of their classmates' entry qualifications; 29% of the FOS students and 19% of the ABI students thought that the academic staff sometimes, or to a certain extent, treated and evaluated the two groups differently (ibid.:21). These findings are corroborated by the data for chemistry (Klüver and Krameyer, 1981:56–7). Here, however, it was found that in more advanced semesters (year cohorts 1976–77 and 1977–78), ABI and FOS students integrated quite well in practicals, to the advantage of ABI students, who had less work experience than FOS classmates. However, the new *Brückenkurse* rules which came into operation in 1978 made these compulsory courses socially more divisive; the FOS students are brought together in groups at an early stage, and the personal relationships which develop at this point ensure that the FOS students subsequently tend to stay together for practicals. This is most unfortunate because it militates against a potentially valuable exchange of experience between FOS and ABI students and also helps to perpetuate the possible social 'stigmatisation' of FOS students.

The *Brückenkurse* therefore tend to have negative social consequences on the academic group, and they constitute a very substantial additional burden on the FOS students. It has been pointed out, for example, by Hoffknecht and Intrup (1983:34), that work on the bridging courses can adversely affect a student's performance in normal work. Hesse (1983:101) reports how the founding Senate in Siegen opposed *Brückenkurse* culminating in mandatory formal examinations on the grounds that they were likely to damage students' results in the normal *Grundstudium*, and were contrary to the spirit of integration and equal opportunity which was the *Gesamthochschule*'s original inspiration. In its declaration, the Senate states that the proposed Ministerial decree on entry qualifications and *Brückenkurse* may even jeopardise the success of the integrated *Gesamthochschule*.

In view of these factors, which tend to put FOS students at a disadvantage, it is something of a triumph that these students tend to do very well. Klüver and Krameyer (1981:94) argue that there is no intrinsic need for such compensatory courses; the only justification for maintaining them is that FOS students wishing to transfer from the GHS to a traditional university may be barred from doing so unless they can demonstrate that they possess the formal equivalent of the *Abitur*. If the *Brückenkurse* are to be maintained, then Klüver and Krameyer (ibid.) plead for a relevant, subject-orientated content. They even suggest (ibid.:95) that, since FOS students give such a good account of themselves at the GHS, they should be admitted without further hesitation to certain courses at traditional establishments of higher education.

As we have seen, about 80% of GHS students succeed in achieving transfer to the long, university-type courses. Some critics of the GHS have sought to detract from this success by suggesting that standards in the *integrierte Studiengänge* are lower than those in conventional universities. Although this cannot definitely be confirmed or refuted, there appear to be differences between Hesse and NRW in the respect accorded their *Gesamthochschulen* in the academic world. Gieseke and Eilsberger (1977:13) believe that the *Gesamt-hochschulen* in North Rhine-Westphalia have been more successful than the GHS in Kassel in achieving parity of esteem with traditional universities. They attribute the disappearance of scepticism and mistrust to the fact that the NRW institutions now have sufficient staff and resources whereas the degrees at Kassel fall between two stools (FHS and 'traditional' university) both in terms of duration and quality.

It has sometimes been found that GHS students wishing to pursue their studies at another university have difficulty in securing credit transfer (Cerych et al., 1981a: 59). This may be due to a number of factors: the GHS is relatively new on the educational scene, and ignorance about its structures and standards may engender caution or mistrust in other institutions; the *integrierte Studiengänge* are more rigidly structured than is usual at German universities and GHS undergraduates may find it hard to adapt to more loosely structured courses elsewhere. There is, however, another equally convincing explanation: a traditional university which refuses to accept a GHS student may be trying to safeguard its own prestige by blocking attempts at access on the part of those outside its system; by doing this it is helping to maintain its own 'purity' by erecting barriers against academic intruders or 'parvenus'.

Attitudes of Staff and Students The psychosocial dimensions of students' performance in the *integrierte Studiengänge* have been explored by Miller (1980), who carried out an empirical study of 1,600 students at the Duisburg and Wuppertal *Gesamthochschulen*. Some were studying electrical engineering and economics in integrated degree courses, and others were doing mathematics and physics in degree courses which were still under development. The research took place in 1977–80. Miller (ibid.:58), like the authors already cited above, finds little objective difference in academic achievement between FOS and ABI students. Indeed, by the fourth term, the FOS students are further advanced in their work than the ABI students. He believes, however, that there is more to academic success than 'results' and sets out to investigate psychological and social parameters which are usually ignored by higher education planners and teaching staff.

As regards motivation, he finds that students who have won their university places the hard way (e.g. FOS students) are usually more highly motivated than those who have had an easier passage (ibid.:38–9). *Abitur* holders are less motivated than FOS students, and their initial motivation drops slightly in the middle of their course, before rising as the point of termination of studies approaches. FOS students begin with higher motivation than their ABI classmates, and this already high motivation rises slightly during the degree course so that the differences between FOS and ABI groups are accentuated still further.

Many of the non-*Abitur* holders have come from the world of work, and experience a greater degree of achievement anxiety than ABI students. This is most probably due to their lack of experience of academic life (ibid.:41). ABI students initially suffer more feelings of social rejection than FOS students. ABI students are a little more likely to feel vulnerable, misunderstood, unliked, inferior and to have difficulty in making contact with other people. These feelings fade somewhat for ABI students as the degree course proceeds, whereas for the FOS students they increase. Miller (ibid.:45) attributes the initial differences between ABI and FOS students to the fact that the latter have already notched up some practical experience of life, while the former are obliged to derive their self-esteem almost exclusively from their role as students, and are perhaps predisposed to think more critically about this role and about the function of study. It is also possible that when ABI students come to the GHS, they are already suffering from the effects of competition in the *Oberstufe* (upper secondary level) – a factor which may contribute to their initial tension. However, ABI students generally experience a greater degree of self-realisation in their studies than FOS students (ibid.:46). The latter may tend to regard their studies in purely instrumental terms, and the difference between the two groups may also suggest that university life is more geared on the whole to ABI than to FOS undergraduates. Nevertheless, FOS students are generally more satisfied with life, both at home and at the GHS, than their ABI classmates (ibid.:50). Miller attributes this to the fact that FOS students have been admitted to a course of study which they see as enhancing their prestige. Unfortunately, for both groups the level of satisfaction sinks as the course progresses – an indication that the pressures of study affect the private as well as the public domain.

Miller (ibid.:58) concludes that the admission of FOS students to the *Gesamthochschule* unleashes great reserves of motivation and ambition, and that the interaction of ABI with FOS students fruitfully develops the links between theory and practice. The development of further reform is in the students' interests. The *Gesamthochschule* ought not, he feels, to be forced into a competitive struggle with the traditional universities, since this would rebound particularly on the FOS students who are already working under difficult conditions. In his view (ibid.:59), the *Gesamthochschulen* should seek to develop and realise their distinctive reform objectives – above all equality of opportunity.

So far as staff attitudes are concerned, the study by Klüver and Krameyer (1981) shows that both *Fachhochschule* and university lecturers believe that students 'used' to be better than they are now. The ex-FHS lecturers look nostalgically back to the vocationally experienced, rigorously selected students whom they used to teach in the *Ingenieurschulen*, while university teachers believe that the old classical *Gymnasium* gave a much better preparation in the natural sciences than the new-style sixth form, and that today's *Abiturient* lacks general culture and the motivation to work hard. So neither the students with *Abitur* nor those without it measure up to the lecturers' expectations on entry to the GHS! Of the *Abiturienten*, only about half have taken special advanced courses in school mathematics or natural sciences, while less than 40% have taken such courses at upper secondary level in chemistry (ibid.:49). And so the dream picture cherished by many university lecturers of highly motivated and subject-specialist *Abiturienten* turns out to be a fiction.

Lecturers from the university tradition tend to associate FOS students with DI, and ABI students with DII, but students' final decisions do not, in fact, conform to this pattern. In the end, FOS and ABI students do not gravitate to the DI and DII tracks respectively. It is interesting to note that professors from the university tradition 'think' that ABI students must be superior to FOS students in the domain of language, and are therefore likely to do better. This supposition is probably a means of buttressing their enduring conviction that the *Abitur* holders must be superior at least in some respects, because at that point the good performance of the FOS students in chemistry, physics and mathematics was already common knowledge (Klüver and Krameyer, 1981:25–6). The apparent negative attitude of teachers from the university tradition towards FOS students is brought out again by Endemann and Klüver (1983:66). The 'university' professors who permit themselves a verdict on the subject tend to believe that the *Abiturienten* at the GHS have a greater aptitude for study and that students at classical universities are more 'suited to study' (presumably than students at the GHS). The 'university' professors tend to be concerned about the maintenance of academic standards, whereas the FHS professors want above all to see the maximisation of educational opportunity for both ABI and FOS students. The former, therefore, tend to emphasise academic values, whereas the latter emphasise social ones.

In the Essen study of attitudes among chemistry students, it was found that students felt it very important, as a matter of principle and not just for them personally, to keep the decision to take DI or DII open until the end of the *Grundstudium* (Klüver and Krameyer, 1981). Staff, however, differ in their views on keeping options open. *Fachhochschule* professors want to keep full integration at least until the end of the fourth semester, whereas university professors want differentiation much earlier on. The former care more about equal opportunity and realising the reform aims of the *Gesamthochschule*, while the latter wish, above all, to attain high academic standards with their students. This finding is corroborated for economics by Endemann and Klüver (1983:90), who found that the primary concern of professors with a university background was to ensure comparability with conventional universities.

Theory and Practice

We have already seen how, in the nineteenth century, the German spirit ran counter to the utilitarian *Zeitgeist*. Such was the scepticism about relevance and usefulness that Fichte had suggested dividing the curriculum into theoretical and practical parts, only the first of which was to be done at university. Idealist philosophy contributed to a neglect of practical, vocational education. This 'idealist' quality in German education has been so extremely long-lasting and pervasive that in 1977, the International Council on the Future of Universities (ICFU) noted (apparently with some surprise) that:

> The subjects which are the principal centres of student radicalism . . . are taught in a highly ideological way. Students are not expected to engage in the more time-consuming sorts of work, whether it be close statistical analysis, fieldwork or exact philology. . . . The old feeling survives from the Humboldt university that the university ought to be a place where the student undergoes a sort of spiritual revolution, 'finds himself'. The university is a kind of moral holiday from the generally hard-working and highly efficient German society. (ICFU, 1977:115)

Nevertheless, a drive for career-oriented university education had already begun in the 1920s and represented a radical counter-movement to the Humboldtian concept (Lüth, 1983:165). In the late 1960s both the students and the BAK had called for a less abstract and more practical model of higher education which would wean individuals away from self-involvement, and bring them into a creative, fruitful relationship with society. The Wissenschaftsrat gradually changed its position regarding the practical orientation of education (*Praxisbezug*). In 1963, it tended to take the view that *Praxisbezug* was not appropriate for university-type institutions, but as numbers increased and the universities were gradually obliged to cope with a larger spectrum of the population, respect for the vocational gained ground; in 1966, the WR renounced the aim of training every student to do research and in 1970, stressed the need for universities to develop a sense of social responsibility (Lüth, 1983:150); it called upon the universities to produce graduates who had received a general education for various professional activities, and who would be mobile and flexible in the world of work (WR, 1970:73). Although there was some resistance to this principle in the traditional universities, the *Gesamthochschulen* were committed to the promotion of links between theory and practice as a reform objective. Some of the most notable atttempts to introduce applied degree courses were embodied in vocational placements and in the concept of the *Projekt* at Kassel; there has been significant development of teacher education both in North Rhine-Westphalia and Hesse.

Projects and Placements

At Kassel, the *Projekt* was intended to be a powerful means of integrating theory and practice, and achieving social relevance. The educational rationale of the *Projekt* has already been described above in connection with the notion of learning-through-research developed by the Bundesassistentenkonferenz (BAK, 1970b). It was intended to be emancipatory; to promote intrinsic motivation; to help students integrate scholarly theory with social praxis; and to contribute to their political socialisation. There was to be a possibility of interdisciplinary group work, if appropriate. *Projekte* were to be based on professional problems, and to be carried out independently and autonomously by the students (Winkler, 1979:52). They were meant to help engineers, for example, to achieve a deeper understanding of the social implications of their work, thereby enabling them to transcend the basic subject content of their course (Neusel, 1981:76). From the beginning, the *Projekt* was conceived as an essential part of the integrated degree courses.

In practice, it has proved difficult to realise all these worthwhile objectives. Winkler (1979) draws attention to the many practical problems which have arisen in the supervision of *Projekte*; it can be difficult to find the financial resources and materials to do them justice; students often find it hard to come to terms with group work and to accept a group mark; not the least of the problems is the inexperience of staff in giving guidance to students undertaking *Projekte*; usually they have not been part of the educational experience of university tutors, and many are at a loss to know how best to supervise them.

A further attempt to link theory and practice at Kassel is the work-study placement, which is now one of the most successful and widely appreciated features of the *Kasseler Modell*. Like the *Projekt*, these periods of vocational experience (*Berufspraktische Studien* (BPS)) are a fruit of the student movement of the 1960s. They have been in existence at the GhK since the late 1970s, and are a feature of more than ten degree courses (Freimann, 1988:3). They are intended to provide social experience in a professional field, and to link the world of work with university study, juxtaposing the traditional structures of the former with critical scholarship (ibid.:4). About one thousand Kassel students undertake BPS every semester; since employers now welcome them, and claim to benefit from the arrangement, there are obviously advantages on both sides. The BPS have become a service which the GhK offers to the region. Since each subject grouping has developed its own distinctive model for placement, the degree structures are not uniform. Usually, there are two periods of work-study, but in economics there is only one six-month placement, after the fourth semester (ibid.:5).

Despite the fact that the BPS have been enshrined in law and are regarded as the hallmark of the integrated degree courses, it is still difficult to enlist the participation of sufficient appropriately trained supervisors to make the whole exercise as worthwhile for the students as it ought to be (Neusel, 1981:88). Part of the problem is that work of this type does nothing to enhance the scholarly reputation of academics, which depends on research and publications rather than placement supervision. Freimann (1988:8) states frankly that lecturers' preparation and supervision of the BPS often leaves much to be desired. He believes that research is now a higher priority for most university staff than the realisation of reform objectives, and anticipates that the BPS may in future be downgraded by being made pre-sessional or voluntary. Freimann (ibid.:9), however, also sketches a more encouraging, alternative scenario: he discerns in certain sectors of the population a growing discomfort at the effects of big business, science and technology and an increasing interest in social and ecological matters, which may help build support for a humane, enlightened concept of professional education. If this change in the spirit of the age gathers momentum, it will offer higher education a second chance to realise the reform ideals of the 1960s and the comprehensive universities will be particularly well placed to contribute to a renaissance of applied degree courses.

Teacher Education

The teaching profession in Germany is characterised by deep-lying, historically determined status disparities between teachers in dif-

ferent school types. In keeping with their general mission of maximising equality of opportunity and achieving *Praxisbezug*, the *Gesamthochschulen* set out to reform teacher education by designing new
course structures to make it more practical and to overcome traditional divisions within the profession. To understand the basis of the
hierarchy, it is necessary to examine the origins and ethos of the
different school types in Germany, since these exercise a powerful
influence on the self-images, social standing and salary levels of
teachers in each type.

The birth year of the most prestigious and 'academic' secondary
school (*Gymnasium*) was 1810, for it was in that year that Wilhelm
von Humboldt introduced the *Examen pro facultate docendi*, a state
examination for secondary school teachers which required them to
measure up to Humboldt's ideal of *Bildung*. It loosened the hold of
the Church upon the teaching body, and enabled *Gymnasium*
teachers to enjoy the respect which society accorded to academics.
Its effect was to make teaching an important career in its own right,
capable of attracting people who had a vocation for the work and
were not merely clergymen who had failed to secure a living (Ringer,
1969:24–5). In 1812, new rules were drawn up which fixed the
course of preparation for university study. This was the origin of the
Abitur examination, which could only be done at institutions offering
a full quota of Latin and Greek. In time, the curriculum came to be
dominated by ancient languages and was marked by an anti-
modernistic outlook.

About the middle of the eighteenth century, the need had begun
to be felt for a more practical curriculum which would cater for the
needs of people in commercial and administrative walks of life, and
it was in response to this need that the *Realschule* developed. '*Real*'
implies a concern with practical matters, and its intentions were
characterised by the '. . . realistic and practical point of view, the
interest in actual life, coupled with a profound aversion to pedantic
scholarship and the abstruse speculations of academic philosophers
and theologians' (Paulsen, 1908:104– 5). The ethos of the University of Halle profoundly influenced the development of the *Realschule*.
It was at Halle that the name *Realschule* seems first to have been
used, and the first school of this type to be successful and prosperous
was founded by J.J. Hecker who had studied at the University of
Halle. The values of the University – assimilation of modern
science and philosophy, adoption of the principle of free thought and
research, use of German rather than Latin as a teaching language –
were taken up and embodied in the *Realschule*.

It is obvious that there is an incompatibility between the spirit of the *Gymnasium* and that of the *Realschule*. The 'pure' values of the former clashed with the 'applied' values of the latter, which classical scholars sought to discredit. The conflict between classicism and modernism took on the character of a war in which the *Gymnasium* stood for conservatism and élitism while the *Realschule* became associated with the lower middle classes. Nevertheless, the cause of modernism in education continued to make progress. The Prussians became increasingly dissatisfied with several aspects of the *Gymnasium* curriculum and in the mid-1920s, the Richertsche Reform reorganised the secondary school curriculum so as to give a greater role to modern studies. Latin was to be pruned so as to give more space for German; modern languages, history and civic instruction were to be emphasised. The effect of these reforms was to enhance the status of the *Realschulen*, to help their recruitment and to make them a more highly valued part of the education landscape. It would, however, be fair to say that they have never attained parity of esteem with the *Gymnasien*.

The elementary school in Germany was originally called the *Volksschule* and is now divided into the *Grundschule* (equivalent to primary school, years 1–4) and the *Hauptschule* (lower secondary school, years 5–10). Frister (1976) argues that the name *Hauptschule* ('main school') is a misnomer, since only a minority of the school population go there. He condemns it as a dead-end school, attended by only lower-class Germans and the children of guest workers. Its problem has been to shed its inherited character as the senior section of the elementary school, and to establish its own identity as a separate form of secondary education (Hearnden, 1976:80).

The origins of the *Volksschule* in Germany are bound up with the Church, and in fact, elementary school teachers used to do duty as church sacristans; the history of their progress towards dignity and professional independence is synonymous with their progressive liberation from Church influence and domination (Bungardt, 1965; Pritchard, 1986a). The state did little to improve the position of elementary school teachers because it was ambivalent about the extension of education to a broader stratum of the population. Too much education carried with it the potential danger of making the people discontented with their station in life. Thus, Frederick the Great wrote to his Minister von Zedlitz in 1779 that ' . . . it is enough if the people in the countryside learn a bit of reading and writing. If they know too much, they will start pouring into the towns wanting to become clerks or something like that' (Bungardt, 1965:13). In the early part of the nineteenth century, teachers were inspired by the ideas of Pestalozzi, which encouraged them to become more critical and reflective about what they were doing; however, the authorities feared that they might become a potentially subversive force and so in 1824, a directive laid down that their political trustworthiness must be ascertained before they were offered employment – prizes, promotion and increased salaries were to be offered to the politically 'reliable' (ibid.:31).

Despite these pressures, teachers continued to press for a measure of liberation; they were supported by their leaders, Adolf Diesterweg (born in Siegen), and Friedrich Wilhelm Wander, both of whom did much to raise teachers' consciousness and aspirations. In the year 1848, Wander drafted a document entitled *Aufruf an Deutschlands Lehrerschaft* ('Call to the Teachers of Germany'), in which he proclaimed the essential unity and common interest of all school teachers. Diesterweg drafted the education section of a new constitution which guaranteed free primary education and freedom from denominational or sectarian influence. The assembly at the Paulskirche in Frankfurt also decided on the separation of Church and school, with the result that the general political climate appeared favourable to the liberation of elementary school teachers (see Bungardt, 1965:ch. 4).

As it turned out, the 1848 Revolution was short-lived. Elementary teachers soon experienced reactionary forces. They were accused of fomenting social discontent and poisoning people's minds. In 1854, the notorious *Stiehlsche Regulative* were introduced which, in effect, cut teachers off from intellectual life by permitting them nothing but religious studies; this ensured that they were denied personal or pedagogical education and were thrown back upon mere practice of teaching skills or 'tricks of the trade'. These restrictions, which were not removed until 1872, greatly damaged the prestige of elementary school teachers – as of course they were intended to do.

To this very day, teacher education is marked by controversy and divisions. In Nazi times, education of *Volksschule* teachers was downgraded to the level of seminars, supervised by the school authorities (Oehler, 1985:85). In the Weimar Republic, the *Länder* acted independently in the development of education for elementary school teachers; the Weimar Constitution laid down that the education of all teachers was to be organised according to the principles valid for higher education generally, but this was not implemented owing to financial difficulties. After 1945, the situation was dichotomous; the high-status *Gymnasium* teachers received an academic education lasting for a minimum of four years (usually exceeded), and followed by a two-year period of school-based teacher training. They were then remunerated as high-ranking civil servants. It was assumed that good subject-knowledge was quite adequate for their needs; therefore, as undergraduates they received little pedagogical training. The education of elementary school teachers lasted for about two years (not usually exceeded), but was not *wissenschaftlich* since it took place at sub-university institutions. Even when some of these establishments received recognition as institutions of higher education in 1958, the curriculum tended to emphasise pedagogy rather than subject study, and the duration of courses remained shorter than at universities.

Historically conditioned inequalities of pay and prestige have thus persisted well into the twentieth century. The vested interests inherent in these disparities have, despite the work of some of the teachers' unions, served to buttress vertical divisions in the German school system. The fact that they are so strongly entrenched has contributed towards preventing comprehensive secondary education from becoming widely accepted and popular in the Federal Republic. The comprehensive universities, however, have attempted not only to provide a more practical education for future teachers, but also to democratise the structure of teacher education.

At the beginning of the 1970s, there was a major movement for the unification of the teaching profession. The Deutscher Bildungsrat (1970) initiated many new ideas in education, and put forward proposals to overcome the old class distinctions in the teaching profession. It seemed an economic and political necessity to ensure that all teachers from the *Grundschule* upwards should receive an 'academic' (*wissenschaftlich*) education (Heipcke and Messner, 1981:266). It was hoped by this means to make teaching more attractive to high calibre recruits. The reform concept upon which teacher education was based was that of the *Stufenlehrer*, in which teachers are educated to work with a particular age range (*Stufe*) rather than to teach in a particular school type. Teachers for all *Stufen* (including intending primary teachers) were to study at *wissenschaftliche Hochschulen* for a basic three years which could be extended to four. A higher salary would depend not on the type of school in which the teacher was employed, but on educational qualifications. The trade union, the Gewerkschaft für Erziehung und Wissenschaft (GEW), was strongly in favour of this proposal, since it would establish uniform conditions of service and salary for teachers at all levels in the system. Hearnden (1976) points out that the quarrels over the interpretation of the Agreement between those *Länder* which wished to make it the basis of a much more egalitarian system (SPD) and those that did not (CDU/CSU) were very divisive, and threatened to impede the mobility of teachers within the

Federal Republic. This would have been disastrous since it was 'just such restrictions on inter-*Land* mobility that much of post-war educational policy had been designed to remove or avoid' (ibid.:139–40). Lack of finance, however, was to result in the new model only being adopted in a piecemeal way.

North Rhine-Westphalia and Hesse both adopted the *Stufenlehrer* model, and the Kassel *Gesamthochschule* in 1970 wished to pioneer a concept of teacher education which was more radical than was the norm in the Federal Republic. A forecast of teacher shortage was propitious to reform; at the time, Hesse was divesting itself of its one- and two-teacher schools, and had begun to introduce comprehensive schools, to operate in conjunction with a cycle of guidance and orientation (Heipcke and Messner, 1981:266). The general financial situation was favourable; the Federal Government, the Kultusministerkonferenz, the political parties, the teacher training colleges, the GEW and the Bundesassistentenkonferenz all approved of the concept of the *Stufenlehrer* (ibid.: 264–5).

The Kassel concept of teacher training for *Stufenlehrer* was developed in the summer of 1971 by a group of newly appointed university staff from a number of subject disciplines, and from that of Education. Interdisciplinary co-operation of this kind was rare and not subsequently maintained (ibid.:269). It was agreed that the degree course should last eight semesters for all *Stufen* (a six-semester common course, followed by two further semesters) and that all students should undertake a *Projekt*, either subject-related or interdisciplinary in nature. The aim of the course was to encourage students to look at the whole complex of school and society in a critical and constructive manner, which would reach deeply into their personality and life history (ibid.:277).

Unfortunately, it proved difficult to achieve a streamlined co-ordination between the other subjects and Education, and this has turned out to be a persistent problem (ibid.:270). There were also difficulties with the *Projekt* which should have constituted an integral part of the course, but tended to become marginalised to the status of an option. However, the protagonists were convinced that the Kassel teacher education concept stood for the principles of democracy, emancipation, subject integration and practical orientation. The name of Wander was invoked; the aspirations of 1848, and the hated *Stiehlsche Regulative* were recalled; people felt that their present struggles were a way of keeping faith with those who had struggled so hard for teacher liberation in the past. In the early days, the students as well as the lecturers participated in curriculum development, especially in social and educational sciences, language, literature and art courses. They believed that by such joint promotion of reform activities, they were helping to confer an identity upon the new institution and raise its profile (ibid.:271). Their aims were to unify the teaching profession, and democratise the educational system. Where better to do this than at a new comprehensive university, where the theory–practice link could be reinforced by collaboration with colleagues from the *Fachhochschule*? (ibid.:264).

In 1973–4, however, came the oil crisis. This had a financial effect which sent an exocet through the original concept of the *Stufenlehrer*. The most radical part of the programme, politically and sociologically, was the unitary concept of the four-year programme for teachers in all school types. If it had been implemented, it would have dissolved the duality of the German teaching profession, and united the two historically divided traditions. Unfortunately, the Ministers of the *Länder* decided that upgrading the education and salaries of the elementary school teachers was more than could be afforded, given the new financial situation. In April 1974, they decided that the teaching profession was to undergo a division, with *Primarstufe* and *Sekundarstufe I* candidates on one hand studying for six semesters, and *Sekundarstufe II* candidates on the other, studying for eight semesters (ibid.:268). This set the parameters within which further development was to take place. There was a violent clash in Hesse between the Kassel *Gesamthochschule* (GhK) and the Ministry of Education, which had produced a draft of a proposed structure for teacher education (*Eckdatenentwurf*). Although in keeping with the suggestions of the *Länder* Ministers, the draft was widely perceived as subverting the Kassel concept of teacher education. The Foundation Council of the GhK declared that it intended to stick to its own model, and the students too protested that the *Eckdaten* would perpetuate hierarchical status differences between teachers. When the text of the ministerial decree was published, the students issued the following 'death notice': 'Our common laborious way through life was abruptly ended. After long, patiently borne suffering, our *Stufenlehrer* departed this life, suddenly but not unexpectedly, at the age of 5 semesters. Its life was one long struggle – we struggle on' (quoted by Scheuerer and Weist, 1981:98).

The objectives for which the GhK had striven in teacher education were a microcosm of the reform objectives for the institution as a whole – interdisciplinarity, practical orientation, democratisation – and failure here raised the fear of failure on a much broader scale. Despite many interventions and objections, the Hesse Ministry insisted on bringing its own structure into force, on grounds of cost and the need to ensure compatibility between all *Länder* in teacher education.

Although the model which eventually prevailed at Kassel was not as egalitarian as some people wanted, it had several interesting and progressive features. Instead of founding the core curriculum on the foundation discipline of education, the new programme was based on four interdisciplinary thematic complexes, which focused on the socio-political context of schooling. In order to make them realise how they had themselves been influenced by family and school, students were led to reflect on their own educational and social history. Later, they built outwards to the study of educational theory, and learned to analyse their own actions in the school context. In teacher education, 'work-study placement' became 'school placement', and the GhK claims to be the first institution in the Federal Republic to have involved future *Gymnasien* teachers in this activity. All universities in the *Land* have now added such practical experience to their teacher training programmes, and the GhK can justly claim to have been the trailblazer for the general introduction of school placements throughout Hesse (Heipcke and Messner, 1981:282). Despite these achievements, it has proved difficult to prepare, place and supervise large numbers of students, and impossible to link the practical work done at pre-service level with the following phase of teacher training leading to the Second State Examination. The achievement of a link between the undergraduate and postgraduate phases of teacher education has always proved elusive in Germany.

Notwithstanding its limitations, the *Stufenlehrer* model of teacher education developed at Kassel is unusually progressive, to a degree which has sometimes threatened to isolate it. An attempt has been made to democratise teacher education as far as the present laws and practices in other *Länder* will allow. The Kassel reforms seek to make good the defects which had emerged in the Humboldtian-inspired type of education, and go a fair distance to meet the demands of students and junior university staff in the 1960s and early 1970s.

Like Hesse, North Rhine-Westphalia was particularly anxious to introduce the concept of the *Stufenlehrer*. Since it is the most populous of the federal states, with about 17 million inhabitants and about 28% of the total school-going population in the Federal Republic, this was a momentous decision. Its implementation was complicated by the fact that secondary education is still organised according to different school types, not along comprehensive lines. Teacher education in NRW is structured as follows: the *Primarstufe* prepares teachers for primary level (classes 1–4), *Sekundarstufe I* (SI) for lower secondary level (classes 5–10) in *Hauptschule, Realschule, Gymnasium* or *Gesamtschule* (comprehensive school). The *Sekundarstufe II* (SII) prepares for upper secondary level (classes 11–13 in *Gymnasium,* vocational school or free-standing *Kollegstufe*) (source: Handbuch NRW, 1986:93). Ninety per cent of all SII teachers do a supplementary examination in SI. NRW is proud of the fact that its comprehensive universities were the first institutions in the *Land* at which the new concept of the *Stufenlehrer* was fully implemented (MWF NRW, 1979:52).

A particularly important experiment in the field of teacher education has been the *Wuppertaler Modell*, which represented an attempt to do justice to the special mission of the *Gesamthochschule* in integrating theory and practice (Böversen (ed.), 1989; Kunsmann, 1978:219). Under the *Wuppertaler Modell*, school placements were arranged for students aiming at careers in *Realschulen, Gymnasien* and vocational schools. This experiment began very tentatively with three schools in 1973–4, initial diffidence being due to the fact that the organisers were not sure whether their work enjoyed the support of the Ministry. A new law relating to teacher education was awaited, and there were some people who doubted the value and standing of practical placements in the first phase of teacher education (Hegele, 1978:200). Certain financial problems had to be overcome, and there was an acute awareness that the schools were already overburdened by probationers, teacher shortages, pressure on space and the restructuring of the sixth form.

The results of the first small-scale trial were, however, extremely favourable with the result that Professor Dr Gruenter, the founding *Rektor* of Wuppertal, invited representatives of schools and the area seminars to a meeting, at which the Working Party for Teacher Education in Wuppertal (Arbeitskreis Lehrerbildung in Wuppertal (AKLW)) was formed. The AKLW reached agreement about the objectives and organisation of the experiment, which in 1974–75 was extended to eight schools (ibid.:201). In January 1975, the Ministry of Education formally showed its approval of the AKLW's work by issuing a decree in which it legitimised the school placement experiment for a period of three years, and requested local schools to facilitate it, wherever possible. Owing to increased enrolments at Wuppertal, the AKLW decided to reduce the placement period from five to four weeks and in 1977, 159 schools, varying in level from *Kindergarten* to *Volkshochschule*, were involved. The firm legal footing for the placements now helped to clear up uncertainties about their status and general acceptability. There are still practical difficulties and deficiencies in the attempt to offer and supervise school experience to all intending teachers at undergraduate level (see Bohnsack, n.d.), but the principle of placement has now been enshrined in the examination regulations for the entire *Land* (*Lehramtsprüfungsordnung* (LPO), 18 November 1985: para. 5a).

The *Wuppertaler Modell* was influential, and copies of the reports of its activities were frequently requested by other institutions, both within and outside North Rhine-Westphalia. It proved that the traditional barriers between school types and teacher training institutions could be overcome, even though there was still a fundamental incompatibility between vertical and horizontal grouping. It was not just the 'results' that counted but the spirit of co-operation engendered by the project. It was important in a narrow sense as a worthwhile curriculum development, and in a broader sense as a contribution to the realisation of the *Gesamthochschule* mission (Kunsmann, 1978:219).

Research

While it may be true that in Germany, *wissenschaftliche Hochschulen* are assumed to be equal in rank (Wissenschaftsrat, 1985:10), it is essential that the *Gesamthochschulen* should demonstrate beyond all argument that they are indeed *wissenschaftlich* in status, especially so far as their university-type courses are concerned. The *Gesamthochschulen* need strong research records in order to be able to measure up satisfactorily to the various performance indicators which the *Land* authorities and other bodies might apply to them. Typical examples of such indicators are success in obtaining research funding from external sources, and admission to membership of the prestigious Deutsche Forschungsgemeinschaft (DFG).

A number of factors have made it difficult for the comprehensive universities to develop satisfactory research policies and impressive research records. In the early years, academic staff at *Gesamthochschulen* were disadvantaged because the new institutions were not yet fully equipped with laboratories, libraries and the other appurtenances of scholarly activity; it sometimes happened that a professor who had been in receipt of a research grant at a traditional university moved to a GHS, and found that the grant-awarding body was unwilling to transfer the grant to the newly established institution, lest the facilities there should prove inadequate for the successful completion of the project.

Part of the problem was that there existed an inherent tension between the reform objectives of the GHS, and the traditional values upon which prestige and money depended. Prior to the reforms demanded by the students at the end of the 1960s, many professors had tended to devote their energies to research at the expense of teaching. An objective of the *Gesamthochschulen* was to improve the quality of teaching, but in Germany (as in many other countries where the German model has taken root), the intense emphasis upon research as the criterion of academic quality has the effect of down-grading the status of teaching. This is frankly admitted by the Wissenschaftsrat (1985:20, 21–2), which states that in the present German system of higher education there are no material incentives to take on extra teaching, and since one's scholarly reputation cannot really be enhanced through excellence in teaching, there are no other forms of motivation to make the individual especially committed to it (ibid.:21). Staff who seek to do justice to the reform objectives of the comprehensive universities by putting a lot of time and energy into the supervision of placements and small group work find it difficult to sustain their own research output.

In the early years of building up credibility, the new *Gesamthochschulen* needed a degree of commitment from their staff which drained away time and energy normally available for research. It is this dilemma which prompts Teichler and Klophaus (1981:301) to quote a remark frequently heard among their academic colleagues, that 'their *Habilitation* is the *Gesamthochschule* of Kassel' – this indicates the speaker's pride in the development of the *Hochschule*, but is a tacit excuse for not having done much research. A problem for the comprehensive universities is that in Germany the system of appointment and promotion loosens one's attachment to the institution in which one works. It is only by receiving a 'call' (*Ruf*) to move to a different institution that a scholar can attain a Chair or a better position; one must have built up considerable prestige and a substantial research reputation to be considered worthy of such a 'call'. Normally in-house promotions are not permitted in universities, and this is regarded as a very important principle in maintaining the quality of staff; it also helps to ensure fairness and objectivity in the appointments system, since it is reasoned that there is a danger of individuals being able to 'pull strings' to gain promotion within their own institutions. This system is a major instrument for maintaining high academic standards in research and teaching, but it has the undesirable side-effect of increasing individualism and decreasing institutional loyalty. Whereas the comprehensive universities claim to encourage co-operation, the promotion system encourages competition and self-centredness. If individuals know that they can only 'get on' by 'getting out' of the institution that employs them, then they are less likely to dedicate themselves to furthering its wellbeing.

The comprehensive universities have a special commitment to applied research and to 'relevance'. However, the type of research which is most prestigious and most likely to pay off in career terms is usually theoretical or 'pure'. The criterion of 'relevance' is a controversial one; some people neglect it and may be accused by reformist colleagues of betraying the ideals of comprehensive higher education, while others cultivate it and may be accused by traditionalist colleagues of neglecting quality in their work. The pressures for achievement are such that progressive ideas are sometimes not given a fair chance. For the more orthodox academics, membership of a *Gesamthochschule* may conflict with membership of the scientific community and with their personal career ambitions. Having said this, however, we should add that many professors have joined the *Gesamthochschulen* out of conviction that its reform objectives are worthwhile, and have succeeded both in contributing to the realisation of these reform objectives and in making a good name for themselves in the scholarly world.

So far, the difficulties associated with research in the GHS have been discussed mainly from the viewpoint of the individual scholar. Now it is time to examine research policy in the GHS at institutional level. In 1979, the Ministerium für Wissenschaft und Forschung in North Rhine-Westphalia (MWF NRW) emphasised the need to develop research at all the comprehensive universities, and stressed that research-led teaching was particularly important for the integrated degree courses. It indicated its intention of deciding on research priorities (what is currently termed 'selectivity' in the United Kingdom) and listed the criteria which would be used to determine such priorities (MWF NRW, 1979:58). These were as follows: relevance to teaching, innovative characteristics, social relevance, distinctiveness, compatibility with official research planning in the *Land* NRW, 'rarity value', and modernity. It listed the specialist research areas for each *Gesamthochschule*, and went on to spell out the implications of this concentration for teaching. Co-operation between the comprehensive universities was to be encouraged, especially between Duisburg, Essen and Wuppertal, which are all situated close to each other. Such inter-institutional collaboration was to facilitate the offering of a large spectrum of subject choices to students, and the notion that each GHS should necessarily teach *all* subjects was, therefore, correspondingly discouraged.

The service function of research has recently been highlighted by the *Land* of North Rhine-Westphalia which has set its universities the goal of ecological and economic renewal of the region. Technology transfer is strongly emphasised, and a national budget of 6 million DM for the financial years 1985–88 has been allocated for co-operation between the *Hochschulen* and industry (Handbuch NRW, 1986:105, 109). An earlier and successful experiment in putting research at the service of the community was the 'science shop' (*Wissenschaftsladen*) (Herrmann and Schmidt, 1983). This idea originated in the Netherlands in the mid-1970s, as a result of calls for social relevance in higher education during the student move-ment of 1968 (ibid.:52). The first *Wissenschaftsladen* (WL) in the Federal Republic was opened in 1981 in Essen, and is still in existence. It solicits applications for expert help in some field of activity, screens them and links up clients requiring advice with scientists or academics qualified to give it. Clients might, for exam-ple, be small nurserymen with micro-ecological problems, or per-haps factory committees or housing groups. The work of the WL gives a new meaning to 'regionalisation' by using the scientist's qualifications to help solve the problems and interests of ordinary citizens, thus making science more acceptable to a broad sector of the community (ibid.:51). The social objectives of the WL are to reduce alienation arising from division of labour and inequality of opportunity, and to bridge the gap between the people and the hierophants of science. It is *Praxis* with a social conscience – an excellent way of serving both individual citizens and the local region.

At Kassel, a selective research policy has also been adopted but, before agreement was reached on the choice of the areas of priority, the GhK, like its sister institutions in NRW, had to cope with a number of difficulties – some of them of a psychological or social rather than of an economic or academic nature. Teichler and Klophaus (1981) describe the tensions which arose during the early years in their institution. The Humboldtian principle of unity of research and teaching was accepted, and the GhK was therefore faced with the task of establishing and developing a research tradi-tion. There was hardly any equipment, the newly appointed staff mostly had relatively little experience in the field of research, and many years were to elapse before Kassel was in a position to recruit research staff from among its own graduates. The fact that the teaching staff consisted of people from two different traditions ought to have been hailed as a great opportunity, but the immediate difficulties seemed to loom larger than the opportunities (ibid.:300). The university staff were very conscious of the need for them to be fully accepted by the scientific community, and it was partly this which led them to distance themselves from the FHS lecturers. The latter, in their turn, felt somewhat insecure because they were now expected to undertake research, and suggestions meant to help them achieve good results (such as training in research methodology) were perceived by some as expressions of discrimination against them.

In view of all these adverse factors, it is not surprising that it was some time before research began to flourish. The new *Gesamthochschule* accepted in broad terms the desirability of interdisciplinary and applied research. Towards the end of 1972, it was agreed that university teaching methods, planning in higher education and school planning should be regarded as special focuses for research (Teichler and Klophaus, 1981:304). It was also agreed that, rather than relying heavily on state initiatives, the *Hochschule* itself would assume increased responsibility for the planning and promotion of research. At first, the natural sciences, particularly physics and chemistry, were much more successful than other subjects in their applications for institutional research funds. This highlighted the need to widen the spectrum of research activity. Since the success of the new institution depended so much upon success in building up a good research record, the second founding President of Kassel, Ernst von Weizsäcker, declared that the development of research would be his most urgent and pressing task (ibid.:306). He strongly rejected the notion that the Kassel GHS should be merely a teaching institution, but he was realistic enough to admit that his institution was going to have difficulty in competing with established universities for resources. He believed that the GhK needed to develop a distinctive profile, building on its special strengths, such as the practical experience of the *Fachhochschullehrer* (ibid.:307).

In his report, the President emphasised three principles relating to research: (1) the special practical orientation of the GhK; (2) the necessity to promote traditional research at the highest level; (3) the role of interdisciplinary centres and working parties in promoting practice-oriented research. Subsequently the Gewerkschaft für Erziehung und Wissenschaft proposed fifteen themes as the major focus of research in the Kassel GHS. This list stimulated much discussion and controversy; some people rejected its implicit criterion of relevance, others felt that it gave insufficient emphasis to science and technology and did not take account of existing research potential (ibid.:309). The fifteen suggested topics, however, assisted progress towards the development of a research policy, even if there was still disagreement about giving financial priority to interdisciplinary work rather than to research in particular subject disciplines.

In 1978, the Hesse Law for Higher Education called for a policy of research selectivity and for the setting up of research centres. In the same year, two such centres were founded: one for research into vocational and higher education (Wissenschaftliches Zentrum für Berufs- und Hochschulforschung (WZI)) and one for psychoanalysis, psychotherapy and mental health (Wissenschaftliches Zentrum für Psychoanalyse, Psychotherapie und Psychohygiene (WZII)). The foundation of these centres helped to establish a discrimination of focus in the young institution; interdisciplinary work grew, and with it the participation of ex-FHS teachers in research; in 1976–78, the Kassel GHS tripled the amount of funding which it was able to attract from external sponsors; at last the social sciences came into their own – in 1980, they were able to bring in more external funding than engineering and the natural sciences, which at first had commanded the lion's share of available resources (ibid.:311).

Despite this initial success, certain problems still remained to be faced. In 1979, resources became scarcer, and the introduction of level funding made competition for existing resources very much sharper. The technology sector had expanded, and its claim to a larger share of the 'cake' constantly brought it into conflict with the natural sciences. Scarce resources were being increasingly used to attract teaching staff of high quality, and this policy was not always compatible with that of selective allocation of money for research. It became difficult to sustain the policy of interdisciplinary priority research areas (ibid.:314). It also seemed clear, by about 1980, that practice-oriented research was especially vulnerable to political controversy. In 1979, the GhK failed to achieve membership of the Deutsche Forschungsgemeinschaft, and blamed the contraction of resources as a major reason for its exclusion. The initial failure was, however, later retrieved, and the GhK has now been accepted as a member of the DFG.

At Kassel, as at the other comprehensive universities, it is not easy to reconcile the need to concentrate research resources with the need to fund and equip all teaching staff and departments adequately. There is a permanent tension between concentration and diffusion. Just as individual scholars have to reconcile their need to build up their own reputations within the scientific community with their commitment to the reform objectives of the institution which employs them, so each particular *Gesamthochschule* has to walk a tightrope between realising its own distinctive objectives and achieving acceptability within the German higher education system as a whole. To fail in the latter aim would be to disadvantage its students and this would be just as serious a betrayal of its mission as would the abandonment of its reform goals.

This chapter has concentrated on three major areas: the integrated degree courses, the commitment to the theory–practice link and the development of a research policy in keeping with the special character of the *Gesamthochschule*. Achievements in the first two areas have been substantial. University-level degree courses have been opened to a wider range of students than would traditionally have had access to them. Non-traditional students perform well academically. The goal of social justice is promoted. *Praxisbezug* has been widely welcomed and valued; the example set by the comprehensive universities in this respect has influenced other traditional universities, which have sometimes distanced themselves from the Humboldtian model and become more community-oriented in their outlook. It is the third area – that of research – which seems most problematic for the *Gesamthochschulen*. The pressure to achieve institutional respectability by demonstrating high levels of research prowess cannot but serve to deflect the comprehensives from their reform objectives; such pressure tends to push them increasingly in the direction of traditionalism. This is greatly to be regretted, when one reflects that the original objective of the comprehensives was to break the mould of the classical university rather than to adjust to it.

−6−

Staff and Students

The Integration of Staff

Inherited Attitudes

A major objective of the *Gesamthochschule*'s reform philosophy was to weld the academic staff into a functionally unified body (Handbuch NRW, 1986:13). As we have seen, the feeder institutions from which the GHS academic staff were drawn differed considerably in background and status. The defence of power and status by staff from the university tradition within the *Gesamthochschulen* has been a phenomenon of central importance in the history of the new institutions.

Weber (1948) analyses the composition of power in sociological terms, and suggests that it depends on three factors: class, status and party. 'Class' is determined by money, and specifically the presence or absence of property. Ellwein (1985:129) notes that many of the *Akademiker* in the nineteenth century were not especially well-off, and often had to wait for a long time before they could establish their own households. But they still belonged to the upper social stratum; like the nobility and the landed bourgeoisie, they formed part of the ruling class. In Weber's terms, their power depended not on 'class' but on 'status'. He uses this word to denote social prestige, and the terms 'status' and 'prestige' will be used interchangeably in the present study. 'Status' depends upon honour, rather than legal agreement; it is based on the respect or deference freely accorded an individual or office. Being honorary, it is at once strong and weak: strong because it is voluntarily ascribed, and weak because it disappears if the social consensus which creates it is withdrawn or destroyed. Weber's third determinant of power is 'party'; this term refers to political power and depends on the structural forms of social domination. So far as 'party' is concerned, the power of universities lies in their right to award degrees which affect the life chances of individuals, thus affecting the social reproduction of society. Bell (1973:410) shows that it is the universities (and not the schools) which are increasingly arbiters of social position and asserts that: 'As the gatekeeper it [the university] has gained a quasi-monopoly in determining the future stratification of society'.

Many of the professors appointed to the new *Gesamthochschulen* from the university system engaged in the most spirited defence of their power in all its aspects – class, status and party. This involved refusing to accept colleagues from the *Fachhochschulen* as their peers. In beating off a challenge from below, they were continuing a long historical tradition. Surveying the German university in the nineteenth century, Ellwein (1985:120–1) perceived it as fighting a 'war on two fronts'. On the one hand, it was utterly determined to retain its exclusive right to grant doctorates; on the other, it insisted on its right to decide what constituted *Wissenschaft*. For a long time, it tried to fend off the attempts of the *Technische Hochschulen* to establish themselves as fully academic institutions, and at first was even reluctant to recognise the claims of the natural sciences as high status disciplines alongside philosophy. It used the distinction between applied and theoretical knowledge to exclude non-university institutions from the ranks of the fully 'academic' *Hochschulen*, and subjects taught at the *Technische Hochschule* (TH) of Berlin, such as food chemistry, architecture, meteorology, surveying, shipbuilding and electrical engineering, were not mentioned in the same breath as *Wissenschaft* (ibid.:128). Important innovations in scholarship such as physical chemistry, physiological chemistry, and the social sciences were only grudgingly acknowledged, if at all, and Ben-David (1972) notes that the result of this conservatism was that intellectual leadership in many of the newer fields passed to Britain and the United States. The result of the German university's attempt to defend its monopoly was the development of new disciplines outside the university system, beyond its control and authority. Its monopoly was eroded, as the *Technische Hochschulen* carved out a new niche and identity for themselves. Finally, at the end of the nineteenth century, the Emperor of Prussia gave the TH of Berlin the right to award doctorates. Ultimately, the university was not powerful enough to mount a successful defence of the boundaries which it had tried to construct around *Wissenschaft*.

A battle of the same kind was fought in the 1950s and 1960s when the *Pädagogische Hochschulen* started clamouring for university status. Hennis (1982:7) states that: 'Every conceivable legal device was employed to interpret the concept of *wissenschaftliche Hochschule* as applying only to universities of the traditional kind', and reminds his readers of the resistance of the Westdeutsche Rektorenkonferenz in the 1950s to the founding of new universities. This resistance was based on vested interests. Status was defended by legally defining the 'essence' of the university in an extremely narrow, 'exclusivist' way. Of the three major institutions which have contributed to staff of the *Gesamthochschulen* – classical university, *Fachhochschule* and *Pädagogische Hochschule* – the PH ranks immediately after the university in terms of prestige. Its status has varied considerably, however, with some *Länder*, like Hamburg, according it far more respect than others. The status of individual PHs varies too, according to their resources and academic distinction. Thus, Peisert and Framhein (1980:30) list eleven PHs which are not entitled to award doctorates (data for 1977). Nevertheless, the PH is less open to disparagement by the university than the *Fachhochschule*. Reviewing historical precedents, such as the resistance of the universities to the colleges of technology being upgraded to full academic status, Schmithals (1982:41) finds every reason to assume that the universities will continue to disregard the aspirations of the *Fachhochschulen*. He states that:

> Today it is the question of the (non-academic) education at the '*Fachhochschule*' and the university that meets with strong resistance on the part of the universities ... An 'Open University' as developed in Britain would be in flat contradiction to nearly everything that could qualify as a living tradition in the development of German higher education.

Clearly, in view of the traditional German universities' defence of boundaries and privileges, the creation of a unified staff structure at the *Gesamthochschulen* was likely to encounter major problems. But there were compelling educational reasons for pushing ahead. The desired synthesis of theory and practice could be achieved in the integrated degree courses only if university and *Fachhochschule* teachers co-operated closely and harmoniously; only thus could they achieve a cross-fertilisation of their different traditions, and make their distinctive forms of expertise and experience available to their students.

Development Towards Integration

First reactions of the Fachhochschullehrer At first, the progress of the *Fachhochschullehrer* towards full university status seemed to proceed unchecked. The initial stages passed almost unnoticed, and it was only gradually that they became aware of their changed situation.

The first of the changes that preceded the establishment of the *Gesamthochschulen* was the upgrading of the *Ingenieurschulen* to *Fachhochschulen*. Hermanns (1982:45–6) stresses the relative passivity and acquiescence of the teaching staff in this development. They had not planned the change, determined its direction or decided how quickly it would come about. All of this had been settled by the education authorities. The reform gave the institution a new name, and put the teachers in new pay categories; their teaching loads were reduced from twenty-four hours to eighteen hours a week, and they were given access to a committee structure with increased resources. The practicalities of their daily lives had changed little, however, and they had little awareness of having undergone a 'status-passage' (Glaser and Strauss, 1971). The process which upgraded their status almost took them unawares.

The new *Fachhochschule* lecturers were now given academic freedom, and could use it to make of their new opportunities what they wished. No state authority controlled or supervised them. They could involve themselves actively in the new committee structures, but were not obliged to do so (Hermanns, 1982:46); they could use the extra time from reduced teaching loads to prepare their lectures more thoroughly or to bring themselves up to date on the latest technical developments; if they wished, they could exert considerable influence on the structure and organisation of the merged institution; alternatively, they could use their new free time for purposes which had nothing to do with professional activity. No-one kept an eye on them. This effectively removed the need to come to terms formally with their new conditions of service, and any who disliked the change could easily deny that a status-passage had taken place (ibid.:47–8).

Gerhard Rimbach, himself a former *Fachhochschule* lecturer and subsequent *Rektor* of the Siegen GHS, has carried out both empirical and theoretical research on the role of the *Fachhochschule* teachers in the merged institutions. In an essay (Rimbach, 1983) dealing with integration of various categories of staff, he stresses that many teachers at the old *Ingenieurschule* had mixed feelings about its promotion to third-level status, and points out that the interval between transition to *Fachhochschule* and integration within the *Gesamthhochschulen* did not allow sufficient time for a new self-image to develop.[1] He distinguishes three main complexes of attitudes at the stage of the first upgrading (from *Ingenieurschule* to *Fachhochschule*):

(1) A first group missed the familiar hierarchical structures of the *Höhere Fachhochschulen*, and were reluctant to accept upgrading beyond the *Akademie* level;

1. Hermanns (1982:44, note 1) points out that the *Ingenieurschule* in Kassel became a *Fachhochschule* on 1 August 1971, and on 2 August 1971 was transferred to the *Gesamthochschule* – so the transition time was 24 hours! In NRW, it was two years.

(2) A second group emphasised that the newly won prestige of *Fachhochschule* status depended upon the *Fachhochschule*'s remaining recognisably different from the *wissenschaftliche Hochschulen*;

(3) A third group wanted convergence of the existing types of *Hochschulen* and integration of the *Fachhochschulen* within the *Gesamthochschulen*.

The next phase in the upward movement of the *Fachhochschulen* was, of course, their absorption into the new *Gesamthochschulen*. (It should be noted that, in *Länder* where no comprehensive universities were founded, the *Fachhochschulen* developed as independent, freestanding units.) The second transition brought many changes for the better – for example, a great increase in accommodation, personnel and resources (Hermanns, 1982:49). The trade union of the FHS teachers, the *Hochschullehrerbund*, kept a low profile during all these happenings, mainly because their members stood to better their situation, in both salaries and status.

It was decided to introduce the integrated degree courses, and to replace the old FHS courses with new ones specially designed for the *Gesamthochschule*. FHS teachers were now *required* to participate in planning, and had no further choice in the matter. Important issues, such as implementation of the new reform goals, design of the new curricula, or establishment of the new research infrastructure, were all turned over to them. They were 'in on the ground floor', and since it was some time before university teachers were 'called' to the new institutions, FHS teachers exercised considerable power and responsibility.

Predictably, some people were far more active than others in building up the new institution, and the Ministry in NRW decided to offer incentives to those who were actively pushing things in the desired direction. It allocated to the faculties a number of the more highly paid posts, intending them to go to the longest-serving *Fachhochschule* teachers, who would otherwise have had no opportunity of reaching these pay scales.[2] This was a demonstration of

2. Leuze (1985:26) states that this giving of promotions for long service infringed the principle of rewarding merit. In its judgement of 16 February 1979 the Münster Oberverwaltungsgericht (Administrative Court of Appeal) put an end to the practice and forced the NRW Ministry to make promotions depend on merit 'even' for *Fachhochschullehrer*. Hermanns (1982:55 footnote) refers to a similar but earlier verdict given on 22 May 1974 by the Verwaltungsgericht (Administrative Court) in Cologne which also had the effect of ending the practice of promotion by length of service. He further points out (ibid.:53, (1)) that, at the *Ingenieurschulen* and subsequently at the *Fachhochschulen*, lecturers moved almost automatically from one pay scale to another (A13 to A14). Although FHS teachers at *Gesamt-*

good faith and goodwill towards the FHS teachers (ibid.:53). Since the *Gesamthochschule* was the only institution at which they could have improved their status in this way, it also helped to win their support for the reforms. Hermanns (ibid.:54) reports that the FHS teachers, whose attitudes he surveyed, felt fully on a par with university teachers, and did not anticipate conflict. They expected to enjoy collegial rapport and co-operation with the university professors 'called' to their faculties.

It was the appointment of the new professors from the university tradition which brought the first real problems. There were two stages in the process: first, a subject area was selected for the establishment of a new post; secondly, a person was chosen to fill it (ibid.:62). The FHS teachers could decide to do one of two things: appoint to a subject area in which FHS teachers were already represented, or appoint to a wholly new subject area in which no FHS teachers would operate. The advantage of the first option was that a university professor appointed to an existing subject could bring in resources and equipment from which the FHS teacher could benefit – given a positive and co-operative relationship between them. (If, on the other hand, a bad relationship developed, obviously jealousies and tensions might arise.) The advantage of the second option was that the FHS would not be involved, and therefore would not be challenged. The FHS teachers already in post had a major influence on the decisions taken. The less secure tended to appoint to new subject areas, to reduce the chance of rivalry. Secure and well-established FHS teachers could take the 'risk' of appointing to existing subject areas, because they did not easily feel threatened.

The next stage after deciding whether to appoint to existing subject areas or open up new ones, was to choose a suitable candidate for the post. Hermanns (ibid.:64–5) points to a major paradox here. An FHS teacher who was himself entirely unenthusiastic about the whole concept of the *Gesamthochschule* might still insist upon a candidate who was known to be strongly in favour of the GHS and its reform goals, feeling that such a person would probably be liberal-minded, and therefore prepared to work closely with the FHS staff, without undermining their position. In working out arguments of this kind, FHS teachers became increasingly aware of potential conflict between different categories of staff. Their situation was no longer as clear-cut as it had been (ibid.:64). Another relevant factor

---

hochschulen were appointed at scales which matched the top scales at the *Ingenieurschulen*, progress from one pay scale to the next was not automatic, and so the proposed advantage to FHS teachers at the comprehensives was less than intended.

was whether the new staff member had an essentially practical or theoretical background. If the former, the newcomer would rival the FHS teacher on his/her own ground, leaving him/her with no distinctive contribution to make. If the latter, there was a danger that the FHS teacher might be hived off and encapsulated, on the grounds that theory and practice were too far apart for any real co-operation to be possible (ibid.:65). The situation was obviously a threatening one.

Rimbach (1983:63) reveals that only a minority of the *Fachhoch-schullehrer* were in favour of the *Gesamthochschule* at this time. The galloping pace of development had left the majority sceptical and dissatisfied. The formal granting of the right to the title of 'Professor' (on 6 November 1973) did little to improve matters. Although there were more *Fachhochschullehrer* than university professors in the early years, the FHS people still felt disadvantaged, and were in fact under-represented in key committees. Most of them had not been encouraged to undertake research in their previous institutions, and had no doctorates (ibid.:65). (This situation changed with time; 67.4 % of the FHS professors teaching on integrated degree courses in Siegen, for example, did hold doctorates by 1982 (ibid.:76).) At first, many of them were apprehensive at the thought of doing research, and did not want this included in their duties. They saw professors appointed from established universities, and were amazed at the resources which these new appointees could command in terms of money, staff and equipment (Hermanns, 1982:67). Even if they assumed that all of this represented the university norm, they still felt themselves members of an underprivileged caste (ibid.:68), particularly since they were obliged to perform certain 'humble' tasks (like conducting practicals) in person, whereas university professors could always delegate (ibid.: 78).

At this point, the *Fachhochschule* teachers' attitudes had shifted from positive to negative. At first, they had confidently expected university-level status and conditions of service, and had done much of the basic hard work in setting up the *Gesamthochschulen*. Now, they faced developments alienating them from the institutions which they were striving to make a success – and worse was to follow.

The Law Steps In The FHS teachers were already suffering from feelings of inferior status and insecurity, when a new development made their position even more difficult. On 29 May 1973, the Constitutional Court (Bundesverfassungsgericht) in Karlsruhe gave a judgement (commonly known as the 'Higher Education Verdict' or *Hochschulurteil*) which caused a structural division in the teaching body of the *Gesamthochschulen*, and made it virtually impossible to achieve an integrated staff structure. The original dispute centred on the joint decision-making procedures which had been developed in the *Gruppenuniversität*, mainly as a result of the student revolt of the 1960s. A group of university professors in Lower Saxony challenged the Interim Law (*Vorschaltgesetz*) of 1971, claiming that joint decision-making at universities contravened section 5(3) of the Basic Law (*Grundgesetz*), which guaranteed freedom of research and teaching – a seemingly innocent and uncontroversial provision. On the basis of this article, the Court ruled that university teachers must be guaranteed a form of organisation that would facilitate the carrying-out of their scholarly activities (Nagel, 1981:445–6). In view of their qualifications and experience (which students, research assistants and, presumably, teaching staff without doctorates lacked) professors were to have the decisive say on research and appointments to Chairs. In matters relating to teaching they were to have at least 50 % of the votes, and in all decisions affecting research and teaching, the 'undifferentiated participation' of non-academic staff was to be avoided. The higher education teachers on committees which dealt with research and teaching matters were to form a homogeneous group (that is, were to be selected on criteria which distinguished them clearly from other groups). University teachers were put in a special position. Only those qualified by *Habilitation* or some other qualification to teach and research independently belonged to this group. The lawgiver was enjoined to take appropriate measures to protect scholarly activity, and such measures were eventually incorporated in paragraph 38 of the 1976 *Hochschulrahmengesetz* which gave professors an absolute voting majority in matters pertaining to research, artistic development projects, teaching and appointments to Chairs. Many people saw this as a death blow to the *Gruppenuniversität* and a step towards restoring the old *Ordinarienuniversität* of unhappy memory.

Foreigners may well be somewhat shocked at the divisive effects of this ruling on a mixed staff such as exists at the *Gesamthochschulen*, but it was almost inevitable in the German context. The lawyer Dieter Leuze (1985:25), now the Academic Registrar (*Kanzler*) of the Essen GHS, scornfully describes the Law (GHEG, 30 May 1972) for the foundation of the *Gesamthochschulen* in North Rhine-Westphalia as simply 'lumping together' the various categories of staff from the planned donor institutions (for example, university professors, lecturers, *Fachhochschullehrer* and certain 'others'), and making them all *Hochschullehrer*. He condemns this procedure as 'imprecise' and 'superficial' and believes that this melting-pot approach to the integration of GHS *Hochschullehrer* was bound to fail. It should have been clear to the lawgiver that it was impossible to rank academics from the classical university tradition alongside the quite differently educated *Fachhochschullehrer*, and treat them all alike. Leuze is scathing about the lawmakers of the *Land* of North Rhine-Westphalia, calling them 'dilatory' and 'thick-skinned' (ibid.:26) and pointing out that they caused immense problems for the drafters of the *Hochschulrahmengesetz* (ibid.:27). He adds: 'Back in 1975, I concluded for these reasons that the ill-conceived staff structure of the *Gesamthochschulen* had maimed them almost irremediably at birth'.

The straightforward transfer of polytechnic-type staff to university is so foreign to the German mentality that even Dahrendorf had had reservations about it in his Plan (1967), and had suggested some separation of the teaching and research functions; even the normally liberally minded Bundesassistentenkonferenz (BAK, 1971) was against automatic global transfer. The BAK laid great emphasis upon appropriate qualifications, and recommended that every application for transfer should be examined by an appointing committee consisting of representatives of various academic groups within the *Gesamthochschule*. Hermanns (1982:15) suggests that the BAK stressed qualifications to this extent because they were confident that their own members (mainly the *Mittelbau*) would stand up well to any competition offered by *Fachhochschule* teachers.

A crucial part of the *Hochschulurteil* was its definition of the *Hochschullehrer* as an 'academic researcher and teacher, who on the basis of *Habilitation* or some other proof of competence, is entrusted with the independent representation of a discipline in teaching and research'. For some staff at traditional universities, 'proof of competence', in the absence of *Habilitation*, might well take the form of outstanding publications in their field. This possibility is allowed for in the so-called 'genius clause' in section 44 of the *Hochschulrahmengesetz*. *Fachhochschullehrer*, however, were unlikely to satisfy either the normal or the 'genius' definition. None the less, if the whole reform concept was not to fall apart, their legal position had to be defined in a way that legitimised their role in the *Gesamthochschulen*. The solution adopted was to invent two categories of professor. This structure had then to be applied to other institutions too, since the basic framework laid down in section 44 of the 1976 *Hochschulrahmengesetz* was mandatory for the whole Federal Republic, and had to be respected in *Land* legislation. Other institutions, however, were likely to have more homogeneous staffs, so there was less probability of intra-institutional conflict arising when the Law was applied.

Under section 44 of the *Hochschulrahmengesetz*, the conditions for admission to a professorship were the following:

(1) a completed course of study at an establishment of higher education;
(2) pedagogical aptitude, normally reflected in experience of teaching or training;
(3) a special ability for scholarly work, normally demonstrated by the acquisition of a doctorate; and
(4) in addition, as required by the nature of the post,
    (a) other supplementary scholarly achievements, which have been demonstrated by *Habilitation* or scholarly achievements of equal value...(this is the 'genius clause') or (b) special achievements in the application or development of scholarly knowledge and methods, during a period of professional practice of at least five years, of which at least three years must have been spent outside the domain of higher education.

Sub-section 4 of section 44 has been incorporated in *Land* legislation in NRW and Hesse. It forms the basis for a division of *Hochschullehrer* into research-oriented 'a' professors and practice-oriented 'b' professors, with 'a' professors on C4 (highest) and C3 pay scales, and 'b' professors on scales C3 or C2. (The 1985 amendment to the *Hochschulrahmengesetz* speaks of phasing out the C2 category, but this will take time.) Some of the former FHS professors have in fact succeeded in transferring to the 'a' category but they are a tiny minority. Otherwise, FHS professors who satisfy the provisions of 4b above are b-1 professors, while those who do not are b-2 professors (Hermanns, 1982:39). The fact remains that they are all 'b' category staff. Their terms and conditions of service are inferior to those of 'a' professors, as are their voting powers and representation in certain university affairs. They are not supposed to undertake basic research, and study leave is granted on the understanding that they will use it either to do applied research, or to sharpen their practical expertise by going back to work in industry for some months. A 'free' term like this is referred to as a 'research semester' if taken by an 'a' professor and a 'practice semester' if taken by a 'b' professor. Most seriously of all, 'b' professors have a much heavier teaching load than 'a' professors. In NRW, FHS professors who work in integrated degree courses are supposed to do twelve hours teaching a week, while in Hesse the load is set at fourteen. FHS teachers who work in polytechnic-type courses in *Gesamthochschulen* have to do the same number of hours (eighteen) as their counterparts outside the GHS.

The 'a' professors, on the other hand, are only expected to do eight hours teaching a week, and occasionally do no more than six in practice. As a rule of thumb, the 'a' professor's weekly workload is made up roughly as follows: eight hours lecturing, eight hours preparation, four hours administration and twenty hours research. This is an approximate norm, but the number of teaching hours which each category of staff has to give each week is legally fixed. (A mere four hours administration may seem low by British standards, but in a system which is subject to considerable state regulation, the state assumes much of the administrative burden, and there is correspondingly less for academics to undertake.)

For a time, the FHS professors' subordinate position in law threatened the stability of the *Gesamthochschulen*. During the debate on the Amendment to the 1976 *Hochschulrahmengesetz* (HRG), one lobby urged that the *Fachhochschulen* be taken 'out' of the HRG, and given their own institution-specific legislation. It was fortunate that this counsel was rejected by the Knopp Kommission, otherwise the standing of the *Fachhochschulen* might well have been irreparably damaged, and the integrative mission of the *Gesamthochschulen* endangered. Another secessionist proposal was made by Cramer (1983) who suggested that FHS courses which were not part of the *integrierte Studiengänge* should be taken out of the comprehensives and 'given' to the nearest *Fachhochschulen* instead. If implemented, this proposal would have seriously weakened, if not altogether wrecked, the *Gesamthochschulen*. A speedy reply to Cramer's article (in the same issue of 'German University Affairs', *Deutsche Universitätszeitung* (*DUZ*), 1983) was penned by Friedrich Buttler, the *Rektor* of Paderborn. Buttler points out that one of the main reasons for Cramer's suggestion is the friction between different staff categories. It is crucial to note, however, that these tensions only arise between FHS and university professors who are teaching on the integrated degree courses. In straight FHS or university-type courses, there is no conflict of interests, and thus no point in taking the FHS element 'out' of the GHS. Buttler goes on to show that the withdrawal of the FHS courses would offer no advantages in terms of law, regionalisation, or optimum future size, and would probably increase costs. The *Gesamthochschule*, he believes, is a place where prejudices should disappear, and it must be allowed to build upon what has already been achieved. He is clearly convinced that attitudinal as well as cognitive benefits can accrue from people working together within a shared academic institution.

These threats to remove the *Fachhochschulen* from the *Gesamthochschulen* have so far been averted but the attempt to achieve an integrated staff structure has clearly not succeeded. There are structural inequalities between different categories, and the 'b' professors operate under very severe constraints. Their heavy teaching load makes it harder for them to do research, and any research they do manage is in the less prestigious 'applied' field. So much for the objective facts about the position of the *Fachhochschullehrer*. Let us now take a closer look at how they feel.

The Attitudes of the Fachhochschullehrer towards their Situation Occupational status is sociologically and psychologically important. Argyle (1969) has argued that self-esteem is based on two main dimensions: status and power on the one hand, and warmth and friendliness on the other. There can be no doubt that status disparities within the *Gesamthochschulen* have been the cause of much personal hurt and unhappiness; Cerych et al. (1981b:67, note 40) report an incident in which a senior staff member of FHS status called a young university lecturer in the same GHS, 'dear colleague', only to be told firmly later; 'Please remember that I am not your colleague'. Rimbach (1983:63) points out that snubbing could be a two-way process. In the foundation phase of the comprehensives, the newly appointed 'a' professors, who represented subject discipline, faced the heavy task of developing the *integrierte Studiengänge*, and bringing in research funding. On arriving, they sometimes met with cooperation from some of those already in post, but they also encountered 'cool reserve and rejection' which they had to try to overcome. Ten years later, levels of co-operation, conflict and mutual respect still vary from subject to subject, faculty to faculty and person to person. However, the violence and the frequency of disputes have diminished somewhat with the years. Leuze (1985:26), like Rimbach, makes it clear that the unpleasantness was not all on one side. The FHS teachers often used their majority in faculty committees to outvote the 'others', although the professors, with the licence delivered to them by the *Hochschulurteil*, were often in their turn haughty or condescending.

Hermanns (1982:74) finds that the FHS teachers do not compare their present position with their earlier situation in the *Ingenieurschule*. If they did, they would have to admit an objective improvement in their circumstances. When they judge within the context of their everyday working life, their overall feeling is one of status loss. In their previous institutions, they had been 'top dogs', setting the standards and determining the direction of development (ibid.:75). Now, however, it is the 'a' professors who have the greatest influence, and the 'b' professors feel alienated. The GHS does not seem to be truly 'their' institution. Measuring themselves against the 'a' professors as a yardstick leaves them with severe feelings of status deprivation. It is in keeping with the findings of social psychologists that the ex-FHS teachers should measure their status using an intra- rather than an inter-institutional comparison, and compare themselves with a superordinate group. Festinger (1954) postulates a unidirectional upward drive in the standards by which we measure ourselves. Our self-concept depends on comparison with others, but both individual and occupational groups tend to compare themselves with those who are slightly above them rather than with those below them.

The way in which staff cope with their professional tensions and conflicts has an effect upon the cohesion of the courses which they deliver. According to Hermanns (1982:76–8), the FHS teachers use three main strategies to cope with status deficit. They may attempt to ape the 'a' professors by keeping standards as high as possible and pushing the students very hard; this effort to prove that they are essentially the 'same' as the 'a' professors does nothing to overcome institutional status barriers and may be an inappropriate way of handling students in DI. Alternatively they may play upon their own distinctiveness, for example, by emphasising the special value of *Praxisbezug*, and trying to give their students qualifications which will be acceptable to regional employers. They create their own fields of activity, leaving it to the 'a' professors to concern themselves with the status of DII in the scientific community. Within their self-defined fields of reference, the status question becomes irrelevant, because they are no longer using the 'a' professors as their prime comparator. This second option seems the most attractive, but it is far removed from the synthesis of theory and practice which the co-operation of professors from different traditions was meant to bring about. There is a risk of its deteriorating into a form of academic apartheid, and it comes perilously close to Hermanns' third strategy – resignation, and withdrawal to the kind of teacher's role which typified the old *Ingenieurschule*. The result here is, of course, that the individual staff member dissociates himself from the administration and from the organs of academic self-government, thus frustrating the development of a democratic political culture within the institution. None of the three alternatives is very healthy either for the individual 'b' professor, or for the academic community within which he works.

In an empirical survey of FHS teachers' attitudes within the GHS, Rimbach (1974b) found that only 3.5% of his sample were 'satisfied' with their situation, while 41.9% were dissatisfied, and

29.3% were only moderately satisfied. Most of the dissatisfied staff had 5–10 years of service, including service prior to joining the GHS. Asked which institution they would join if they were choosing again, more than half (56.2%) opted for an institution other than the *Gesamthochschule* (*Ingenieurschule* 21.9%; *Fachhochschule* 34.3%). About one third (38.8%) chose the GHS, and the rest did not answer the question. Asked how they compared their present professional situation with that in the *Fachhochschule*, 33.9% judged the change negative, while only 6.3% judged it positive. Most felt that their professional situation had worsened in recent years. Asked what staff reforms they would like, 34.6% called for a homogeneous teaching body, while only 4.8% demanded better promotion opportunities. Recently there has been a legal change in the amendment (1985) to the *Hochschulrahmengesetz*, of which section 45(2) now removes the prohibition on in-house promotions for *Fachhochschullehrer*. This should go some way towards removing the promotion blockage for FHS teachers, but it still does not remove their feeling of relative status deprivation.

Rimbach's survey was conducted in 1974; we may well ask whether there has been any improvement in staff relations since then. It is important to note that on 20 October 1982, a judgement (1BvR 1467/80) was delivered by the Constitutional Court which improved the position of the 'b' professors in comprehensive universities. It refers to section 49, paragraph 1, no.4b of the Law for Higher Education of North Rhine-Westphalia, and states that it is in no way a contravention of the Basic Law to treat appropriately qualified FHS professors as members of the 'a' group if they teach on integrated degree courses in a GHS. This was greeted by *Kanzler* Leuze as a 'blow for freedom'. Nevertheless, the same judgement re-emphasised that the 'b' professors teaching on FHS-type courses cannot be regarded as the equals of staff in *wissenschaftlich* courses or institutions of higher education. Many of the professors from outside the university tradition, therefore, continue to feel stigmatised, and with just reason. Recently interviewed by the writer, a 'b' professor in business management at the Essen GHS made a number of forceful points which help to throw light on the present situation.[3] The first point is a positive one, concerning the synthesis of theory and practice; the others relate to the staff structure in the GHS.

(1) The 'a' professors in business management go to far more trouble over practical aspects of the course than professors at traditional universities (e.g. by inviting visitors from the business

---

3. Personal interview conducted with a professor in Business Management at the Essen *Gesamthochschule* on 26 April 1985.

world and supervising practical work). Conversely the 'b' professors are at pains to provide a deep theoretical background to their work – more so than professors at the ordinary *Fachhochschulen*. This is very good for the students, and is clearly a result of the reform policy underlying the *Gesamthochschulen*.

(2) The work climate is soured by competition. The FHS teachers may not have had such good material resources in the old *Ingenieurschule* as they now enjoy at the GHS, but at least they got on well together. A harmonious work climate is much more important than elaborate equipment; it also promotes efficiency and is therefore conducive to good work. In the present 'class-war' conditions, people waste energy fighting one another, and this is bad both for the institution and for the students.

(3) Asked whether 'a' and 'b' professors had different mentalities and values in relation to their work, the interviewee (who had served as Dean of his faculty for some years and was therefore well-placed to judge) claimed that 'a' and 'b' professors were in no way polarised by differences in mentality or outlook concerning the intrinsic nature of their work. The disputes which arose never centred on matters of professional judgement, but always on the 'damned question of status'.

(4) Asked to identify the worst features of his working situation, he replied: 'the unequal starting conditions. That under unequal conditions, we are expected to produce equal achievements. . . . I would like to be as good as an "a" colleague. I really do not want to be a second-class professor or to be perceived as such by the students.'

(5) There are no special problems, so long as staff of different categories do not have to co-operate on the same courses. The 'a' colleagues working together with 'b' colleagues on the integrated degree courses have to struggle to maintain an academic status that will stand favourable comparison with that of colleagues in traditional universities like Münster or Cologne. Where staff are not mixed, this problem does not arise.

It is apparent that far from having become 'normalised', the question of status in the comprehensive universities is still a running sore, and looks likely to remain so for the foreseeable future. The violence of the early rows may have abated, and people may have become 'used' to having two categories of professors, but this does not make the distinction any less invidious if one happens to be a 'b' professor.

The Attitudes of 'a' Professors towards their Situation So far, we have looked at the integration of the teaching body from the standpoint of the *Fachhochschule* teachers, and have seen that there are structural barriers to their progress within their institution. But the situation is not entirely satisfactory for the 'a' professors either – and again for reasons which have to do with status. The union of university teachers, the Hochschulverband, had not welcomed the advent of comprehensive universities, regarding them as a possible threat to academic standards and a means of diluting a hitherto cohesive professional body. Hermanns (1982), who worked for many years at Kassel, sketches the career of an imaginary 'a' professor of engineering, newly appointed to the *Gesamthochschule*. The negative picture which he presents may not always be applicable in all cases, but vividly highlights the problems which 'a' professors may encounter.

The appointment should be the climax of the new professor's career but even the Board which appoints him contains former *Fachhochschule* teachers – i.e. people whose status is less than the status he will have, if appointed to the post. The fact that he is not appointed entirely by his peers makes him feel that he is not, in fact, entering an academic élite (ibid.:79). The élite is, so to speak, adulterated – it is not quite exclusive enough.

When he takes up his post, the young scholar experiences various problems. His status is not quite as assured and authoritative as he had expected. He is not pleased that research fellows and assistants who have successfully completed their post-doctoral theses are still in the *Mittelbau*, while 'b-2' staff who have not even done their doctorates are among the professors (ibid.:83). He encounters administrative and organisational difficulties – rooms which will only become available when rebuilding takes place, delays which occur in supply of equipment, contact with workshops which is more complicated than he had thought, faculty finances which take an inordinate amount of time and effort to obtain. The research infrastructure seems unsatisfactory, and the new professor is regarded as 'reactionary' if he wants a secretary and telephone in the antechamber to his office.[4] When he wants faculty funds for research, he is given to understand by his 'b' colleagues that these funds are really for those (like themselves) who have no external funding. Colleagues in other institutions to whom he complains simply tell him that he should have known better than to accept the job in the first place (ibid.:84). It is very difficult to convince people in well-established institutions

4. Rechtien and Bierbaum (1980) also refer to the lumbering bureaucracy in the *Gesamthochschulen*, which sought to combine academic and state administration in one system, for the purpose of promoting institutional autonomy, freedom and democratic values. They believe that hierarchical structures at the top of the pyramid limit flexibility and reduce commitment lower down.

that the GHS, although 'different', is just as admirable. 'Our' engineering professor despairs of ever achieving parity of esteem for the GHS, and so begins patterning everything he does on the *Technische Universitäten*, thus, unfortunately, negating the distinctive features of the GHS (ibid.:87).

After a while, he begins to realise that his supposed 'teething troubles' are actually permanent features of his present situation. His daily routine seems weighed down by a mass of trivialities (ibid.:88). Above all, the staff structure is a constant source of conflict. The main bones of contention are: the foundation of 'institutes', the allocation of resources, the nature of the DII degree course and the right of former FHS teachers to teach and examine at DII and at doctoral level (ibid.:87). Of course, some 'b' professors are meritorious, but exceptions cannot be made for individuals. Conversely, it must be admitted that some 'a' professors are not fully up to the mark, but the line must be held, and one cannot start picking and choosing from the 'other side' ('X should be allowed to teach in DII, but Y should not'). Any compromise might jeopardise the 'a' group's hegemony, and thus lower the prestige of the 'academic' courses in the eyes of the outside world (ibid.:89). The 'a' professor, who works hard to show the academic community at large that the GHS takes teaching and research very seriously, thinks that the 'b' professors should honour his efforts (obviously in the common interest) and give him the respect he deserves. These hopes are disappointed. He is insufficiently respected by his 'b' colleagues, and his efforts on behalf of the GHS as an institution are undervalued.

Little by little, however, he begins to support the institution where he now works, because he realises that his own future is bound up with it. Criticism of the GHS by peers in other universities rebounds on him and taints his own reputation. He must try to make something of this *Gesamthochschule*, because if its reputation sinks, so does his own along with it. Thus, he passes from 'victim' to 'champion'. Even if the 'a' professor has decided to leave the GHS, he must still consolidate his research record in order to make himself more marketable. This may very well involve bringing in external funding for research, in which case, of course, the reputation of the GHS is strengthened (ibid.:86).

Hermanns' picture is painted in strong colours and needs a little diluting. First of all, it must be said that not all 'a' professors are dissatisfied, and not all of them antagonise or patronise their 'b' colleagues. The *Gesamthochschulen* have attracted some 'a' professors of exceptional distinction, and Rimbach (1983:73) suggests that the higher an 'a' professor's reputation is, the easier it is for 'b' colleagues to work harmoniously with him (presumably because his self-confidence and professional reputation are totally secure). A person in this position has no need to score cheap victories over those beneath him in the hierarchy. Thus harmony can and sometimes does exist between the two groups, but the fact remains that the career progress of the 'b' professors is very seriously circumscribed. (Even 'b' professors with doctorates are not automatically entitled to supervise doctoral students independently.) The obstacles to movement are not just attitudinal but structural, and their legitimacy has been confirmed by the highest court in the land.

Nevertheless, the mixed staff seems to cause the 'a' professors to suffer from 'prestige contagion' arising from contact with the lower-status 'b' professors. It was Benoit (1966) who coined the term 'prestige contagion'. He argues that

> close association with those of markedly lower prestige tends to degrade. These facts explain in large part the ceaseless struggle of those of low prestige to lessen the physical and a fortiori social distance separating them from those of high prestige; and the no less determined efforts of those of high prestige to avoid physical and a fortiori social propinquity with those of lower social prestige. (ibid.:7)

Hermanns' study indicates that not only 'b' professors but also 'a' professors are disappointed in their status aspirations. The mixture of staff causes 'prestige contagion' to the 'a' category and 'status deprivation' to the 'b' category, to the disadvantage of each and to the misfortune of the institution as a whole.

'Classification' and 'Framing'

The presence of both *Fachhochschule* and university professors on the staff of the GHS is intended to facilitate the integration of theory and practice in the curriculum. The fact that there is a fissure in the staff structure has implications for curricular integration.

From quite an early stage, there has been a tendency to push FHS teachers towards teaching on the DI branch of the Y-model, on the grounds that DII is likely to enjoy more public esteem if taught exclusively by 'university' professors. The GHS is obliged to struggle for status, and FHS teachers who insisted on teaching in DII courses could be accused of injuring the long-term reputation and acceptability of GHS degrees. It has even been argued that students would have a right to complain if DII were not taught by teachers of full university standing and qualifications (Hermanns, 1982:56). In the interests of the greater good, there has been a tendency to 'shunt' FHS teachers into the DI branch, which effectively streams GHS staff into 'more prestigious' and 'less prestigious' courses (see Klüver and Krameyer, 1981:74; Hoffknecht and Intrup, 1983:35). This parallels the formal division of staff into 'a' and 'b' professors, and helps to perpetuate status inequalities, as well as undermining the synthesis of theory and practice which is one of the *Gesamthochschule*'s reform objectives.

Integration between theory and practice does take place, but is less developed than it should be, and teachers from the two main traditions in the integrated courses have different conceptions of what it involves. For FHS teachers, *Praxis* means industrial or vocational experience, whereas for university (UNI) teachers it means research or laboratory experience (Klüver and Krameyer, 1981:68). In general, the FHS teachers take polytechnic-type courses as their model for DI work in the GHS (ibid.:82), whereas UNI teachers adopt the traditional university model (ibid.:79). The UNI teachers are quite satisfied that the goal of *Praxis* is already sufficiently realised in the *Grundstudium*, whereas some of the FHS teachers feel that the applied aspects of the subject are drowned by the theory. The FHS teachers feel that the UNI staff are betraying the reform goals of the GHS, and regret that so little integration has taken place. In fact, there is no GHS where complete commonality of study is maintained for as long as four semesters (ibid.:80), and this means that the Y-model is under constant pressure to become more like a V-model. In the case of the consecutive model at Kassel, the pressure is towards earlier specialisation and differentiation. Klüver and Krameyer (ibid.:69–70) state that integration of content is not seriously attempted, let alone realised, in the *Grundstudium*, and that there is little reciprocal influence between the two branches in the *Hauptstudium* (ibid.:88).

Failure in achieving staff integration is correlated with failure in achieving curricular integration. This could have been predicted from Bernstein's work (1971) on 'classification' and 'framing' in educational knowledge. Bernstein uses the word 'classification' to denote the degree of boundary maintenance between different elements in a curriculum. Boundary strength refers to the division of labour in educational knowledge. Strongly insulated boundaries between different types of course content point to what Bernstein calls a 'collection' type of curriculum, whereas reduced insulation points to an 'integrated' type (ibid.:49). Previously insulated subjects or courses become 'integrated' when they are subordinated to some relational idea which blurs the boundaries between them.

'Framing' refers to what may be transmitted, and what may not.

Strong 'framing', from the students' viewpoint, occurs when they have little control over the content of what they have to learn. The 'frame' is often weakened for the purpose of controlling social deviancy, the idea here being that a link is needed between the practical concerns of the pupil and the abstract concerns of the school, if the latter is to retain any power over the former (ibid.:58). 'Framing' becomes weaker as one moves up the educational system; in Germany, the curriculum requirements at primary and secondary level are fairly rigid, compared with the ideal of *Lernfreiheit* at tertiary level. We should note, however, that 'framing' is stronger in the *integrierte Studiengänge* than in many traditional German university degree courses. This is because educational planners are very conscious that some of the students do not have traditional entrance qualifications, and wish to ensure that the final degree standards (allowing graduates to proceed from DII to doctoral study) will in no way be compromised. Strong 'framing' in the *Gesamthochschulen* could therefore be seen as the product of institutional insecurity.

The nature of 'classification' and 'framing' affects the professional identities of those who work within the educational system, and the authority and power structure which controls the dissemination of educational knowledge (ibid.:54). In the 'collection' type of curriculum, knowledge is regarded almost as private property, with its own structure and market value (ibid.:56). It plays a crucial part in forming and maintaining the identity of the knowledge-bearer (or seeker, as the Humboldtian ideology would have it). Any change in 'classification' thus affects the identity of those involved in the educational transaction, and it is this threat which causes resistance to any change in the educational code.

Now, it is clear that the reform objectives of the *Gesamthochschule* imply a move away from the 'collection' towards the 'integrated' type of curriculum. The idea on which 'integration' is based is that of linking theory and practice in the interests of increased social relevance. Strong 'classification' creates a strong sense of belonging to a specific class (ibid.:54), and many of the university teachers 'called' to the GHS from more traditional institutions are undoubtedly accustomed to the psycho-social and intellectual security which it offers. The same applies to lecturers with long years of teaching experience in well-established *Ingenieurschulen*. 'Classification' in the GHS tends to be weak because of the commitment to interdisciplinarity and the integrated degree courses. This reduces people's sense of security, threatening the identity of *Fachhochschule* and university teachers alike by blurring their areas of authority and forcing them into a 'power-sharing' situation. Bernstein (ibid.:64) points out that since they weaken specific identity, 'integrated codes' need a high level of moral consensus to make them work. When successfully realised, 'integrated codes' should lead to new collegial relationships which are horizontal rather than vertical, because they are no longer dictated by the old subject hierarchy (ibid.:62). In the *Gesamthochschulen*, however, the consensus needed to facilitate the achievement of Bernstein's 'integrated code' is lacking because of disagreement on educational goals and, above all, because of the structural division of the teaching body into 'a' and 'b' professors. Some compensation needs to be offered for the loss of a strong subject-based identity – for example, socially rewarding relationships with colleagues, or the possibility of engaging in prestigious and successful collaborative research. At present, however, there seems to be no adequate 'pay-off' for loss of identity, or at least none sufficient to command universal allegiance to the 'integrated' code within the GHS. Many members of staff react by strengthening the 'classification' and re-establishing the 'collection' code. This, of course, has the effect of tearing the *integrierte Studiengänge* apart, thus undermining the very core of the GHS reform concept.

The Students

Regionalisation and Social Class

Although Germans often assure foreigners that there is no question of a 'league table' of German universities, one inevitably suspects that some institutions are none the less more prestigious or popular than others. The very struggle of the *Gesamthochschulen* for recognition in the academic community seems to imply a need to succeed 'institutionally', as well as offering 'respectable' subject courses. One measure of such institutional success is student preference, reflected in the ability to recruit and keep enough students to assure 'organisational health'. In a contracting economic climate, it is also vital that each of the *Gesamthochschulen* should be able to demonstrate the need for its existence.

A major point of policy in the foundation of the *Gesamthochschulen*, and of post-war universities generally, was to ensure a more evenly distributed provision of study opportunities throughout the country. It was regarded as especially important for the encouragement of people who had hitherto not gone on to higher education that such provision should be on a regional basis, since this was likely to make it cheaper and less intimidating for working-class students. Cerych

(Cerych et al., 1981a) points out that emphasis on the GHS's function in promoting 'equality of opportunity' has now somewhat lost out in popularity, in favour of an emphasis on its 'output' in terms of qualified manpower, contribution to the cultural life of the region and prestige accruing from research. Nevertheless, since regionalisation was central to the original reform concept, we shall consider it here, as it is important both for the enrichment of individual students and for the continuing viability of the *Gesamthochschulen*.

Various points regarding the siting of the *Gesamthochschulen*, and new universities generally, are made by Framhein (1983) in her book *Alte und Neue Universitäten*. She outlines the arguments and counter-arguments which were weighed in choosing locations for the new universities. The basic conflict was between 'regionalisation' and 'urbanisation'. Those who supported the policy of regionalisation believed that new foundations should be sited in peripheral, isolated regions, so as to compensate for deficits in the infrastructure, and make the locations more attractive. It was hoped that new universities would boost commercial life, and offer employment to local people, thus helping to prevent out-migration into other towns or regions. The supporters of urbanisation felt that universities should not be used as 'aid to under-developed regions', and found it economically preferable to build up existing population densities and conurbations by centralising rather than decentralising resources. They advocated the foundation of second and third universities in attractive large cities. In the end, however, the policy of regionalisation won out, and new university locations were chosen instead of expanding existing ones. This result was a much more finely meshed net of higher education establishments, with a correspondingly greater likelihood of competition between them.

Most of the *Gesamthochschulen* are, in fact, situated in very densely populated areas, and are close to such older and well-established universities as Bonn, Marburg, Cologne and Göttingen. One might suppose that these 'old' universities would attract students away from the new foundations, thus making it more difficult for the latter to become viable. Framhein (ibid.:94) provides figures indicating student preference for 'old' versus new universities based on a survey of student freshmen (N=14,341). These show that the character and atmosphere of a city (or town) do a great deal to attract students. It is interesting to note that the children of 'academics' (children whose parents have been to university) are keener on 'old' universities than are working-class students (those whose parents have been educated only to *Hauptschule* level). The higher the socio-economic status of a family, the greater the desire to send their children to a university in an attractive town (ibid.:98). However, the overwhelming majority (86%) of students are pleased with their particular *Hochschule* and only 1% have come to it unwillingly. Most students do not care whether they attend old or new universities. Framhein's conclusions would thus seem to be generally encouraging to new foundations, such as the *Gesamthochschulen*, in their attempts to attract students.

In fact, there is as yet no special conflict between 'old' and new universities. Both have expanded as a result of the increase in the size of the age cohort eligible to attend university. Originally the idea had been to accommodate the extra student numbers in the new foundations, but the older universities themselves trebled in size between 1960 and 1982. It is thus clear that the development of new universities has not blocked that of the 'old' (Framhein, 1983:22). Reduced funding has, however, led to increased competition. If the space available for teaching and research is taken as an indicator, then most universities today are overcrowded. At the end of the 1970s, however, the new universities were using only 92% of their capacity, whereas the 'old' universities were using 138% (i.e. were coping with 38% more students than they had been designed to accommodate; ibid.:26). In 1981, the Westdeutsche Rektorenkonferenz complained of unbalanced and irresponsible development of the new universities at a time when the 'old' ones were overcrowded; they called for the allocation of increased resources for the 'old' institutions. Some went so far as to demand the closure of new universities, whereas others argued that funds should be poured into them to build them up and make them attractive. By 1982, however, the new universities were also overcrowded (on average by 30%), which meant that the 'old' universities could no longer complain that the new ones were under-used. They could, however, show that overcrowding was running at 'only' 30% in the new universities, compared with 60% in the 'old' ones (ibid.:27). Framhein's data (ibid.) clearly show that the *Gesamthochschulen* are in no danger of being accused of under-using space. Duisburg is the most overcrowded of all the new foundations (although at the time of writing, new buildings are being constructed), with Paderborn in second place, Kassel in third and Essen in fourth (jointly with Oldenburg). Siegen and Wuppertal, too, have far more students (over 40% more) than they were designed to accommodate (data for 1982 taken from Wissenschaftsrat, 1983). Only a handful of the traditional universities (such as Berlin, Munich, Bonn, Mainz and Cologne) are more overcrowded than the *Gesamthochschulen*.

Framhein (1983:400) defines a catchment area (*Hochschulregion*) as a circle in which at least 25% of the local students are enrolled in a particular local *Hochschule*. The efforts of the comprehensives to bring in students from their local regions have met with a high degree of success. (Figures for regional recruitment at the *Gesamthochschulen* are given, in approximate percentages, in the Handbuch NRW, 1986.) In Duisburg, about two-thirds of the students come from the city itself, the neighbouring towns of Mülheim/Ruhr and Oberhausen or the districts of Kleve and Wesel. About 70% of them live within a radius of 20 kilometres. About 70% of the students at the Essen GHS come from the Ruhr district and 30% live in the city of Essen itself. Some 80% of the Paderborn students come from within the *Land* NRW, of whom 50% live in Höxter, Lippe, Hochsauerland, Soest and Paderborn. In Siegen, it is reckoned that about two-thirds of the students come from the city or its close environs. Wuppertal recruits 30% of its intake from within the city itself, and a further 25% come from the four adjoining regions. At Kassel, about three-fifths of the students come from North Hesse (GhK, *Bericht des Rektorats*, 1977:30). These data obviously indicate a high degree of regional appeal for the *Gesamthochschulen*, and therefore, success in achieving a reform objective.

As far as student recruitment is concerned, the viability of the *Gesamthochschulen* seems assured – for the present at least. It is essential, however, that they should continue to attract students in healthy numbers. The accusations concerning under-utilisation of space, although unjustified, show that they do not lack enemies. Framhein shows that the older universities' catchment areas are becoming smaller – in fact they have shrunk by about one third (1983:68). This is at least partly due to the impact of the new universities. Münster, for example, is now surrounded by a crescent of such foundations (ibid.:70). Many of the new *Hochschulen*, particularly in the North West, have narrow, overlapping catchment areas (ibid.:45). When the *Gesamthochschulen* were founded, they were urgently needed to take the load off the older institutions, and were not in competition with them. However, when student numbers drop in the 1990s, there may be a fight for survival between the universities, forcing the newer ones to recruit outside their natural catchment area. Owing partly to factors beyond their control (e.g. the general attractiveness of the towns or cities in which they are located), this may prove difficult; they do not have the 'pull' of some of the older universities, and the range of subjects which they teach also tends to be narrow, which means that many local students are forced to go elsewhere to study a particular subject (ibid.:83). It would, therefore, be unwise for the *Gesamthochschulen* to become complacent about student recruitment. If, as Framhein's research (1983) would suggest, students have no a priori loyalties, and weigh various alternatives before deciding where to study, difficult times may be in store for the *Gesamthochschulen*.

As regards the social composition of the *Gesamthochschulen*, the available data indicate that the percentage of students from working-class homes is over 20%, i.e. double the normal percentage in North Rhine-Westphalia, Hesse and the Federal Republic as a whole (Handbuch NRW, 1986:497–8; GhK, *Bericht des Gründungspräsidenten*, 1977:30–1). The *Rektor* of Siegen notes that the percentage of students receiving financial support (loans under the BAföG scheme[5]) at his GHS is 48.3% (1982) compared to 33% for the FRG as a whole. He concludes from this that the Siegen GHS is playing an important role in enabling young people from poor families to go on to higher education (SGHS, *Rechenschaftsbericht des Rektorats*, 1983/4:24). The *Gesamthochschulen* have, therefore, been very successful in bringing in students from working-class backgrounds and have genuinely contributed to a broadening of educational opportunity.

One positive feature of the comprehensive universities is their favourable staff–student ratio, which at Siegen is 1:11 (Woll, 1980:58); according to Cerych et al. (1981a), the ratio at Kassel is the same as that at Siegen, and in the comprehensives in North Rhine-Westphalia it is 1:13 (excluding the distance university at Hagen and the medical faculty at Essen). In Framhein's investigation (1983), students in Siegen and Paderborn cited as one of their reasons for choosing those particular *Hochschulen* 'contact with academic staff'. Only students in Osnabrück had stronger expectations of personal contact of this kind, whereas students in Münster anticipated very little contact with their university teachers. It has been stated by Scheuerer and Weist (1981) that students at the Kassel GHS feel that the atmosphere at a *Gesamthochschule* differs in positive respects from that at a traditional university. Men and women who have attended both types of institution claim that students at Kassel experience less interpersonal alienation and a

5. BAföG is the abbreviation for *Bundesausbildungsförderungsgesetz* (Federal Law for the Promotion of Education). All persons with appropriate levels of motivation, inclination and ability have the right to education, and if they, their spouses or parents are not in a position to finance it, then the state will give them aid. The BAföG scheme first came into operation in 1971; pupils received aid in the form of non-repayable grants, and this is still the case; aid for students consisted at first of a combination of grants and loans, but from autumn 1983 non-repayable grants were stopped, and needy students must now repay their loans.

higher degree of social integration than at other *Hochschulen* (ibid.:119). The achievement of a climate of communication between staff and students was a major reform objective of the BAK and the SDS in the 1960s, and on present evidence it would seem that the comprehensives have been reasonably successful in promoting such a climate.

Despite their achievements in serving the local community and democratising education, the comprehensive universities find it difficult to win universal approval. They lay themselves open to public criticism if they fail to cultivate their regional and social roles, yet are equally vulnerable, in a different way, if they do so. If they fail in their duty to the region, they are accused of neglecting one of the most important reform objectives of the *Gesamthochschulen* – promotion of equal opportunity. As we have seen, they have had a considerable degree of success in doing this. Their very success, however, may be used to stigmatise them as 'working-class' institutions failing to provide the cultural and social 'mix' which is needed for real *Bildung*. Their 'local' mission co-exists uncomfortably with the aim of winning 'national' and 'international' recognition. By concentrating on regionalisation, they may be unwittingly relegating themselves to a low status in an invisible prestige hierarchy, yet by reaching out beyond the regions, they are perhaps departing from their original goals. Most of the *Gesamthochschulen*, however, are trying to have it both ways by building up their international and their regional roles.[6] It remains to be seen whether, having chosen the middle road, they will be attacked from both sides.

Job Prospects of GHS Graduates

Empirical evidence concerning the employment record of GHS graduates is hard to find. However, Hitpass et al. (1983) have carried out a longitudinal study of about 1,000 students in integrated degree courses in Essen; their sample consisted of people from various social classes (including a high proportion of working-class students), who entered with different entrance qualifications (some with, some without *Abitur*); after the same period of study, the

6. At present, all the *Gesamthochschulen* are cultivating international links with care and enthusiasm. About 4.7% of their students are foreigners (Handbuch NRW, 1986:483–5), and this percentage is about equal to that in universities, *Technische Hochschulen* and *Sporthochschulen* in North Rhine-Westphalia generally (5%, ibid.:477). The *Gesamthochschulen* have partnership arrangements with a wide variety of universities all over the world, and encourage their staff to build up international contacts by inviting foreign guest lecturers to visit and travelling abroad themselves to teach and examine.

different groups attained comparable academic success, and after a two-year period in the world of work, achieved similar salaries. There was, however, a difference in the career expectations of DII and DI students. The former were materialistically oriented, and sought prestige; the latter were more socially and personally oriented (ibid.:39). Once they entered professional life, the DII graduates were more satisfied with their jobs than the DI graduates, and experienced less of a gap between their expectations and the reality of working life. This might imply that the hopes of DI students for an improvement in their position through the medium of education were pitched unrealistically high.

Klüver and Krameyer (1981) included questions relating to the job prospects of GHS students in their survey of chemistry students. The main focus was on students' perceptions of their career chances. What they wanted from their future jobs was not so much financial reward or status as an interesting occupation and a good work climate. There was no difference in the motivation of ABI (*Abiturienten*) and FOS (*Fachoberschule*) students. The impression that today's youth is not particularly concerned to achieve high social status is corroborated by a survey carried out for the BMBW (1985b) in which a cross-section of youngsters were asked what values were worth living for. Money and professional success (chosen respectively by 48% and 52% of the sample) were rated as much less important than friendship (82%) and freedom (82%). It therefore looks as if many young Germans today are now rejecting materialistic, task-centred objectives in favour of more affective objectives.

Klüver and Krameyer (1981:89) found that very few students began their course with a clear view of what career they wanted. Many of them, particularly DII students, have vague aspirations to do independent research, but realise as time passes that opportunities for this are limited, and that a job in industry is much more likely. DI students, however, from the beginning, envisage themselves working in small or medium-sized industrial concerns. DI and DII students are initially both afraid of unemployment, but their optimism grows as their course proceeds, and towards the end of it, the majority are reasonably sure that they will find an acceptable post when they leave the GHS. Doctoral students are even more convinced than undergraduates that everything will turn out well. Klüver and Krameyer attribute this self-assurance to increasing confidence in the quality of the education they are receiving at the GHS (ibid.:90). Some students, however, feel that a *Fachhochschule* would have given them equally good prospects with less investment of time and money. DII and doctoral students both consider it unlikely that the choice of a *Gesamthochschule* has had negative effects on their employment chances.

The actual experience of GHS graduates in the world of work seems to be in line with the chemistry students' expectations. DI students are equated with FHS graduates and have no trouble in finding employment. The Essen DI students benefit from the good reputation of the old *Ingenieurschule* and any reservations which industry may have had regarding GHS graduates have been overcome by positive experiences (ibid.:91). It appears that the question of whether one has attended a conventional university or a *Gesamthochschule* is less important than a particular *Hochschule*'s reputation, a student's marks and his/her performance at interview. Job experience prior to study (e.g. as a laboratory assistant) is also invaluable.

At first, both lecturers and DII students believe that the students' value in the labour market will be inferior to that of university graduates, but both parties later revise their opinions in a more optimistic direction. Lecturers teaching in the *Hauptstudium* do not anticipate problems in placing their graduates, as long as high standards are maintained. Interestingly, both lecturers and students anticipate fewer problems in their 'own' branch than in the other branch of the Y-model. In other words, both the DI and DII groups believe that they have got the best of the bargain! Lecturers and students both believe that personal achievements and qualities are extremely important in obtaining a post, and the reputation of a doctoral supervisor is regarded as more significant than that of the *Hochschule*. The standing of the individual university teacher is given much more weight than that of the institution. Teachers in DII regard it as absolutely vital, for the purpose of overcoming any residual scepticism on the part of employers, that the courses should at least equal, and perhaps surpass, comparable courses at a university. This constitutes yet another source of pressure on the GHS to conform to university norms, rather than to follow a distinctive path.

All in all, then, the picture which emerges is that the *Gesamthochschulen* are held in high regard by their students and serve them well, both socially and vocationally.

–7–

The Fate of the Comprehensive Universities

State Power in Innovation

The role of the state as an educational innovator in Germany is time-honoured, and its importance is undiminished today. At a recent symposium in Bonn, the Chairman of the Wissenschaftsrat reminded his listeners that Humboldt had accomplished his reforms without the direct co-operation of a single professor, and stressed the current importance of state–university partnership in bringing about change (Heckhausen, 1985:34). The exercise of state power was essential for the foundation of the *Gesamthochschulen*. Left to their own devices, the institutions of higher education involved in the realisation of the comprehensive ideal would probably never have resolved the tension between innovation and traditionalism. It was widely accepted that the university system was incapable of reforming itself from within, and the state therefore acted as an agent of change. The state authorities defined comprehensivation as a desirable objective, and set up mechanisms to investigate the best way of bringing it about. The most important instrument for this purpose was the series of exploratory studies carried out under the joint auspices of the Federal Government and the Federal States.

The Pilot Studies

The Bund-Länder-Kommission (BLK) arranged, under the framework agreement of 7 May 1971, to set up pilot studies to determine how best to implement a policy of comprehensive higher education. The BLK itself issued a concise summary of the main findings from six of the studies in 1977; two years later, a very thorough analysis of the pilot projects was published by Winkler (1979). Projects were mounted in Aachen, Bremen, Hamburg, Karlsruhe-Pforzheim, Kassel, Osnabrück, Stuttgart and Ulm-Ostwürttemberg. Objectives differed somewhat from one experiment to another, but they generally related to:

— structure and re-organisation of higher education;
— reform of courses;
— study support systems (for example, counselling, media);
— measures to increase efficiency in higher education. (Winkler, ibid.:93)

The projects involved such activities as: longitudinal study of integrated degree courses in Hamburg and Ost-Württemberg (ibid.: 147, 279); quantitative analysis of demand, and availability of student places; design of a social work course to be taught jointly by two institutions; investigation into the use of space across campuses in Stuttgart (ibid.:259–60).

Most of the pilot studies were begun in 1972–73 and were concluded by about 1975 (in Hamburg somewhat later). Staff were specially employed to work on them, sometimes full-time, sometimes part-time, usually six to ten in number for each project. The findings focused upon two main areas: first, evaluation of pilot studies *per se* as a tool for educational planning; second, assessment of the feasibility of comprehensive higher education. Although the BLK (1977:48) claimed that the pilot studies had provided a whole series of important decision-making aids, their effect was to highlight the disadvantages rather than the advantages of comprehensive universities. The apparent negativity of the results was at least partly a reflection of organisational difficulties encountered by the project leaders.

For one thing, problems concerning the conditions of service of potential employees made it hard to attract suitable staff. The jobs were short-term and their duration was sometimes uncertain. High-calibre people with extensive experience of curriculum development and evaluation were needed, but individuals in this category were usually neither able nor willing to accept short-term jobs. This made recruitment problematic. In Aachen, for example, five posts were available but not all could be filled, and the project began with only two staff (ibid.:108). In Osnabrück too, it was difficult to attract staff to work on the project, because the jobs were short-term, the appointment procedures cumbersome, and the budget small (ibid.:235). Similarly in Stuttgart, it was only young, relatively inexperienced people who seemed to be interested. These difficulties were sometimes overcome by releasing permanent academic staff from some of their normal teaching duties, so that they could engage part-time in project work. Some *Fachhochschule* staff in Bremen were employed on these terms (ibid.:133), but found it almost impossible to do justice to their normal work and to the demands of the pilot study research. The leader of the Aachen pilot study, who was also professor of electrical engineering and head of an important institute, was able to devote only a limited amount of his time to the project, and was criticised for not pulling his weight (ibid.:113–14).

Unsatisfactory conditions of employment meant that committee work was sometimes inefficient. In Hamburg, Plander (1975) reports that the members were ill-informed about their task and too few in number, while the continuity of their work was disrupted by frequent changes in the composition of the team. Staff had varying concepts of their roles and some suffered from 'goal ambiguity'. Many continued to give their personal or subject interests priority, and some were half-hearted in their commitment to the project because they were secretly opposed to comprehensive higher education.

Winkler (1979:393) concludes that it is a basic error to form project groups at institutional level only, because their work needs to be co-ordinated with other planning enterprises on the level immediately above. He also points out that planning groups must be large enough to include specialists from various fields (for example, budgeting, law, organisation theory, architecture, building and curriculum development). There must be liaison between all of these – it is no good if building is not considered in conjunction with student numbers, or if changes in entry requirements for integrated courses are out of phase with changes in secondary education (ibid.:397). His research makes him doubt the value of pilot studies as an instrument of state planning. The *Bund*, the *Länder* and the BLK all had the sincere intention of setting up comprehensive universities when the pilot studies were launched, but this was not enough to guarantee success. Certain objective conditions were needed to establish the *Gesamthochschulen*, and pilot studies could neither create nor promote these conditions. So many complex economic, social and political factors had to be taken into account that planning machinery which was unable to exert macro-political influence usually ended up endorsing the status quo (ibid.:387).

The principal factors identified by the researchers in the pilot studies as likely to impede the development of comprehensive higher education were:

— lack of clarity about the structure and rights of the teaching body;
— problems about admission requirements for the integrated degree courses;
— uncertainty about the status and acceptability of terminal qualifications. (Winkler, 1979:174).

The controversial nature of the integrated study courses is illustrated clearly by the battle fought over chemistry between the University of Ulm and the *Fachhochschule* of Aalen (see Winkler, 1979:285). The FHS wanted recognition of four semesters joint *Grundstudium*, whereas the University wanted only two; the FHS wanted a common examination board, whereas the University thought that each institution should conduct examinations independently; the FHS wanted equal treatment for all lecturers involved in teaching the course, whereas the University wanted 'clarification' of the structure of the teaching body, and particularly of the rights and powers of the FHS teachers. Despite the fact that both the Ministry of Education and the staff conducting the pilot study sided with the FHS, the differences between the two parties proved unbridgeable, and the experiment failed.

This example shows how vested interests could wreck any possibility of co-operation between institutions. Winkler (ibid.:177) reports that some of the staff actively involved in promoting the *Gesamthochschule* none the less wanted it to be 'reversible'. Sometimes component institutions of the same type in a proposed merger had divergent interests – witness the curious spectacle, in the Osnabrück pilot study, of one *Pädagogische Hochschule* (PH Osnabrück) actively seeking integration within a comprehensive university, and the other (PH Vechta) trying to retain its autonomy, within or outside of an integrated structure. Far from always striving to upgrade their status by supporting the GHS, staff at non-university institutions were often concerned to preserve their institutional identity. The Pforzheim FHS, for example, rejected the 'GHS-Karlsruhe' blueprint for several reasons, one of them being dislike of the name, which incorrectly (and unacceptably) suggested that only *Hochschulen* actually in Karlsruhe itself were involved. The BLK (1977:52) notes that, although it was obviously vital that inter-institutional conflicts should be clearly articulated, it was particularly difficult to bring them out into the open.

It is enlightening to compare the stances of the BLK and the *Land* of Hamburg in their respective attitudes towards state power. The BLK (ibid.:54–55) highlights the essential role of the state in bringing about comprehensivation. It claims that this is a long-term, gradual process, and that the first step is exploration of the possibilities of co-operation between institutions. Nevertheless, it concludes that the *Hochschulen* cannot be expected to achieve integration, or resolve difficult structural issues by themselves, particularly if their own vested interests are threatened by new developments (ibid.:50). Although the institutions of higher education must be actively involved in innovation, state–university collaboration is essential in achieving results (ibid.:55). The BLK is painfully aware of the difficulty of integrating a mature, fully functional university into a *Gesamthochschule*, and pinpoints staff attitudes as the main obstacle to merger.

Whereas the BLK (ibid.:35, 40, 50) lays great stress on state power in promoting new developments, the Hamburg education authorities emphasise that legal and other state measures are not, in themselves, sufficient to establish comprehensive higher education; they believe that what is needed is grassroots consensus, and real co-operation between staff in different types of institution (ibid.:7). Yet even in Hamburg, a liberal *Land*, where the state took an active role in innovation, and where the comprehensive ideal enjoyed a high degree of public support, a political decision not to push ahead with the plan to found *Gesamthochschulen* had to be taken. The Final Report on the Hamburg pilot study points out that, whereas many other *Länder* had complained of an inadequate legal basis for the successful implementation of reform, Hamburg had an excellent legal basis for the first stage of development towards a comprehensive university (Hamburger Abschlußbericht, 1977:3). This should have facilitated various joint courses of study, but negative attitudes of subject departments ensured that very few such developments took place. Progress towards comprehensivation was further hampered by the enormous pressure of student numbers on existing organisational, staff and financial resources (ibid.:3), and it was thought unwise to strain these resources still further by demanding radical reorganisation. The Final Report stresses that inter-institutional co-operation must be voluntary: 'There is absolutely no intention of forcing the *Hochschulen* into a comprehensive system of higher education against their will. . . . All participants in the *Hochschulen* must work together towards overcoming their mutual mistrust and their status-consciousness, so as to be ready, of their own accord, to achieve sensible co-operation' (ibid.:6).

The failure of the comprehensive ideal in Hamburg illustrates a paradox. The successful implementation of innovation in Germany apparently necessitates the active deployment of state power; Hamburg's very liberality, however, resulted in its being unwilling to resort to *dirigiste* methods, and this militated against the introduction of *Gesamthochschulen*.

Because of traditional expectation in Germany that progressive measures will be introduced from above, it is sometimes argued that the Federal States which fail to take a strong proactive role are, to all intents and purposes, adopting a reactionary stance. In his analysis of the pilot study in Baden-Württemberg, Winkler (1979:312) complains that the Ministry of Education did not apply sufficient pressure for the introduction of comprehensive higher education, and claims that its *laissez-faire* attitude amounted to the adoption of conservative policies by default. In *Länder* where the government was reluctant to act in a prescriptive way, the process of innovation was retarded. Basic course development in North Rhine-Westphalia took ten months, but in Hesse, where the Ministry was less directive, it took three and a half years (Cerych et al., 1981a:105). At first glance, the Hesse Ministry's less interventionist approach may seem more 'democratic', but it actually exposed the institution to damaging and time-wasting political controversies. As we have seen, the BLK (1977) emphasises the role of state power in successful innovation. The following are matters which, it believes, ought to be taken away from the universities and settled by the state: framework for course syllabuses, specification of terminal awards, entry requirements, the number of student places for various subjects, and the organisational framework for the institution. This would give the state a role far in excess of that considered proper in present-day Britain. Nevertheless, the state in the Federal Republic is an essential agent of change, and it would hardly be going too far to claim that the success of an innovation is directly related to the extent to which the *Land* governments have, in fact, given a strong lead. This is in keeping with a long historical tradition. The role of state power in introducing reform (in Bismarck's Germany, for example) was crucial in the formative stages of Germany's emergence as a nation-state in the nineteenth century, and is still crucial today.

The Law and Innovation

It is interesting to compare policy and law-making in the two *Länder* in which comprehensive universities were successfully introduced. North Rhine-Westphalia adopted a much more directive policy than Hesse, and laid down the general parameters for development. It was the Ministry for Higher Education which initiated the establishment of the five *Gesamthochschulen* in NRW, and worked hard to bring them into being, devoting considerable financial and specialised manpower resources to the project. A legal framework was provided at the outset: the *Gesamthochschulentwicklungsgesetz* (GHEG) of 30 May 1972. The institutions were given considerable scope in developing courses and no attempt was made to prescribe definite models. It did, however, set out clearly the manner in which the various official bodies and authorities were to lead, support, and finance the enterprise (Cerych et al., 1981a:101). The Law was well received and provided a good framework for future development. Later that year (21 December 1972), the Ministry issued the so-called Christmas Decree, in which the Y-model was selected for the integrated degree courses; entry conditions, length of degree course, intermediate examinations, and conditions for transfer between courses were all laid down (ibid.:102). Despite resentment in some quarters that the model was 'imposed' from the top downwards, the decree ensured that course content and examination procedures could be designed quickly and efficiently.

An important factor in the successful establishment of the NRW *Gesamthochschulen* was that each was given a Foundation Senate, consisting of up to ten members from the donor non-university institutions which formed the nucleus of the GHS, and eleven staff newly appointed to the GHS. These eleven members, commonly known as *Eckprofessoren*, were nominated by the Minister – a procedure unique in the history of German higher education (ibid.:101), but one which ensured close collaboration between the Foundation Senate and the Ministry. The *Eckprofessoren* had special rights, and received extra pay for their work in helping to establish the new institutions. The positive side of strong ministerial control in the early stages of development lay in the fact that it enabled administrative functions to be devolved to the institutions relatively quickly; the link between the Ministry and the professors ensured for the most part that the fledgling institution was spared debilitating bouts of internecine wrangling, which would simply have dissipated energies. The negative side of the close association between the Ministry and the *Eckprofessoren* was that the latter were perhaps too acutely attuned to the wishes of the Ministry – a condition which was not calculated to enhance their innovative potential in developing courses or in co-operating with *Fachhochschule* lecturers.

In Hesse, the separation between academic and state administration was much greater than in NRW. The legal basis for the establishment of the GhK was the *Errichtungsgesetz* of 1970, which gave some general guidelines, and made it possible to form the first Council. At Kassel, the newly appointed professors had no vote and no seat on the Foundation Council – and this led to tensions between them and the external members (Cerych et al., 1981a:111). The first Foundation Council was eventually dissolved by the Hesse Minister of Education, and a second one constituted, this time consisting entirely of members from Kassel rather than from outside. A decree of 28 August 1972 gave the Second Foundation Council certain powers (to form a Senate, set up various committees

and choose a President), but the Minister retained the most important decision-making and ratifying powers, including the right to set
up curriculum development groups, to allocate posts and funds, to
approve course outlines and examination regulations, and to set up
commissions to select new professors (Nagel, 1981:45). The planning machinery was such, however, that the *Hochschule* needed the
Ministry's agreement in matters of everyday detail. This went on for
some years and resulted in a dependency-syndrome, in which the
GhK was 'over-protected' by the Ministry. In Hesse, the legal and
administrative framework created by the state was not as all-
embracing as in NRW, but the Hesse Ministry intervened quite a lot
in day-to-day planning (Cerych et al., 1981a: 118). A number of
initiatives to provide a legal basis for the future development of the
GhK were mooted in the debate preceding the Landtag election
campaign of 1974, and nothing came of them (ibid.: 112). In the
next few years, two opposing factions emerged in the GhK: the
'conservative' majority and the 'progressives', who belonged to the
Gewerkschaft für Erziehung und Wissenschaft (GEW). The conflict
between them came to a head when the Ministry refused to ratify the
Hochschule's choice of a new President in 1980 (ibid.:113). To this
day, the GhK remains strongly politicised, with the GEW retaining
a substantial power base.

The Hesse Law for Higher Education (*Hessisches Hochschulgesetz*
(HHG)) of 1970 had anticipated that there would be a special law
for *Gesamthochschulen* in due course, but three factors militated
against this: as has already been indicated, the 1974 draft of a GHS
law became a casualty of the election; the Karlsruhe Verdict of 1973
made it impossible to achieve an integrated staff structure; and the
Hochschulrahmengesetz (HRG) of 1976 neither made the integrated
GHS the normative model for higher education, nor obliged the
Länder to develop new institutions of higher education according to
the IGHS model. Legislation in Hesse had to take account of these
legal developments, and when the Hesse law on higher education
was adapted to the HRG, no specific provision was made for the
GhK; it was treated instead as a fifth *Land* university.

After long hesitation, the Foundation Council of the GhK accepted the unwelcome fact that the comprehensive university was to
be given no special legal position (Nagel, 1981:50). The absence of a
specific GHS law had certain negative implications for the GhK.
First, it implied adaptation of the GhK to traditional universities
rather than re-orientation of the latter to the new GHS model.
Second, since the law said nothing of the comprehensive universities' special mission, the constant question became: Which takes

precedence – the traditional university model or the reformist GHS model? (Brinckmann, 1981: 133, 126). Once the chill winds of financial adversity began to blow through the system, antagonism towards the GhK gathered momentum. Its foundation absorbed resources coveted by the rest of the system, and the Minister's suggestion, in the mid-1970s, that money freed when posts became vacant at traditional universities should be used to fund new posts at the Kassel *Gesamthochschule* did nothing to win it friends. The lack of a specific GHS law also made it harder for the GhK to retain its distinctive qualities. This is greatly to be regretted, since the GhK was in fact the most reform-oriented of all the comprehensive universities.

The BLK (1977:47) notes that the early concepts of comprehensive universities were based on abstract models. It was not clear at the beginning what tasks and problems would have to be faced, and it was easier to achieve consensus about abstract goals than about practical organisation. A precondition for successful realisation of the GHS ideal is the clear articulation of objectives, and the acceptance of those objectives by the institution of higher education concerned (ibid.:52). Much the same point is made by Klüver (1983) when he argues that the reform goals for the GHS were at first expressive, rather than instrumental. The expressive goals indicated a consensus about the need for reform but, by the time the serious, practical work on reform had begun, the consensus had already started to crumble. If change was to come about, expressive goals needed to be reformulated as instrumental goals, and if this could not be done reasonably quickly, traditional norms and procedures tended to reassert themselves. Even the apparent consensus represented by expressive goals was somewhat vulnerable, because it was dependent on national and international political factors; if these happened to change, then the consensus was in danger of collapse (ibid.:12). The period of agreement about the desirability of comprehensive education was a very brief one. After the student revolt, the will and the energy to achieve reform was certainly present, but only briefly so; for a while the necessary finance, too, was available, but with the oil crisis of 1973–4, the financial climate deteriorated dramatically. By this time, however, the new *Gesamthochschulen* in Hesse and North Rhine-Westphalia had already been founded. If the authorities had not acted so quickly, the new institutions would probably never have come into being.

Changes in the Federal Framework Law

More than anything else, it was the intransigence and status awareness of the university professors which ruined the comprehensive
ideal as a reform model for higher education. Their élitism led them
to maintain the boundaries between themselves and the *Fachhochschule* professors, and this not only obstructed the *Gesamthochschulen*,
but also affected the Federal Framework Law for Higher Education.
The 1976 Law, which had been a response to demands for reform at
the end of the 1960s, was amended in November 1985. The Amendment, however, was in some respects reactionary; it was forced to
take decisions of the Federal Constitutional Court into account, and
to recognise the reality that many of the attempts made to institutionalise reformist ideas in 1976 had failed.

The 1976 HRG had put forward the concept of comprehensive
higher education as the pattern of development for the whole education system. On the advice of the Knopp Commission (1984),
which had been asked to make recommendations for the proposed
updating of the Law, the relevant paragraph was deleted from the
1985 Amendment. Knopp did not give detailed reasons in his report
for taking this decision. The matter had been well aired in public. It
was assumed that the reasons for the recommendation were so well
known as to need no further rehearsal, and it was taken for granted
that it would not arouse undue controversy.

The 1985 Amendment not only scrapped the comprehensive
ideal, but also modified provisions relating to university democracy.
It was stipulated that the *Rektor* or President of a university must be
a professor, and that he was to work for a limited period of office
with a small, high-level committee. This militates against the group
management model possible under the legislation of North Rhine-
Westphalia. It is a move calculated to promote strong leadership in
higher education, and Wildt (1984:74) has suggested that the relatively short period of office (four years in the presidential model, and
two in the *Rektor* model) will have the effect of strengthening the
already considerable power of the *Kanzler* (Registrar – a permanent
employee) still further. He sees in this a weakening of academic
authority and a threat to university democracy. In the committee
which elects the Head of a university, professors must now have a
majority. North Rhine-Westphalia, where professors as an interest
group formerly made up only two-fifths of the total membership,
now has to change its rules so as to comply with the Amendment,
and views this as an erosion of existing democratic structures
(Pritchard, 1986b:592).

The 1976 Law had established academic departments (*Fachbereiche*) as the basic organisational units of universities. This was intended to break the hold of the notorious institutes and faculties, which had served as power bases for certain professors. By 1985, however, it was felt that the new arrangement had disadvantages too. There had been a proliferation of small departments, which tended to become isolated and encapsulated. The 1985 Amendment promoted larger subject groupings, and strengthened research Institutes. Deans were to have *ex officio* representation on Senate, and all professors were to be eligible to vote on new appointments and on doctoral and post-doctoral theses. The effect of this legislation is to make professors as a group more powerful than before, and to reduce the power of non-professorial staff. It is unpopular in SPD *Länder* because it moves away from the *Gruppenuniversität* concept which had emerged from the critique of higher education associated with the student revolt.

The reassertion of more conservative values and structures in higher education has not only tended to isolate the existing *Gesamthochschulen* in the system, but has also led to élitist rather than egalitarian changes in the HRG (Gellert, 1984). The reform period in German higher education was extraordinarily brief, particularly when one reflects how overdue it was and how badly it was needed. Inertia and paralysis were deeply rooted in the system. Change came only as a result of a political upheaval (the student revolt) which for a time put the legitimacy of the state in question. The effects of 1968 were, however, short-lived, and in this respect, the aftermath of 1968 resembled that of 1848. The comparison is not, however, entirely appropriate. Counter-reform in the 1970s and 1980s was much less brutal and deliberate than in the years following 1848. The state had already attempted to innovate before the student revolt, and the process of reform had gathered a certain slow momentum. This accounted for the speed with which the authorities were able to act when it became politically imperative and expedient to do so. It would be wrong to conclude that the state really wanted to sabotage comprehensive higher education; on the contrary, it invested money and effort in the pilot studies and in the attempt to introduce facilitating legislation. The major obstacle to successful merger was the stance adopted by the academic staff of the classical German university tradition. When they were able to harness the Constitutional Court to the defence of their interests, their position became well-nigh unassailable. The fact that the political system permitted them to do so requires explanation and analysis.

The Law and Political Culture

Germany once aspired to be a *Kulturstaat*, was for a time a *Machtstaat*, and now claims to be a *Rechtsstaat*. Its constitution is the Basic Law[1] which is an attempt to secure the supremacy of parliamentary government and bring into being a democratic political culture. The powers of the Constitution have to be exercised within the framework of the law, which means that its provisions have to be subject directly to legal enforcement. This accounts for the primordial importance in German public life of the Law in a general sense, and of the Constitutional Court which has been set up to give an authoritative interpretation of the Basic Law (Smith, 1979:54). The fact that lawyers in the FRG enjoy high status is related to their role as guardians of the nation's democratic structures; their extremely prestigious position in the Establishment contrasts notably with that of lawyers in authoritarian societies, who often suffer severe status deprivation, especially if they are not involved in defending the interests of the state. Thus, Medvedev (1986:42) reports that Soviet defence lawyers are the pariahs of the legal profession, and have very few procedural rights. He cites the comment made by Kaminskaya, one of a small number of prominent defence lawyers in the USSR, on Russian students' legal training: 'If the defense attorney was ever mentioned in lectures, it was only in the role of a wretched, defeated opponent . . . although we had not yet fully realised how abysmally low in status the profession of defense counsel was, we were very well aware of its unpopularity among the public at large'.

Contempt for defence lawyers' role is typical of a one-party state, which lacks the tradition of a loyal opposition. It is significant that the number of lawyers decreased substantially in Nazi Germany (Dahrendorf, 1965: 233) whereas in the Federal Republic more than half of all higher civil servants and about one half of the approximately two thousand incumbents of top positions are lawyers by training (ibid.:234). It is interesting to note that Academic Registrars of universities are normally expected to be trained lawyers, and that there are lawyers who actually specialise in education. The Germans are a litigious people, and many of them regard

1. The fact that the constitution of the Federal Republic is called the 'Basic Law' is due to its assumed provisional status. When it was drafted, the division of Germany was not thought likely to be permanent, and the Law contains an Article (146) to the effect that it shall cease to be in force on the day on which a constitution adopted by a free decision of the German people comes into force. Those who drafted the Law thought they were engaged in a stopgap enterprise, and were unwilling to give the state the permanent hallmark of a constitution (Smith, 1979:4).

sharpening the critical faculties and tolerating, or even encouraging, dissent as very important for the development of a healthy political culture. Because they perceive a link between the rule of law and democracy, they often feel that to resort readily to legal action is somehow to be on the side of freedom. To a certain extent, this is true, but the law now bulks so large in German public life that it is beginning to threaten the democratic ethos which it seeks to promote.

The law impinges on higher education in the Federal Republic in two major ways: it can be used to provide an ordered framework for the establishment and development of institutions; alternatively, it can be used as a non-violent means of managing conflict. The former function could be termed 'normative' and the latter 'regulative'. It was the normative function which facilitated the foundation and early success of the comprehensive universities, and the regulative function which ensured, in the 1973 Karlsruhe Verdict, that they could never be anything more than a flawed realisation of their creators' intentions. Although the state can still operate as a beneficent instrument of reform, as it did in the nineteenth century, the hypertrophy of the law often vitiates its good intentions. The past two decades have seen a flood of laws and rules in higher education. Schuster (1983: 42–5) analyses the factors which have brought this about:

— quantitative expansion, . . . resulting in a system of rules which only experts can fully grasp;
— qualitative extension of the higher education system's tasks (for example, service functions such as technology transfer);
— conflicts in objectives (for example, between mass education and education for the highly gifted; social needs and individual demands; research and teaching), all of which are sharpened by financial pressures;
— the need for state ratification of course outlines and examination regulations;
— the emergence of different interest groups, in response to syndicalist influences (even the use of students as demonstrators can be subject to rigid regulations which have nothing to do with the real needs of the situation).

Pride in the *Rechtsstaat* reflects a desire for justice and democracy. As long ago as 1969, however, Helmut Schelsky was already aware of the possible disadvantages of excessive reliance on law in the university system. He thought it illusory to hope that state law-giving could re-establish the life of the mind and facilitate intellectual communication. Reviewing plans for the *Gruppenuniversität*, he predicted that laws centring higher education on various interest groups would institutionalise rather than dissolve conflict, and that the state would then attempt (ineffectively) to resolve it by renewed and continuous intervention: 'If the laws for higher education do not work, the State will have to intervene more and more in the life of the *Hochschule*' (Schelsky, 1969:121). Schelsky feared that such intervention would undermine the autonomy of the institutions of higher education, and it is interesting that Schuster (1983), writing a decade and a half later, claims this is exactly what has happened. Although the norm of autonomy is as strong as ever in theory, the proliferation of rules, laws and decrees in higher education has undermined confidence in the university's own self-administering structures. Paradoxically, this may lead to even more laws because of the naive belief in some quarters that loss of decision-making power can be remedied by still more legislation (ibid.:46).

The erosion of university autonomy is not the only disadvantage of *Verrechtlichung* (legal (over-) regulation). Excessive readiness to take disputes to court can promote an unhealthy reliance on authority. Citizens lose the ability to manage conflict pragmatically and find solutions for themselves; public discussion is extinguished; instead, problems are referred to the courts, and judgement is delivered from on high. In the struggle for educational innovation, negotiation based on goodwill and common sense is replaced by a dependence on official structures (one thinks of the incident in Wuppertal when the well-intentioned, enlightened attempt to provide school placements for trainee teachers floundered, until the Ministry devised a legal framework for it). Gerstenberger (1976:71) associates over-reliance on legal and state apparatus with the bourgeois revolution in Prussia, which established the bourgeois mode of production, but not its corollary – bourgeois political rule. This, she believes, helped to ensure that the authoritarian ideology could survive almost untouched.

University democracy and the vexed issue of staff structures in the comprehensive universities were essentially a political conflict which was processed as a legal one. This tendency – often referred to as 'politicised legalism' – can be harmful to the body politic, because it leads to a situation in which conflict is managed by people legitimised not by a democratic mandate, but by their technocratic competence as lawyers. Massing (1974) argues that the political character of constitutional jurisdiction should be openly admitted, and claims that the power of the Constitutional Court at Karlsruhe reflects the structural weakness of representational democracy in Germany. The judges at Karlsruhe are 'part of governmental crisis management, operating in a preventative manner, aiming at a prophylactic cure of possible violations of rules. They have to defuse conflict potentials dangerous to the system with the means available to a court, and they have to lower the threshold of conflict to a bearable level' (ibid.:225). Probably the most telling criticism of politicised legalism is that it represents a type of conflict management in which the courts take political risks which should properly be taken by government.

Acceptance of legal formality alone as a universal principle is always dangerous, no matter what concept the law is based on. Thus, Luhmann (1974) points out that when mere legality is accepted as an almost universal yardstick, arbitrariness becomes a central aspect of human social life. This holds good regardless of whether law is explicitly based on moral principles or is divorced from them. If it is taken to have a moral basis, the problem is that the norms and values institutionalised in it may be relativistic and sectional, perhaps serving to enforce sexist, fascist or racist outlooks. The contrary contention, inherent in legal positivism, that the law and morals are not necessarily connected, also has dangers, but of a different order. The philosopher Dworkin (1977) believes that the law should embody both rules and principles, and demonstrates that legal positivism is not an adequate way of making it work effectively. He contrasts positivistic attachment to predetermined legal rules with *principles*, which are dictated by justice, fairness or other moral considerations, and are needed for the resolution of really difficult cases. Legal principles differ from legal rules in that their essential nature is not damaged, even when they do not prevail; because principles are congenitally controversial, anyone who invokes them requires independence of mind; although incompatible with legal positivism, they are necessary to the practical operation of the law, and theories which deny them are not adequate to cope with the complexity and sophistication of modern legal practice (ibid.:65).

Any doctrine which would separate the law and morals has been rejected with particular vehemence by thinkers like Gustav Radbruch, who lived through the Nazi era. Formerly a legal positivist, Radbruch came to believe that the separation of law as it is, from the law as it ought to be, had contributed to the horrors of Nazism, and that the German legal conscience should recognise the demands of morality (Hart, 1963:30–1). A further shortcoming of legal positivism is its contention that correct legal decisions can be logically deduced from predetermined legal rules without reference to social aims, policies and moral standards (ibid.:18). Even at the linguistic level, this argument is flawed. Although there is a core of agreed meaning in the vernacular language of any country, there is also a shadowy fringe of ambiguity, which deductive reasoning is power- less to resolve. This kind of reasoning is unlikely to help in solving complex cases, and can result in mere formalism or literalism. Worse still, it overlooks law's essential social purposes which are of great importance in a wide sense (ibid.:27). This last point is particularly relevant to the fate of the *Gesamthochschulen*. An import- ant element in their *raison d'être* was the promotion of social justice, and the Constitutional Court was unable to take account of this, when it came to deliver the Karlsruhe Verdict. Since it is precisely in the pursuit of social objectives that the GHS has been most success- ful, this is inevitably disturbing.

The danger of relying too much on legislation to protect the structures of democracy, without doing enough to promote its spirit, is inherent in the *Rechtsstaat*. There is a risk that the drive for greater freedom and equality may be lost in technocratic concepts of reform, and that the operation of legal and administrative machinery may eventually stifle the original living impulse. This is why Habermas et al. (1961:15) talk of liberty's being formalised into a set of rules, which then become a fetish. It is one of the ironies of German higher education that it is the state authorities which deserve the main credit for introducing reform, and yet it is often those same auth- orities which later become instrumental in restricting reform or rolling it back. Since legislation is an important aspect of state power, it is no coincidence that the law often sets up a framework for reform, which it subsequently stifles or reverses.

Have the *Gesamthochschulen* Done What They Set Out To Do?

The reasons for the failure of the comprehensive ideal to achieve widespread acceptance in the Federal Republic have already be- come obvious. But what of the existing comprehensive universities? How far have they achieved the aims set out for them? Are they successful in terms of their avowed objectives?

Nerad (1984) outlines three models which can be used to deter- mine whether institutional goals have been effectively implemented. The first is the evolutionary or learning model, in which the original programme is being modified all the time; goals change and there is uncertainty as to whether they have been achieved. The second is the interaction or bargaining model, in which the importance of goals is minimised, and the focus is on the negotiating process at different levels between different actors. The third is the planning-control or managerial model, which accepts goals as initially formulated, and measures results against them. This model has several shortcomings: by viewing organisations synchronically, it runs the danger of failing to treat them as living entities which change and grow; it is based on a hierarchical concept which assumes, usually unjustifiably, a high degree of compliance on the part of implementers; and it tends to view implementation as the transmission of policy in a linear progression of consequential actions, whereas a more realistic approach would be to regard policy 'as a series of intentions around which bargaining takes place and which may be modified as each set of actors attempts to negotiate to maximize its own interests and priorities' (Barrett and Fudge, 1981:4).

No evaluation model is perfect and, despite its shortcomings, the 'managerial model' has certain strengths which have led to its being widely used in judging the success of organisational innovations. It is, of course, true that such judgements always contain a considerable degree of subjectivity and that 'success' lies in the eye of the beholder. Nevertheless, the fact of insisting, as the managerial model does, on assessing outcomes in terms of initial explicitly stated objectives provides a hard clear line against which to reach a verdict; this helps to eliminate prevarication and establish rigour. Given the melancholy truism that most achievements in human life fall notoriously short of intentions, the use of the managerial model is much more likely to result in unsympathetic than in laudatory judgements; the merits of an innovation must, therefore, be rated all the more highly if they can be demonstrated to exist even when judged against a somewhat harsh criterion. Mindful of these considerations, let us therefore proceed to utilise the managerial model for the present study by taking the aims of the *Gesamthochschulen* as formulated in chapter 4, and examining the extent to which they have been fulfilled.

(1) *Organisational merger.* Formally a number of different institutions have indeed been merged, and now have corporate autonomy. The great failure has been that an integrated staff structure has not been achieved, and this has inevitably had negative effects both on the integrated degree courses and on the effort to synthesise theory and practice. Nevertheless, the legal verdict of 20 October 1982, which stated that professors who are similarly qualified and who teach together in the integrated degree courses must be considered equal in rights and status, lays the basis for a real co-operation.

(2) *Social justice.* A large number of university places have been

made available in previously under-provided areas. The comprehensive universities have strengthened and stimulated the regions where they have been established, and there is evidence that they have attained great regional popularity. Access to university-level study has been broadened, and degree courses have been made available to those who would not normally be qualified to enter them, especially from working-class backgrounds.

(3) *Compensatory education.* The *Gesamthochschulen* have succeeded in achieving good educational standards with students who do not have *Abitur.* Like the British Open University, they give those without the usual formal matriculation qualifications the chance to prove themselves. In NRW, bridging courses have been provided as an explicit form of 'remedial' education; since, however, the evidence suggests that they are not functionally necessary, they are quite rightly no longer so demanding in terms of student hours as they used to be; in Hesse, they are not required at all. If one had a criticism, it would be that the comprehensives require too much credentialling for entry rather than too little; they are still very far removed from the open admissions policy which is characteristic of the 'strong' definition of comprehensive higher education. None the less, the authorities are slowly coming to see that they could afford to take greater 'risks' in admissions without compromising educational standards. This has already been helpful in introducing a welcome element of flexibility into German universities, and will become even more important in the future.

(4) *Promotion of applied and vocational studies.* Much progress has been made in attaining this objective, and the comprehensive universities have stimulated other universities to emulate them. It is unfortunately true that the applied and vocational elements of degree programmes are often under threat because they are costly to set up and supervise; nevertheless, it is vital to ensure that educational ground gained here is not lost – placements and practical studies are very much part of a modern approach to higher education and are a necessary corrective to the over-theoretical orientation which had become characteristic of German universities. Applied research, too, has proved controversial, but despite constant tension between traditional values and reformist objectives, the *Gesamthochschulen* have successfully demonstrated academic 'quality'.

(5) *New degree courses with flexibility of transfer between them.* The comprehensives have devised and defended new academic paradigms which have opened up new opportunities to students. The short courses have not, of course, proved attractive in their own

right, nor was it ever probable that they would do, given the fact that the German civil service tends to 'stream' people into channels according to the level, quality and quantity of their education. To have such an unrealistic expectation of the short courses would be like expecting a British Ordinary degree to be as 'attractive' as an Honours degree. Most students have been able to leapfrog upwards, and although this was not what was originally planned, it offers a way of overcoming earlier setbacks and enabling young people to make the most of their talents. The *integrierte Studiengänge* stimulate a productive interchange between theory and practice and provide a new avenue of upward mobility to young people from non-university traditions.

The *Gesamthochschulen* have made strenuous attempts to live up to the comprehensive ideal which was the inspiration of the 1976 Federal Framework Law. Their outstanding successes have been achieved under the rubrics of 'social justice' and 'applied and vocational studies'. They have been creative in curricular terms; they are popular with their students; they have no difficulty in recruiting; they have served their regions well, and have done much to democratise access to higher education. All of this constitutes a very considerable achievement. Their development has, unfortunately, been stunted by the way in which the law has operated to perpetuate status differentials between the academic staff from different backgrounds; this, however, is not their 'fault'; it is due to specifically German factors, and need not be a handicap in other countries wishing to introduce institutions similar to the GHS.

Neo-Conservatism and Comprehensive Higher Education

Since universities are social institutions, it is not irrelevant to consider the future of the *Gesamthochschulen* in the present socio-political climate of the Federal Republic. Since about 1979 there has been a renaissance of conservative creeds in many parts of the developed world, and several countries in Western Europe are now under conservative régimes. Although in Germany there has been a CDU/CSU/FDP coalition since 1982, neo-conservative policies are more muted there than in the United Kingdom. This is partially due to the fact that the heterogeneous nature of a coalition necessitates compromise (and therefore a softening of the hard lines of policy); it is also due to an acute awareness of the past and an acceptance of certain imposed democratic forms. However, it is still true to say that in both countries there has been a move towards competition and capitalism which has important implications for education.

German conservatism[2] after the War was grounded in Christian Democracy. In the 1950s, the 'Christian' basis of its ideology was not clearly elaborated (since this might have given rise to controversy and thus lost voters), but its values, which were articulated at a fairly high level of generality, were broadly those of order, personal-authoritarian political sentiment, anti-modernism, and consciousness of individual liberty (Grande, 1988:58). It tended to place more emphasis upon religious affiliation than upon economic theory, and espoused traditional social and confessional values rather than monetarism. The 1980s, however, have seen a transformation in the outlook of the German Christian-Democratic parties. They have become more willing to admit openly that they are, in fact, conservatives; they have turned away from their former anti-modernism, and now encourage capitalist growth.

The implication of these political trends is that the principles of competition and vocationalism are now being generalised throughout the education system. Most important of all, the introduction of market forces into higher education represents a major break with European educational tradition and brings it closer to the American model. In Darwinian terms, market forces apparently ensure the survival of the fittest (or most popular) institutions and individuals. They are, however, useless for promoting the social purposes of education such as levelling out patterns of discrimination or promoting access from under-privileged groups. The harsh effect of market-based policies in education is intensified by conservative neglect of social welfare. The family is at the centre of neo-conservatism, and is conceived as a self-help unit which relieves demands on the public budget, in the wake of the dismantlement of the welfare state (Grande, 1988: 65–6). This means that children from strong financial and cultural backgrounds are likely to be advantaged compared with equally able but less privileged members of society, thus frustrating an important aim of comprehensive higher education.

The impact of market forces on university access is particularly worrying when one considers the avowedly élitist orientation of

2. It is questionable whether it is strictly correct to call the present German government 'conservative' at all. Grande (1988:56) points to the difficulty of defining German conservatism theoretically: 'Since the Second World War there has been no political party which defines itself as conservative and on whose politics and policies research could focus; and even individual politicians and intellectuals were often reluctant to label themselves as "conservative". Yet, there is a substantial literature in which the post-war history of West Germany is seen as being shaped mainly by conservative forces.'

conservatism. The beliefs now associated with modern conservatism were first propounded in reaction to the French Revolution, during which egalitarianism threatened the pre-eminence of the traditional aristocracy. Then, as now, élitism and a defence of privilege served 'to differentiate conservatives from liberals on the unconscious or unwritten level even when, as so often today, their programs agree on the conscious or written level' (Viereck, 1956: 22). Part of the mission of the German comprehensive universities is to help democratise education by increasing access from under-privileged groups and regions, and as we have seen, they have been very successful in doing so. In the future, however, neo-conservative values are likely to make it more difficult for them to sustain this initial success.

Neo-conservatism in an unusually prosperous society such as the Federal Republic is conducive to materialistic values; these, in turn, can lead to complacency (hence inertia), and militate against the drive of the *Gesamthochschulen* to introduce greater flexibility into higher education. Materialist complacency often combines with a strong bureaucracy to stifle creativity and push universities towards conformity. Yet flexibility and diversity are desperately needed and are at a premium. The vertical divisions in the German higher education system are formidably strong, and it is difficult to move from one level to another without 'paying ' by putting in (a sometimes unnecessary amount of) extra time – this, in a country which is already troubled by the excessively long periods taken by its young people to complete their courses (WR. 1986). It is not normally sufficient for a student to demonstrate academic or technical competence through good performance; he or she is asked to fulfil the letter of the law even if this means undertaking a substantial period of additional study. Increased *Durchlässigkeit* would tighten (not loosen) the system by saving time and money, maximising individual talent, and ensuring that a particular educational track, once embarked upon, never became a cul-de-sac. Yet the attempts of the *Gesamthochschulen* to achieve this encounter formalistic and legal barriers, which are buttressed by centralist structures. Normally it is socialist governments which are thought of as 'centralist', but conservative materialism and support for market forces can, paradoxically, co-exist with a strong emphasis on state power. A key distinction between conservatives and liberals is that the former assume that men are not born naturally free or good, and are prone to evil, error and depravity. Hogg (1947:13) writes that '. . . nothing is more clearly taught by all human history and experience than the fact in human nature which our forefathers simply described as original sin'. In order to cope with effects of original sin, it is necessary to put man inside a secure institutional or ideological framework which will help keep his nature ethical (Viereck, 1956:14). Willingness to make ruthless use of the state apparatus on occasion is a natural corollary of mistrust of the individual, and therefore entirely in keeping with conservative thinking.

The disposition of conservatives to have little confidence in the sound judgement or intrinsic goodness of humankind manifests itself in a desire to control dissent (admittedly a practical necessity for all governments but, for ideological reasons, particularly congenial to conservative ones). During the student movement of the 1960s, social criticism was regarded as a proper, even necessary feature of university life, and the educational ideas associated with it had a direct influence on the foundation of the *Gesamthochschulen*. Now, however, neo-conservative monetarist policies make people less secure in employment, and less confident about exercising their right to freedom of speech. Fear of unemployment tends to stifle radicalism and has helped subdue not only trade unions, but also student activism which, although not without its unpleasant side, was a major factor in bringing about educational reform throughout Europe. Caute (1988:401), reflecting on 1968, believes that the triumph of the capitalist ethos in the advanced nations during the past twenty years has led to a constant cultural neutering of dissent, in which all ideas are treated as short-lived merchandise, market forces are idolised, and the profit motive reigns supreme.

The application of a marketing ethos to higher education distorts the critical functions of *Gesamthochschulen* (and other university-type institutions) by inducing them to *accept* societal values rather than question them. If, in order to survive, they are forced to sell their 'services' to whomsoever will pay for them, they can no longer take the search for truth as their primary duty. They must look for sponsors, but where are sponsors to be found who want to purchase social criticism or disturbing, unorthodox ideas? Yet these are as necessary now as they always were to the progress of science and of society. Luria and Luria (1970:78), drawing attention to the danger of the modern American multi-university perpetuating the least desirable features of society, write: 'Passive acceptance of the goals and values of society deprives the university of the claim to intellectual leadership and encourages its involvement in ventures of dubious ethical and intellectual value.'

For their part, students in Germany and elsewhere are disappointed with the outcome of the reform aspirations of the 1960s. Many young people have become impatient with the plodding pace of democratic forms and procedures, and despair of ever obtaining results by means of participatory democracy. As Daalder points out (1982:502): 'The long drawn-out nature of the process of reorganising university government has done much to dampen enthusiasm for reform, both within the universities and in the wider political arena.' However, despite the powerful political, economic and legal forces militating against change, students now hold some trump cards in their fight for a liberal, humane educational system. First, there is a demographic crisis among native Europeans, which results in labour markets screaming for young well-qualified entrants and effectively places the young in a powerful position. Secondly, now – as once before in the 1960s – gross overcrowding of universities is making German students dissatisfied, and they are again beginning to protest. A recent publicity pamphlet (January 1989) to rally support for a lecture boycott in the University of Erlangen states the following:

> We are striking for sensibly-structured courses, for creative forms of learning and teaching, for equality, for collaboration between the humanities, the social sciences and the natural sciences. In order to achieve this, we need real joint decision-making and increased resources; the social situation of students must be improved, women must at last achieve true liberation, and the right to free choice of educational subject and institution must be guaranteed.

These are precisely the demands that the *Gesamthochschulen* were set up to satisfy. The reasons that have inhibited them from being totally successful in doing so are attributable more to factors inherent in the nature of the larger society than in the institutions themselves. The new student protests set an agenda for reform, during which Germany may yet look with pride to the experience and example of its comprehensive universities.

Bibliography

ABRC (Advisory Board for Research Councils), *Science and Public Expenditure 1985*: A Report to the Secretary of State for Education and Science from the Advisory Board for Research Councils, London, April, 1985

Aiken, H.D., *The Age of Ideology: The Nineteenth-Century Philosophers*, New York: Mentor, 1956

Albert, W. and Oehler, C., *Die Kulturausgaben der Länder, des Bundes und der Gemeinden, einschließlich Strukturausgaben zum Bildungswesen*, Hochschul-Informations-System (HIS), Reihe Hochschulplanung, Bd. 24, Hanover: HIS, 1976

Altbach, P.G. (ed.), *Comparative Perspectives on the Academic Profession*, New York: Praeger, 1977

Anrich, E. (ed.), *Die Idee der deutschen Universität*, Darmstadt: Hermann Gentner, 1956

Argyle, M., *Social Interaction*, London: Tavistock Publications in association with Methuen, 1969

Armytage, W.H.G., *The German Influence on English Education*, London: Routledge and Kegan Paul, 1969

AUT (Association of University Teachers), *A Recipe for National Decline – The Government's Green Paper on Higher Education*, London: AUT, November 1985

BAK (Bundesassistentenkonferenz), *Kreuznacher Hochschulkonzept*, Schriften der Bundesassistentenkonferenz I, Bonn: BAK, 1968

——, *Überlegungen zur Gesamthochschule: Materialien der Bundesassistentenkonferenz 4*, Bonn: BAK, 1969

——, *Bergneustädter Gesamthochschulplan: Schriften der Bundesassistentenkonferenz 8*, Bonn: BAK, 1970a

——, *Forschendes Lernen – Wissenschaftliches Prüfen: Schriften der Bundesassistentenkonferenz 5*, Bonn: BAK, 1970b

——, *Reform der Lehrkörper- und Personalstruktur: Schriften der Bundesassistentenkonferenz 3*, Bonn: BAK, 1970c (2nd edn)

——, *Wissenschaftsfreiheit durch Mitbestimmung*, Bonn: BAK, 1970d

——, *Die Überleitung des Lehrkörpers: Materialien der Bundesassistentenkonferenz 7*, Bonn: BAK, 1971

Balfour, M., *West Germany: A Contemporary History*, London: Croom Helm, 1982

Ball, C. and Eggins, H., *Higher Education into the 1990's*, Milton Keynes and

Bristol, USA: Society for Research into Higher Education and Open University Press, 1989

Barrett, S. and Fudge, C., *Policy and Action*, London and New York: Methuen, 1981

Bauss, G., *Die Studentenbewegung der sechziger Jahre in der Bundesrepublik und Westberlin*, Cologne: Pahl-Rugenstein, 1977

Becker, C.H., *Gedanken zur Hochschulreform*, Leipzig: Quelle und Meyer, 1919

Becker, H., 'Retrospective View from the German Side', in: Hearnden, A. (ed.), 1978: 268–82

Beckhough, H., 'The Role of the British University Control Officer in Post-War Germany', in: Phillips, D. (ed.), 1983: 76–89

Bell, D., *The Coming of Post-Industrial Society. A Venture in Social Forecasting*, Harmondsworth: Penguin, 1973

Ben-David, J., 'The Universities and the Growth of Science in Germany and the United States', *Minerva* 7, 1–2, 1968–69: 1–35

———, *American Higher Education*, New York: McGraw-Hill, 1972

Benoit, B., 'Status, Status Types, and Status Interrelations', in: Biddle, B.J. and Thomas, E.J. (eds), 1966: 77–80

Bernstein, B., 'Classification and Framing', in: Young, M.F.D. (ed.), 1971: 47–69

Beyme, K. von (ed.), *German Political Studies* (German Political Studies Volume 1), London: Sage, 1974

———, *German Political Systems: Theory and Practice in the Two Germanies* (German Political Studies Volume 2), London: Sage, 1976

Biddle, B.J. and Thomas, E.J. (eds), *Role Theory: Concepts and Research*, New York: Wiley, 1966

Bird, G., 'The Universities', in: Hearnden, A. (ed.), 1978: 146–57

Birley, R., 'British Policy in Retrospect', in: Hearnden, A. (ed.), 1978: 46–63

Blackbourn, D., 'The Discreet Charm of the Bourgeoisie: Reappraising German History in the Nineteenth Century', in: Blackbourn, D. and Eley, G., 1984: 159–292

———, and Eley, G., *The Peculiarities of German History*, Oxford: Oxford University Press, 1984

Blase, K.O., 'Eine über 200 Jahre alte Kunsthochschule in einer 10 Jahre jungen Gesamthochschule', in: Kluge, N. et al. (eds), 1981: 217–41

Blaug, M., 'Cost-Benefit Analysis Applied to the Concept of Economies of Scale in Higher Education', in: Goodlad, S. (ed.), 1983: 9–22

Bleuel, H.P., *Deutschlands Bekenner: Professoren zwischen Kaiserreich und Diktatur*, Bern: Scherz, 1968

BLK (Bund-Länder-Kommission für Bildungsplanung), *Bildungsgesamtplan, Bd. I and II*, Stuttgart: Klett, 1973

———, *Bericht der Arbeitsgruppe 'Modellversuche im Hochschulbereich' über die Modellversuche zur Gesamthochschulentwicklung (Drs. 1 54/1977)*, October, 1977

———, 'Rahmenvereinbarung zur koordinierten Vorbereitung, Durchführung

Bibliography

und wissenschaftlichen Begleitung von Modellversuchen im Bildungswesen, 1971', in: *Informationen über die Bund-Länder-Kommission für Bildungsplanung und Forschungsförderung*, Bonn, January, 1984

BMBW (Der Bundesminister für Bildung und Wissenschaft), *Hochschulrahmengesetz vom 26. Januar 1976*, Bonn: 1976

——, *Grund- und Strukturdaten*, Bonn, 1986/87

——, *Bericht der Expertenkommission zur Untersuchung der Auswirkungen des Hochschulrahmengesetzes (HRG)*, Bonn, 1984

——, *Weiterentwicklung der Studienangebote an Fachhochschulen, Studien: Bildung und Wissenschaft, 14*, Bad Honnef: Bock, 1985a

——, *Werthaltungen, Zunkunftserwartungen und bildungspolitische Vorstellungen der Jugend 1985*, Bonn, 1985b

——, *Drittes Gesetz zur Änderung des Hochschulrahmengesetzes vom 14. November 1985*, Bonn, 1986a (referred to in the text as 'the 1985 Amendment' of BMBW (1986a))

——, *Hochschulpolitische Zielsetzungen der Bundesregierung*, Bonn: Schriftenreihe Grundlagen und Perspektiven für Bildung und Wissenschaft 12, 1986b

Böckh, A., *The Public Economy of the Athenians* (trans. by G.C. Lewis), London: John Murray, 1828 (first published 1817)

Bohnsack, F., 'Schulpraktische Studien: Ergebnisse und Folgerungen', *Essener Hochschuljournal* (n.d.)

Böning, E. and Roeloffs, K., *Three German Universities – Aachen, Bochum, Konstanz, Case Studies on Innovation in Higher Education*, Paris: OECD, 1970

Bourdieu, P. and Passeron, J.-C., *Reproduction in Education, Society and Culture*, London and Beverly Hills: Sage, 1977

Böversen, F. (ed.), *Lehrerausbildung in Wuppertal*, Wuppertal: Bergische Universität Gesamthochschule, 1989

Brinckmann, H., 'Die Gesamthochschule Kassel als Universität des Landes Hessen', in: Kluge, N. et al. (eds), 1981: 124–35

British Council, *International Guide to Qualifications in Education*, London: Mansell, 1989

Brosan, G., Carter, C., Layard, R., Venables, P. and Williams, G., *Patterns and Policies in Higher Education*, Harmondsworth: Penguin, 1971

Bruford, W.H., *Germany in the Eighteenth Century: The Social Background of the Literary Revival*, London: Cambridge University Press, 1935

——, *The Idea of Bildung in Wilhelm von Humboldt's Letters*, in : *Essays Presented to James Boyd*, Oxford: Blackwell, 1959, 17–46 (no editor's name given)

——, *The German Tradition of Self-Cultivation*, Cambridge: Cambridge University Press, 1975

Bungardt, K., *Die Odyssee der Lehrerschaft*, Hanover: Schroedel, 1965

Burn, B.B., Altbach, P.G., Kerr, C. and Perkins, J.A., *Higher Education in Nine Countries*, New York: McGraw-Hill, 1971

Burrow, J.E. (ed.), *The Limits of State Action by Wilhelm von Humboldt*, Cambridge: Cambridge University Press, 1969

Busch, A., *Die Geschichte des Privatdozenten*, Stuttgart: Enke, 1959

——, 'The Vicissitudes of the *Privatdozent*: Breakdown and Adaptation in the Recruitment of the German University Teacher', *Minerva* 1, 3, 1963: 319–41

Butler, E.M., *The Tyranny of Greece Over Germany*, Boston: Beacon, 1935 (4th edn, 1935)

Buttler, F., 'Kooperation statt Kapitulation: Bemerkungen zu Hellmut Cramers Vorschlägen aus Paderborner Sicht', *Deutsche Universitätszeitung* 7, 1983: 24–6

BW (Bildung und Wissenschaft), Nr. 1–2(e), *Into the Future by Tradition: Higher Education in the Federal Republic of Germany*, Bonn: Inter Nationes, 1987

Carter, C., 'A Comprehensive System', in: Brosan, G. et al., 1971: 156–61

——, *Higher Education for the Future*, Oxford: Blackwell, 1980

Caute, D., *Sixty-Eight: The Year of the Barricades*, London: Hamish Hamilton, 1988

Cerych, L., Neusel, A., Teichler, U. and Winkler, H., *Gesamthochschule – Erfahrungen, Hemmnisse, Zielwandel*, Frankfurt: Campus, 1981a

——, *The German Gesamthochschule*, Amsterdam: European Cultural Foundation, 1981b

CM 114, *Higher Education: Meeting the Challenge*, London: HMSO, 1987

CMD. 9703, *White Paper on Technical Education*, London: HMSO, 1956

CMND. 2154, *Higher Education Report of the Committee appointed by the Prime Minister under the Chairmanship of Lord Robbins 1961–63*, London: HMSO, 1963

CMND. 3006, *A Plan for Polytechnics and other Colleges. Higher Education in the Further Education System*, London: HMSO, 1966

CMND. 7130, *Report of the Working Group on the Management of Higher Education in the Maintained Sector*, London: HMSO, 1978

CMND. 9501, *Academic Validation in Public Sector Higher Education*, London: HMSO, 1985

CMND. 9524, *The Development of Higher Education into the 1990s*, London: HMSO, 1985

COM (86) 257 final, *Proposal for a Directive on a General System for the Recognition of Higher Education Diplomas Awarded on Completion of Vocational Courses of at Least Three Years Duration*, 7 May 1986

Cowan, M. (ed.), *Humanist without Portfolio: An Anthology of the Writings of Wilhelm von Humboldt*, Detroit: Wayne State University, 1963

Cramer, H., 'Vom Professorenurteil zur Gesamthochschulreform?' *Deutsche Universitätszeitung* 7, 1983: 20–23

Crosland, A., *Speech on the structure and development of higher education*, delivered at Lancaster University, 20 January 1967, in: Robinson, E. 1968: 193–6

Cross, F.L. (ed.), *The Oxford Dictionary of the Christian Church*, London: Oxford University Press, 1958 (first published in 1957)

CVCP (Committee of Vice-Chancellors and Principals), *Report of the Steering Committee for Efficiency Studies in Universities (The Jarratt Report)*, March, 1985

Daalder, H., 'The Sudden Revolution and the Sluggish Aftermath: A Retrospect since 1968', in: Daalder, H. and Shils, E. (eds) 1982: 489–510

——, and Shils, E. (eds), *Universities, Politicians and Bureaucrats: Europe and the United States*, Cambridge: Cambridge University Press, 1982

Dahrendorf, R., *Bildung ist Bürgerrecht: Plädoyer für eine aktive Bildungspolitik*, Hamburg: Die Zeit-Bücher, 1965a (reprinted Wegener, 1968)

——, *Society and Democracy in Germany*, London: Weidenfeld and Nicholson, 1965b

——, (1967) See *Hochschulgesamtplan Baden-Württemberg (1967)*

——, 'Zur Entstehungsgeschichte des Hochschulgesamtplans für Baden-Württemberg 1966/67', in: *Bildungspolitik mit Ziel und Maß*, Stuttgart: Klett, 1974, 138–63 (no editor's name given)

Deutscher Bildungsrat, *Empfehlungen der Bildungskommission: Strukturplan für das Bildungswesen*, Stuttgart: Klett, 1970

Dewey, J., *German Philosophy and Politics*, New York: Putnam, 1942 (first published 1915)

Dworkin, R.M. (ed.), *The Philosophy of Law*, Oxford: Oxford University Press, 1977

EC Journal (Official Journal of the European Communities), No C 197/11, 27 July 1988

Education Reform Act, *Chapter 40*, London: HMSO, 1988

Edwards, A.W.J., 'Two Critical Years in the History of the Rheinisch-Westfälische *Technische Hochschule*, Aachen', in: Phillips, D. (ed.), 1983: 118–27

Eley, G., 'The British Model and the German Road: Rethinking the Course of German History Before 1914', in: Blackbourn, D. and Eley, G., 1984: 39–155

Ellwein, T., *Die deutsche Universität vom Mittelalter bis zur Gegenwart*, Königstein: Athenäum, 1985

Endemann, M. and Klüver, J., *Projekt: Evaluation integrierter Studiengänge an der Gesamthochschule Essen, Untersuchungen im Studiengang Bauingenieurwesen*: Essen, 1981; *Wirtschaftswissenschaften*: Essen, 1983 (two separate volumes)

Evers, C.-H., 'Modell eines neuen Gymnasiums und einer neuen Gesamthochschule', *betrifft: erziehung*, Bd. 1, Heft 3, 1968

——, and Rau, J. (eds), *Oberstufenreform und Gesamthochschule*, Frankfurt am Main: Diesterweg, 1970

Fallon, D., *The German University: A Heroic Ideal in Conflict with the Modern World*, Colorado: Colorado Associated University Press, 1980

Festinger, L., 'A Theory of Social Comparison Processes', *Human Relations* 7, 2, 1954: 117–40

Fichte, J.G., 'Deduzierter Plan einer zu Berlin zu errichtenden höheren Lehranstalt' (written 1807, first published 1817), in: Anrich, E. (ed.), 1956: 125–217

Flechsig, K.-H., Huber, L. and Plander, H., *Gesamthochschule, Mittel oder Ersatz für Hochschulreform?*, Stuttgart: Klett, 1975

Bibliography

Förmer, L., *Technologie und Berufsbildung: ein historischer Aufriß unter besonderer Berücksichtigung des Handwerks*, Cologne, 1987

Framhein, G., *Alte und neue Universitäten: Einzugsbereiche und Ortswahl der Studenten, Motive und Verhalten*, Bad Honnef: Bock, 1983

Freimann, J., 'Das Lehrstück Berufspraktische Studien', *Prisma* Nr. 40, July, 1988: 3–9

Frister, E., *Schicksal Hauptschule: Argumente zugunsten einer sprachlosen Minderheit*, Cologne/Frankfurt am Main: Europäische Verlagsanstalt, 1976

Fulton, O. (ed.), *Access to Higher Education*, Guildford: Society for Research into Higher Education, 1981

Gellert, C., 'Politics and Higher Education in the Federal Republic of Germany', *European Journal of Education*, 19, 2, 1984: 217–32

Gerstenberger, H., 'Theory of the State: Special Features of the Discussion in the FRG', in: Beyme, K. von, 1976: 69–92

Gerth, H.H. and Mills, C. Wright (eds), *From Max Weber: Essays in Sociology*, London: Routledge and Kegan Paul, 1948 (reprinted in paperback 1985)

GhK, *Gesamthochschule Kassel: Bericht des Gründungspräsidenten*, Kassel, 1977

Gieseke, L. and Eilsberger, R., *The Development of the Comprehensive University in the Federal Republic of Germany*, Strasbourg: Council of Europe, 1977

Gillies, A., *Auch eine Philosophie der Geschichte zur Bildung der Menschheit*, in: *Essays Presented to James Boyd*, Oxford: Blackwell, 1959, 61–80 (no editor's name given)

Girvin, B. (ed.), *The Transformation of Contemporary Conservatism*, London: Sage, 1988

Glaser, B.G. and Strauss, A.L., *Status Passage*, London: Routledge and Kegan Paul, 1971

Goodlad, S. (ed.), *Economies of Scale in Higher Education*, Guildford: Society for Research into Higher Education, 1983

Grande, E., 'Neoconservatism without Neoconservatives? The Renaissance and Transformation of Contemporary German Conservatism', in: Girvin, B. (ed.), 1988: 55–77

Green, D., 'Higher Education into the 1990s' in: Ball, C. and Eggins, H. (ed.), 1989: 97–111

Green Paper (1985), see Cmnd. 9524 (1985)

Grundgesetz für die Bundesrepublik Deutschland, Munich: Beck, 1971

Habermas, J., *Towards a Rational Society: Student Protest, Science and Politics*, London: Heinemann, 1971

——, Friedenburg, C., Oehler, C. and Weltz, F., *Student und Politik: eine soziologische Untersuchung zum politischen Bewußtsein Frankfurter Studenten*, Neuwied: Hermann Luchterhand, 1961

Haines, G., *Essays on German Influence upon English Education and Science, 1850–1919*, Hamden, Connecticut: Connecticut College in Association with Archon Books, Monograph No. 9, 1969

Hall, P., 'Time to play the Merger Game', *Times Higher Educational Supplement*, 15 May 1987: 13

Halls, W.D., 'The "German Question" and Post-War Reform in Germany: A Comparative Note', in: Phillips, D. (ed.), 1983: 28–37

Hamburger Abschlußbericht, see: BLK, 1977.

Also: 'Ergänzung zum Abschlußbericht 'Modellversuch Gesamthochschule Hamburg', Freie und Hansestadt Hamburg (n.d.)

Handbuch NRW., *Handbuch Hochschulen in Nordrhein-Westfalen*, Düsseldorf: Der Minister für Wissenschaft und Forschung des Landes Nordrhein-Westfalen, 1986

Hart, H.L.A., *Law, Liberty and Morality*, Oxford: Oxford University Press, 1963

Hartshorne, E.Y. Jr., *The German Universities and National Socialism*, London: Allen and Unwin, 1937

Hearnden, A., *Education, Culture and Politics in West Germany*, Oxford: Pergamon, 1976

——, 'Education in the British Zone', in: Hearnden, A. (ed.), 1978: 11–45

——, *The British in Germany: Educational Reconstruction after 1945*, London: Hamish Hamilton, 1978

Heckhausen, H., Speech at a Symposium held on 17 April 1985 in the Wissenschaftszentrum, Bonn, in: BMBW (ed.), *Humboldt und die Universität heute*, Bonn, 1985

Hegele, I., 'Das Wuppertaler Modell – Der Versuch einer praxisorientierten Lehrerausbildung', in: Hegele, I. (ed.), 1978: 199–204

——, (ed.), *Grundschule Unterricht Lehrerbildung – Festschrift für Fritz Bärmann*, Frankfurt: Arbeitskreis Grundschule E.V., 1978

Heipcke, K. and Messner, R., 'Entstehung, Situation und Perspektiven der Kasseler Stufenlehrerausbildung', in: Kluge, N. et al. (eds), 1981: 262–98.

Heise, K.F., 'Vorspiele zur Gesamthochschule: ein geschichtlicher Aufriß', in: Kluge, N. et al. (eds), 1981: 54–64

Hennis, W., 'Germany: Legislators and the Universities, in: Daalder, H. and Shils, E. (eds), 1982: 1–30

Hermanns, H., *Statuspassagen von Hochschullehrern im Entwicklungsprozeß einer Gesamthochschule – am Beispiel der Ingenieurwissenschaften*, Kassel: Wissenschaftliches Zentrums für Berufs- und Hochschulforschung, Arbeitspapier Nr. 14, August 1982

——, Teichler, U. and Wasser, H. (eds), *The Compleat University: Break from Tradition in Germany, Sweden and the USA*, Cambridge, Mass.: Schenkman, 1983

Herrmann, G. and Schmidt, J., 'Praxisbezug – Forschung für wen?', in: Klüver, J. et al., 1983: 50–9

Hesse, K.-L., 'Soziale Öffnung und Chancengleichheit durch die Gesamthochschulen', in: Klüver, J. et al. (eds), 1983: 98–106

Hitpass, J. and Mock, A., *Das Image der Universität: Studentische Perspektiven*, Düsseldorf: Bertelsmann, 1972

——, Ohlsson, R. and Thomas, E., *Gesamthochschule in der Bewährungs-Kontrolle*,

Cologne: Ministerium für Wissenschaft und Forschung des Landes Nordrhein-Westfalen, 1979 and 1980 (two separate volumes)

——, Ohlsson, R. and Thomas, E., *Studien- und Berufserfolg von Hochschulabsolventen mit unterschiedlichen Studieneingangsvoraussetzungen*, Cologne, August 1983

Hochschulgesamtplan Baden-Württemberg (Dahrendorf Plan), *Bildung in neuer Sicht. Empfehlungen zur Reform von Struktur und Organisation der wissenschaftlichen Hochschulen, Pädagogischen Hochschulen, Studienseminare, Kunsthochschulen, Ingenieurschulen und Höheren Fachschulen*, Kultusministerium Baden-Württemberg: Neckar-Verlag, 1967

Hochschulrahmengesetz (1976), see BMBW (1976)

Hoffknecht, H. and Intrup, R., 'Ist erst die Vorstellung revolutioniert, hält die Wirklichkeit nicht stand! Integrierte Gesamthochschulen: Intention und Wirklichkeit', in: Klüver, J. et al. (eds), 1983: 30–40

Hogg, Q., *The Case for Conservatism*, London: Penguin, 1947

Hüfner, K., 'Differentiation and Competition in Higher Education: Recent Trends in the Federal Republic of Germany', *European Journal of Education* 22, 2, 1987: 133–43

Humboldt, W. von, 'Über die innere und äussere Organisation der höheren wissenschaftlichen Anstalten in Berlin' (1809/10), in: Anrich, E. (ed.), 1956: 375–86

——, *Humanist without Portfolio: An Anthology of the Writings of Wilhelm von Humboldt* (ed. by M. Cowan), Detroit: Wayne State University, 1963

——, *The Limits of State Action* (ed. by J.W. Burrow), Cambridge: Cambridge University Press, 1969

Husemann, H., 'Anglo-German Relations in Higher Education', in: Hearnden, A. (ed.), 1978: 158–73

ICFU (International Council on the Future of the University), *Report on German Universities by the German Universities Commission*, New York: ICFU, 1977

Jarratt Report, (1985), see CVCP (1985)

Jaspers, K. and Rossmann, K., *Die Idee der Universität*, Berlin, Göttingen, Heidelberg: Springer, 1961

Kaehler, S.A., *Wilhelm von Humboldt und der Staat*, Göttingen: Vandenhoeck and Ruprecht, 1963

Kant, I., *Der Streit der Fakultäten*, Königsberg, 1798. Republished Heidelberg, Radsch: 1947

Kerr, C., *The Uses of the University*, Cambridge, Mass.: Harvard University Press, 1963

——, *The Uses of the University with a 'Postscript – 1972'*, Cambridge, Mass.: Harvard University Press, 1972

Kloss, G., 'University Reform in W. Germany', *Minerva*, 6, 3, 1968

Kluge, N., Neusel, A., Oehler, C. and Teichler, U. (eds), *Gesamthochschule Kassel 1971–81. Rückblick auf das erste Jahrzehnt*, Kassel: Stauda, 1981

Klüver, J., 'Zu diesem Buch: Gesamthochschulen – ein hochschulpolitisches Alibi?', in: Klüver, J. et al. (eds), 1983: 7–22

——, Jost, W. and Hesse, K.-L. (eds), *Gesamthochschule – Versäumte Chancen*, Opladen: Leske and Budrich, 1983

——, and Krameyer, A., *Projekt: Evaluation integrierter Studiengänge an der Gesamthochschule Essen. Untersuchungen im Studiengang Chemie*, Essen, 1981

Knopp Report (1984), see BMBW (1984)

Kogan, M., *The Attack on Higher Education*, London: Kogan Page, 1983

Kunsmann, H., 'Zur theoretischen Begründung des Wuppertaler Modellversuchs', in: Hegele, I. (ed.), 1978: 219–30

Kwiatkowski, S., 'The Organisational Problems of Combining Teaching and Research: Humboldt, Weber and the Polish Experience', *European Journal of Education* 15, 4, 1980: 355–61

Lawton, D., *The Politics of the School Curriculum*, London: Routledge and Kegan Paul, 1980

Layard, R. and Verry, D., 'Cost Functions for University Teaching and Research', *Economic Journal*, 85 (337) 1975: 55–74

Lenz, M., *Geschichte der königlichen Friedrich-Wilhelms-Universität zu Berlin Bd.1.*, Halle: Verlag der Buchhandlung des Waisenhauses, 1910

Leroux, R., *Guillaume de Humboldt*, Paris: Ophrys, 1932

Leuze, D., 'Die Gesamthochschule als Ziel – die Rechtslage der Gesamthochschulen heute', *Recht der Jugend und des Bildungswesens*, Heft 1, January/February, 1985: 24–37

Lewis, J., *Introduction to Philosophy*, London: Watts, 1954

Lilge, F., *The Abuse of Learning: The Failure of the German University*, New York: Macmillan, 1948

Lindop Report (1985), see Cmnd. 9501 (1985)

Luhmann, N., 'Sociology of Political Systems', in: Beyme, K. von (ed.), 1974: 3–29

Luria, S.E. and Luria, Z., 'The Role of the University: Ivory Tower, Service Station, or Frontier Post?', *Daedalus*, Winter 1970: 75–107

Lüth, G., *Gesamthochschulpolitik in der Bundesrepublik Deutschland*, Bad Honnef: Bock, 1983

Mann, E., *School for Barbarians*, New York: Modern Age, 1938

Mann, T., *Der Zauberberg*, in: *Thomas Manns erzählende Schriften gesammelt in drei Bänden*, Berlin, 1927

Mark, J., 'The Art of the Possible: The British and the German Universities, 1945–1948', in: Phillips, D. (ed.), 1983: 38–44

Martin, B., 'Martinplan', in: *Akademischer Dienst: Kulturpolitische Informationen*, Nr. 38, 19 September 1968: 430–40

Massialas, B.G., *Education and the Political System*, Reading, Mass.: Addison-Wesley, 1969

Massing, O., 'The Federal Constitutional Court as an Instrument of Social Control: Propaedeutic Sketches for a Critical Functional Form-analysis of Constitutional Jurisdiction', in: Beyme, K. von (ed.), 1974: 215–52

Max Planck Institute for Human Development and Education, *Between Elite and Mass Education: Education in the Federal Republic of Germany*, Albany: State University of New York Press, 1979 (no editor's name given)

——, 'Transatlantic Influences: History of Mutual Interactions between American and German Education', in: Max Planck Institute (1979), Ch. 1: 1–65

——, 'Before and After the "Wirtschaftswunder"': Changes in Overall Educational Policies and Their Setting', in: Max Planck Institute (1979), Ch. 2: 66–82

——, 'The Legacy of the Prussian Enlightenment: The State as the Trustee of Education', in: Max Planck Institute (1979), Ch. 3: 83–106

——, 'Modernizing the School System: The Challenge of Equality and Excellence', in: Max Planck Institute (1979), Ch. 4: 107–32

——, 'The Mighty Midget: The Comprehensive School', in: Max Planck Institute (1979), Ch. 10: 217–35

McClelland, C.E., *State, Society and University in Germany 1700–1914*, Cambridge: Cambridge University Press, 1980

Medvedev, Z., *Gorbachev*, Oxford: Blackwell, 1986

Meeting the Challenge, (1987), see Cm. 114 (1987)

Menke, N. and Ott, M., *Essay about the Way of Studying at German Universities and Fachhochschulen in Comparison to the English System at Polytechnics*, Nottingham, December, 1984

Miller, R., 'Zur Bedeutung der sozialen Struktur, ausgewählter psychosozialer Parameter und der Leistungsentwicklung von Studenten in integrierten Studiengängen', in: Schmidt, J. (ed.), 1980: 23–60

Minerva, 'Recommendations of the Science Council for the Development of Scientific Institutions in Western Germany', *Minerva* 1, 1, 1962: 87–105 (no author's name given)

——, 'Suggestions of the Science Council on the Pattern of New Universities in Western Germany', *Minerva* 1, 2, 1963: 217–25 (no author's name given)

——, 'Recommendations of the Science Council on the Reorganisation of University Teaching Staffs in Western Germany', *Minerva* 4, 2, 1966: 246–53 (no author's name given)

Moodie, G.C. and Eustace, R., *Power and Authority in British Universities*, London: Allen and Unwin, 1974

MWF NRW (Der Minister für Wissenschaft und Forschung des Landes Nordrhein-Westfalen), *Gesamthochschulen in Nordrhein-Westfalen. Materialien zu Aufbau, Entwicklung und Funktion*, Düsseldorf, 1979

Nagel, B., 'Hessische Hochschulgesetzgebung und Entwicklung der Gesamthochschule', in: Kluge, N. et al. (eds), 1981: 43–53

Neave, G., 'The Changing Face of the Academic Profession in Western Europe', *European Journal of Education* 18, 3, 1983: 217–27

——, 'On the Road to Silicon Valley? The Changing Relationship between Higher Education and Government in Western Europe', *European Journal of Education* 19, 2, 1984: 111–29

——, 'Elite and Mass Higher Education in Britain: A Regressive Model?', *Comparative Education Review* 29, 3, 1985: 347–61

——, 'On Shifting Sands: Changing Priorities and Perspectives in European Higher Education from 1984 to 1986', *European Journal of Education* 21, 1, 1986: 7–24

Nerad, M., *Implementation Analysis – A New Magic Tool for Research in Higher Education?*, Kassel: Wissenschaftliches Zentrum für Berufs- und Hochschulforschung, Arbeitspapier Nr. 17, 1984

Neusel, A., 'Das "Kasseler Modell" der integrierten Studiengänge – von innen betrachtet', in: Kluge, N. et al. (eds), 1981: 65–90

Nitsch, W., Gerhardt, U., Offe, C. and Preuss, U.K., *Hochschule in der Demokratie*, New York: Arno, 1977

Oakes Report (1978), see Cmnd. 7130 (1978)

OECD (Organisation for Economic Co-operation and Development), *Reviews of National Policies for Education: Germany*, Paris: OECD, 1972

Oehler, C., 'Die Entstehung der Gesamthochschule Kassel – hochschulpolitische Rahmenbedingungen', in: Kluge, N. et al. (eds), 1981: 15–41

——, *Geschichte der Hochschulentwicklung nach 1945*, Kassel: Wissenschaftliches Zentrum für Berufs- und Hochschulforschung, 1985

Page, C.F., 'Academic Man: Seen Through Novelists' Eyes', *Studies in Higher Education* 3, 1, 1978: 113–21

Paloczi-Horvath, G., *Youth up in Arms: A Political and Social World Survey 1955–1970*, London: Weidenfeld and Nicolson, 1971

Pascal, R., *The Growth of Modern Germany*, London: Cobbett, 1946

Passant, E.J., *A Short History of Germany 1815–1945*, Cambridge: Cambridge University Press, 1959

Paulsen, F., *German Education: Past and Present*, London: Allen and Unwin, 1908

——, *Geschichte des gelehrten Unterrichts*, Leipzig: Veit, 1919

Pedley, R., *Towards the Comprehensive University*, London: Macmillan, 1977

Peisert, H. and Framhein, G., *Das Hochschulsystem in der Bundesrepublik Deutschland*, Stuttgart: Klett-Cotta, 1980

Phillips, D. (ed.), *German Universities after the Surrender: British Occupation Policy and the Control of Higher Education*, Oxford: University of Oxford Department of Educational Studies, 1983

——, 'The University Officers of the British Zone', in: Phillips, D. (ed.), 1983: 51–75

Picht, G., *Die deutsche Bildungskatastrophe: Analyse und Dokumentation*, Freiburg im Breisgau: Walter, 1964

Pingel, F., 'Attempts at University Reform in the British Zone', in: Phillips, D. (ed.), 1983: 20–7

Pinner, F., 'Tradition and Transgression: Western European Students in the Postwar World', *Daedalus* 97, 1, 1968: 137–55

Plander, H., 'Gesamthochschule im Werden – kritisches Resumée bisheriger Entwicklungen in Hamburg', in: Flechsig, K.-H., Huber, L. and

Plander, H., 1975: Ch. 2

Pratt, J., 'Co-ordination in the Public Sector: The Council for National Academic Awards', in: Shattock, M. (ed.), 1983: 116–32

Pratt, J. and Silverman, S., *Responding to Constraint*, Milton Keynes and Philadelphia: The Society for Research into Higher Education and the Open University Press, 1988

Pritchard, R.M.O. 'Reconstructionism – Strategy for a Brighter Future?', *The Northern Teacher* 12, 1, 1975/6: 5–9

——, 'The Status of Teachers in Germany and Ireland', *Comparative Education Review* 27, 3, 1983: 341–50

——, 'The Self-Image of Primary School Teachers: Ireland and Germany', *Studies* 75, 299, 1986a: 295–307

——, 'The Third Amendment to the Higher Education Law of the German Federal Republic', *Higher Education* 15, 1986b: 587–607

Raupach, H., 'Neues Gymnasium, gestufte Gesamthochschule und Hochschulreform', in: Evers, C.-H. and Rau, J. (eds), 1970: 87–108

Rechtien, W., and Bierbaum, C., 'Studienreform und Organisationsstruktur an Gesamthochschulen', in: Schmidt, J. (ed.), 1980: 11–22

Rimbach, G., 'Zum beruflichen Selbstverständnis der Fachhochschullehrer an den Gesamthochschulen in Nordrhein-Westfalen. I and II', *Deutsche Universitätszeitung*, I, 23/1974(a): 981–6; II, 24/1974(b): 1030–5

——, 'Fachhochschule und Universität – Erfolgreiche Integration', in: Klüver, J. et al. (eds), 1983: 60–79

Ringer, F., *The Decline of the German Mandarins*, Cambridge, Mass.: Harvard University Press, 1969

Robbins Report (1963), see Cmnd. 2154 (1963)

Robertson, J.G., *A History of German Literature*, Edinburgh and London: Blackwood, 1959

Robinsohn, S.B. and Kuhlmann, J.C., 'Two Decades of Non-Reform in West German Education', *Comparative Education Review* 11, 3, 1967: 311–30

Robinson, E.E., *The New Polytechnics*, London: Cornmarket, 1968

Rose, H.P., 'Die Rolle der Parteien in der Diskussion um die Bildungsreform', in: Evers, C.-H. and Rau, J. (eds), 1970: 133–45

Rotenhan, E. von, *Krise und Chance der Fachhochschule*, Munich: Kaiser, 1980

Sagarra, E., *An Introduction to Nineteenth-Century Germany*, Harlow, Essex: Longman, 1980

Santayana, G., *Egotism in German Philosophy*, London: Dent, 1916 (new edn 1939)

Sauvageot, J., Geismar, A., Cohn-Bendit, D. and Duteuil, J.-P., *The Student Revolt: The Activists Speak*, London: Panther, 1968

Schelling, F.W.J., 'Vorlesung: Über den absoluten Begriff der Wissenschaft' (1802a), in: Anrich, E. (ed.), 1956: 3–12

——, 'Vorlesungen über die Methode des akademischen Studiums' (1802b), in: Anrich, E. (ed.), 1956: 2–124

Bibliography

Schelsky, H., *Einsamkeit und Freiheit: Die Idee der deutschen Universität und ihrer Reform*, Hamburg: Rowohlt, 1963

——, *Abschied von der Hochschulpolitik oder die Universität im Fadenkreuz des Versagens*, Bielefeld: Bertelsmann, 1969

Schenck, G.V., *Das Hochschulrahmengesetz*, Bad Godesberg, 1976

Scheuerer, A. and Weist, R., 'Reformhochschule und Studentische Politik', in: Kluge, N. et al. (eds), 1981: 91–123

Schleiermacher, F., 'Gelegentliche Gedanken über Universitäten im deutschen Sinn' (1808), in: Anrich, E. (ed.), 1956: 219–308

Schmidt, J. (ed.), *Gesamthochschule: Eine vorläufige Bilanz*, Hamburg: Arbeitsgemeinschaft für Hochschuldidaktik (Blickpunkt Hochschuldidaktik, 60), 1980

Schmithals, F., 'Structural Barriers to Innovation in West Germany', in: Squires, G. (ed.), 1982: 37–42

Schrey, H., *Die Universität Duisburg*, Duisburg: Braun, 1982

——, 'Theoriestudium ohne Praxis – praxis-orientiertes Studium ohne Theorie?', in: Klüver, J. et al. (eds), 1983: 80–97

Schuster, H.J., 'Überregelungen im Hochschulbereich', in: Zöller, O. (ed.), 1983: 41–56

Scott, D.F.S., *Wilhelm von Humboldt and the Idea of a University*, Inaugural lecture published by the University of Durham, 1960

Scott, P., 'Has the Binary Policy Failed?', in: Shattock, M. (ed.), 1983(a): 166–97

——, 'The State of the Academic Profession in Britain', *European Journal of Education* 18, 3, 1983(b): 245–57

SCUE (Standing Conference on University Entrance), London, 29 Tavistock Square, Personal Communication from the Secretary, Dr Clive Wake, January 1987

SDS (Sozialistischer Deutscher Studentenbund), *Hochschule in der Demokratie*, Frankfurt: Neue Kritik, 1961 (reprinted 1965)

Sell, F.C., *Die Tragödie des deutschen Liberalismus*, Stuttgart: Deutsche Verlags-Anstalt, 1953

SGHS, *Siegen Gesamthochschule: Rechenschaftsbericht des Rektorats*, Siegen, 1984

Shattock, M. (ed.), *The Structure and Governance of Higher Education*, Guildford: Society for Research into Higher Education, 1983

Shils, E., 'The Academic Ethos under Strain', *Minerva* 13, 1, 1975: 1–37

——, 'Great Britain and the United States: legislators, bureaucrats and the universities', in: Daalder, H. and Shils, E. (eds), 1982: 437–87

Siebert, H., *Humboldt and the Reform of the Educational System*, Bad Godesberg: Inter Nationes, 1967, 28–51

Simpson, R., *How the Ph.D. came to Britain*, Guildford: Society for Research into Higher Education, 1983

Smith, G., *Democracy in Western Germany*, London: Heinemann, 1979

Snow, C.P., *The Two Cultures: A Second Look*, Cambridge: Cambridge University Press, 1969 (first published 1959)

Bibliography

Snyder, L.L., *The Age of Reason*, New York and Toronto: Van Nostrand, 1955

Spranger, E., *Wilhelm von Humboldt und die Humanitätsidee*, Berlin: Reuther und Reich, 1909 (2nd edn, 1928)

——, *Wilhelm von Humboldt und die Reform des Bildungswesens*, Tübingen: Niemeyer, 1965

Squires, G. (ed.), *Innovation through Recession*, Guildford: Society for Research into Higher Education, 1982

Steffens, H., 'Über die Idee der Universitäten' (1808/9), in: Anrich, E. (ed.), 1956: 309–74

Steinberg, M.S., *Sabers and Brown Shirts*, Chicago and London: University of Chicago Press, 1973

Stewart, W.A.C., *Higher Education in Postwar Britain*, Basingstoke and London: Macmillan, 1989

Sutton, L.H., 'Shuffling Feet: A Discourse on the University of Göttingen', in: Phillips, D. (ed.), 1983: 109–17

Sweet, P.R., *Wilhelm von Humboldt: A Biography*, Columbus: Ohio State University Press, Vol. 1, 1978; Vol. 2, 1980

Swinnerton-Dyer, P., Keynote speech (no title) in: Eggins, H. (ed.), *Restructuring Higher Education*, Milton Keynes and Philadelphia: Open University Press and Society for Research into Higher Education, 1988

Sydow, A. von (ed.), *Wilhelm und Karoline von Humboldt in ihren Briefen*, Berlin, 1906–16 (7 vols)

Teichler, U. and Klophaus, R., 'Forschung, Forschungsplanung und Forschungsorganisation', in: Kluge, N. et al. (eds), 1981:299–319

Tent, J., *The Free University of Berlin: A Political History*, Bloomington and Indianapolis: Indiana University Press, 1988

THES (Times Higher Educational Supplement), 'The Rush to Cement a Union of Minds', 2 Sept. 1988

Thomas, C.R., 'Philosophical Anthropology and Educational Change: Wilhelm von Humboldt and the Prussian Reforms', *History of Education Quarterly* 15, 1973: 219–29

Trow, M., 'Problems in the Transition from Elite to Mass Higher Education', in: *Policies for Higher Education*, Paris: OECD, 1974, 51–101 (no author's name given)

——, 'Comparative Perspectives on Access', in: Fulton, O. (ed.), 1981: 89–121

——, 'Defining the Issues in University–Government Relations: An International Perspective', *Studies In Higher Education* 8, 2, 1983: 115–28

Tymms, R., *German Romantic Literature*, London: Methuen, 1955

URG (University Reform in Germany), *Report by a German Commission*, London: HMSO, 1949

University Statistics 1987–88, Volume One: Students and Staff, Cheltenham: Universities Statistical Record, December 1988

VDS (Verband Deutscher Studentenschaften), *Studenten und die neue Univer-*

Bibliography

sität: Gutachten einer Kommission des VDS zur Neugründung von Wissenschaftlichen Hochschulen, Bonn, 1962

Verry, D. and Davies, B., *University Costs and Output*, Amsterdam: Elsevier, 1976

Viereck, P., *Conservatism*, Princeton, New Jersey: Van Nostrand, 1956

Vossler, O., 'Humboldts Idee der Universität', *Historische Zeitschrift* 175, 1954: 251–68

Weaver Report, *Report of the Study Group on the Government of Colleges of Education*, London: HMSO, 1966

Weber, M., 'Class, Status and Party', in: Gerth, H.H. and Mills, C. Wright (eds), 1948: 180–95

Webler, W.-D., 'The Sixties and the Seventies. Aspects of Student Activism in West Germany', *Higher Education* 9, 2, 1980: 155–68

Weil, H., *Die Entstehung des deutschen Bildungsprinzips*, Bonn: Bouvier, 1967 (first published 1930)

Weinstock, H., *Die Tragödie des Humanismus*, Heidelberg: Quelle und Meyer, 1956

Weizsäcker, E. von, et al., *Baukasten gegen Systemzwänge*, Munich: Piper, 1970

Whitburn, J., Cox, C. and Mealing, M., *People in Polytechnics*, Guildford: Society for Research into Higher Education, 1976

Wildt, J., 'HRG-Novelle steht vor der Tür' *Hochschulausbildung* 2, 1984: 57–77

Williams, G., 'Gentlemen and Players: The Changing British Professoriate', in: Altbach, P.G. (ed.). 1977: 9–22

Wilms, D., 'Der lange Marsch durch die Hochschule', *Die Welt*, Nr. 113, 17 May 1986

Winkler, H., *Zur Theorie und Praxis der Gesamthochschulplanung*, Munich: Minerva, 1979

Woll, A. (ed.), *Anspruch und Realität. Acht Jahre Aufbau der Universität-Gesamthochschule Siegen 1972–1980*, Siegen, 1980

WR (Wissenschaftsrat), *Empfehlungen zum Ausbau der wissenschaftlichen Einrichtungen. Teil 1: Wissenschaftliche Hochschulen*, Bonn, 1960

——, *Anregungen zur Gestalt neuer Hochschulen*, Bonn, 1962

——, *Empfehlungen des Wissenschaftsrats zur Neugliederung des Lehrkörpers an den wissenschaftlichen Hochschulen*, Tübingen: Mohr, 1965

——, *Empfehlungen zur Neuordnung des Studiums an den wissenschaftlichen Hochschulen*, Tübingen: Mohr, 1966

——, *Empfehlungen des Wissenschaftsrates zum Ausbau der wissenschaftlichen Hochschulen bis 1970*, Tübingen: Mohr, 1967

——, *Empfehlungen zur Struktur und zum Ausbau des Bildungswesens im Hochschulbereich nach 1970*, Bonn, 1970

——, *Empfehlungen zur Aufgabe und Stellung der Fachhochschulen*, Cologne, 1981

——, *Empfehlungen zum 13. Rahmenplan für den Hochschulbau 1984–1987*, Cologne, 1983

——, *Empfehlungen zum Wettbewerb im deutschen Hochschulsystem*, Cologne: Wissenschaftsrat, 1985

——, *Empfehlungen zur Struktur des Studiums*, Cologne, 1986

Young, M.F.D., *Knowledge and Control*, London: Collier-Macmillan, 1971

Zöller, O. (ed.), *Wissenschaftsrecht im Wandel?*, Essen: Arbeitsgruppe Fortbildung im Sprecherkreis der Hochschulkanzler, 1983

Index

Index

Index

Index

Index

Medvedev, Z., 202
Menke, N., 137
Messner, R., 151, 154
Metternich, Prince, 60
Miller, R., 142–3
Minerva, 72, 79, 80, 81
Mitbestimmung, 101
Mittelbau, 46, 83, 89, 102, 120
Moodie, G.C., 49
Münchhausen, G. von, 15, 16, 49, 50
Munich, University of, xv
Münster, University of, xv
MWF NRW – Ministerium für Wissenschaft und Forschung des Landes Nordrhein-Westfalen, 130, 158

Nagel, B., 96, 170
Napoleon, 17, 19, 27, 47, 64
Napoleonic War, 59
National Advisory Board for Public Sector Higher Education (NABPHSE, later NABLAHE), 3, 4
Nazis, 26, 34, 95, 150, 202, 209
  influence on German universities, 65–8
  sympathies of Rektor of Regensburg, 83
Neave, G., 4
neo-conservatism and comprehensive higher education, xvii, 209–13
Nerad, M., 206
Network of National Recognition Centres, xvii
Neusel, A., 146, 147
New York, City University of, 11
Nirumand, Bahman, 86
Nitsch, W., et al., 48, 55, 58, 88, 90
North Rhine-Westphalia, 106–10
Notstandsgesetze, 87
Novalis (F. von Hardenberg), 38
numerus clausus, 71, 79
Nüremberg, 24

Oakes Working Group, *see* CMND.7130
OECD – Organisation for Economic Co-operation and Development, 13, 97
Oehler, C., 73, 106, 121, 122, 150
Ohnesorg, B., 86
Ordinarienuniversität, 170
Ordinarius, 45–6, 83, 89–90, 96, 102
Osnabrück, 191–2, 194

Ott, M., 137
overcrowding of German universities, 71–4
Oxford, University of, 49

Pädagogische Hochschulen, 78, 164–5
Paderborn, 108, 185
Page, C.F., 6
Paloczi-Horvath, G., 86
PA Personnel Services, 6
Pascal, R., 60, 61
Passant, E.J., 60
Passeron, J.C., 73, 94, 124, 136
Paulsen, F., 14, 15, 24, 148
Pedley, R., 9
Peisert, H., 77, 81, 84, 95, 126
  Pädagogische Hochschulen, 121, 165
Phillips, D.G., 68
Picht, G., 84
  Die Deutsche Bildungskatastrophe ('The German Education Catastrophe'), 84
Pietism, 14
Pingel, F., 69
Pinner, F., 86, 88
placements, *see Berufspraktische Studien*
Plander, H., 193
politicised legalism, 205
Polytechnics and Colleges Funding Council, 3
Pratt, J., 2, 3
Praxis, 159
  Praxisbezug, 145, 148, 162, 175
Pritchard, R.M.O., 17, 122, 149, 200
Professorenparlament, 61
Projekt, 83, 93, 146
Prussia, 19, 20, 47, 51, 61
  defeat by France, 17–18
  Humboldt and, 13
  repressive measures of Prussian government, 60

Ranke, L. von, 43
Raupach, H., 119, 126
Realschule, 148–9
Rechtsstaat, 56–8, 118, 202, 206
Rechtien, W., 178 n4
Regensburg, University of, 83
Revolution (1848), 20, 201
  failure of, 59–63
Richert, H., 64
Richertsche Reform, 149
Rimbach, G., 117, 169, 174–5, 179
Ringer, F., 21, 34, 55, 65, 87–90, 148

Index

Index